# HAUNTED
# IN AMERICA

## ALSO BY LESLIE RULE

### NOVELS

*Whispers from the Grave*

*Kill Me Again*

### NONFICTION

*Coast to Coast Ghosts: True Stories of Hauntings Across America*

*Ghosts Among Us: True Stories of Spirit Encounters*

*When the Ghost Screams: True Stories of Victims Who Haunt*

*Ghost in the Mirror: Real Cases of Spirit Encounters*

*Where Angels Tread: Real Stories of Miracles and Angelic Intervention*

### TRUE CRIME

*A Tangled Web: A Cyberstalker, a Deadly Obsession, and the Twisting Path to Justice*

# HAUNTED IN AMERICA

## TRUE GHOST STORIES FROM THE
## BEST OF LESLIE RULE COLLECTION

## LESLIE RULE

Andrews McMeel
PUBLISHING®

Andrews McMeel Publishing
a division of Andrews McMeel Universal
1130 Walnut Street, Kansas City, Missouri 64106

www.andrewsmcmeel.com

22 23 24 25 26 RR4 10 9 8 7 6 5 4 3 2 1

ISBN: 978-1-5248-7517-6

Library of Congress Control Number: 2022940267

Editor: Charlie Upchurch
Art Director: Holly Swayne
Production Editor: Jasmine Lim
Production Manager: Julie Skalla

ATTENTION: SCHOOLS AND BUSINESSES
Andrews McMeel books are available at quantity discounts with bulk purchase
for educational, business, or sales promotional use. For information,
please e-mail the Andrews McMeel Publishing Special Sales Department:
specialsales@amuniversal.com.

# CONTENTS

# INTRODUCTION

The stranger was there one moment and gone the next. No one saw him leave. How was it possible for a human being to move so quickly? No one at the Remington employee Christmas party knew the old man. In fact, manager Joey Meyer was the only one who had seen him. "Everyone knew each other," she said. "It was mostly young people, employees, and their families. That's why the old guy stood out." Joey recalled how the stranger in the long, dark coat had quietly observed the party from the edge of the crowd. "He didn't have a drink," she said. "He just stood there, smiling and watching. I thought, *I wonder who he belongs to.*"

She had glanced away for a split second, and when she looked back, he was gone. Curious, she'd searched for him, even running outside to look. He was nowhere to be seen.

By the time Joey told me about this encounter, a few months had passed since the employee party, but she vividly remembered the smiling man, uninvited and so oddly out of place. He had appeared in December 1997 at the Remington Restaurant & Bar in Whitefish, Montana. By now, Joey had concluded that the elderly man was a ghost because her coworkers had also seen apparitions in the historic building.

My visit was in 1998, and I was there to research a book on ghosts. I was in the very beginning stages of the project, exploring a unique idea that I wasn't sure would pan out. My plan was to research the history of haunted places in an effort to identify the ghosts seen. This had been done to some extent, but I intended to dig deeper. I hoped to find something in *forgotten* archives that could shed light on why a particular place experienced paranormal activity.

I was especially interested in locations where apparitions were seen because descriptions would help identify the ghosts. Sometimes spirits have no discernable features, appearing as shadowy figures, but Joey had seen an apparition so solid and real that she hadn't realized he was a ghost until he vanished.

Who *was* the old fellow? What was his attachment to the place? Historical research was the key, but back in the 1990s, the internet was new to the average citizen, and very few records were posted online. The *Whitefish Pilot* had been publishing news since 1904, so I went to their office where they allowed me to search through a century of yellowing newspapers. The papers were stacked on tables, had not been catalogued, and were not in chronological order. Even so, I found a startling clue to the identity of the spirit Joey had seen.

While the Christmas party crasher had appeared out of place, I discovered a report that suggests he was in the *right place,* but at the *wrong time.* He was seventy-five years late to the party!

Marcus Lafayette Prowse had celebrated his seventy-sixth birthday there, seventy-five years earlier on December 12, 1922. Back then, it was Hori's Café, and he had enjoyed a birthday celebration dinner with family in the classy restaurant. He walked home that night along the railroad tracks.

The Great Northern Railway's Passenger Train 44 chugged into Whitefish and rounded a curve at 10:28 p.m. Engineer Fred Kaiding had no time to blow the whistle when he saw the man on the tracks. It was Mr. Prowse, and he was blinded by the train's bright light. Kaiding watched in horror as the old man hesitated and started to turn. A millisecond later, he was struck. He died instantly.

Had Marcus Prowse's spirit returned to the restaurant where he'd last seen his family? Had the Remington party stirred a memory of *his* last party, prompting him to appear? These are the types of questions I ask readers, and it's ultimately up to you to reach your own conclusions after I share what I know.

What *do* I know? While some refer to me as a ghost expert, I insist I am *not.* Only those who have shed their flesh and bones and crossed over to the Other Side are the true experts. I've studied the leading theories embraced by parapsychologists and rely on their decades of research as a general guideline. Any special insights I possess come from collecting my own data. I've noted patterns of paranormal activity at haunted sites. I've interviewed hundreds of people about their spirit encounters. I've slept in haunted hotels and even endured a bumpy ride on a haunted roller coaster in my quest for answers. Yet, my knowledge of otherworldly things is as limited as any other human being's.

I initially chose to research ghosts because I wanted to see proof of their existence. This was never a frightening venture for me. It was exciting. If ghosts exist, then that means that we live on after our bodies die. This is something to be *celebrated,* not feared. It is the reason I set out, a quarter of a century ago, to validate ghost sightings by finding historical documents that matched the scenarios reported in haunted places.

While studying the deaths of the earthbound might seem morbid, it is an integral part of my research. Parapsychologists have long noted that the most active haunted sites tend to be places where traumatic deaths have occurred. Murders, suicides, and accidents are the ultimate ghost makers. Marcus Prowse may be earthbound because his death was sudden and violent.

I included Mr. Prowse's case in my first book on hauntings, *Coast to Coast Ghosts*, published in 2001. I went on to write three more nonfiction books on ghosts, the last published in 2008. My editor, Charlie Upchurch, and I have selected favorite stories from these books to feature in *Haunted in America*. In addition, we've added brand new cases, as well as updates on earlier stories.

While most readers of ghost stories are open to new ideas, we realize there are skeptics in our midst. It's not our goal to change anyone's mind, but we hope all readers will be entertained, regardless of their stance on the paranormal. This is not intended to be a scary book, but we admit some of the stories are chilling. From the case of the slain woman that only a little boy could see, to the antique mirror reflecting ghostly faces, these true accounts come from real people who are willing to admit they are *Haunted in America*.

# 1

## THE EYES
## OF BABES

I can't remember being a baby, but my mother told me that I laughed constantly. "You laughed at *everything*," she said. "You laughed at clouds, and you laughed at trees." Whenever she placed me on a blanket on the grass, I would gaze up at the boughs of the fir trees and giggle hysterically. What was so funny about tree branches? I can't imagine what I could possibly have found so humorous. It occurs to me that I could have been laughing at something or *someone* that my mother couldn't see.

A leading theory among parapsychologists suggests that humans are born with their "third eyes" wide open, but most of us lose our ability to see spirits as we age. Why do we lose this keen sixth sense? *For one simple reason.* We're taught *not* to see!

In our American culture, few adults accept the idea that spirits are around us and that children can see them. Kids know when adults doubt them. They can sense their parents' discomfort, even when the adults don't deliberately shame or ridicule them. Kids want to please their parents, so little by little, their third eyes droop until they are so tightly shut that they can no longer see beyond this world.

In the following story, a group of young cousins witnessed something they were told was impossible. Decades have passed since the frightening episode, and the children who experienced it are now middle aged. But they remember it clearly, and when they compare notes, they realize they did not imagine the madman they encountered in their grandparents' attic.

# Madman in the Attic

When most people remember time spent at their grandparents' homes, their memories are pleasant. Some folks think of fresh-baked cookies, and others smile as they reminisce about grandma's prize-winning tomatoes or the wonderful stories their grandpa told. And almost everyone remembers feeling safe. When Marilyn Covarrubias thinks of her grandparents' house, however, she remembers the scariest moment of her life.

Marilyn was barely school age in the 1950s when she and an assortment of siblings and cousins were often dropped off for long stays with her grandparents in their rented home in Los Angeles, California. "It was an old house," she recalled. "And it was right across the street from Hazard Park." The twenty-five-acre park, with rolling green hills and countless trees to climb, was named for Henry Thomas Hazard, one of Los Angeles' first mayors. The park was enticing to the children, who often sneaked across the road to play there when the adults left them on their own. "We were left alone a lot," she confided.

It was a little spooky, considering that the house made more than its share of odd noises. While old houses tend to creak and groan as the weather changes, the sounds that Marilyn and her cousins heard could not be explained. "We heard a woman and a baby crying," she said and described the eerie, phantom sobs that emanated from an empty room. "One day, my grandma pulled a piece of cardboard off of a hole in the wall and found old clothes inside."

Marilyn watched as her grandmother reached into the wall and extracted old garments—clothing that had once belonged to a woman and baby. Was it hidden in the wall for a sinister reason? Did it have something to do with the ghostly sobbing? Perhaps it was simply insulation. In bygone days, used clothing was sometimes recycled as insulation.

The house was made of heavy wood with plank floors, like many of the homes built in the nineteenth century, and it had probably seen many families come and go. Today, Marilyn can't help but wonder if one of those families left something more than clothing behind. But as a child, she didn't realize anything was off. She enjoyed playing with her gang of cousins in the third-floor attic, an area designated for the grandchildren. "My grandparents kept two big beds up there, and they pushed them together in the middle of the room."

The children loved to jump on the beds and race around the attic. One evening, when Marilyn was six, the kids again found themselves alone. "It was Grandma's bingo night," she remembered. "There were six of us playing in the attic." The bunch ranged in age from her little sister, Karen, who was just a year old, to her cousin Reuben, who was eight. Donny, Reuben, Marian, Marilyn, Tony, and Karen were all happily playing when they heard the familiar sound of heavy footsteps pounding up the stairs. "My grandpa was a big man with size fourteen shoes," said Marilyn. "He always made a lot of noise when he came up those stairs."

The kids were up past their bedtime, so they rushed to get into the beds, pulling the covers up to their chins as they listened to their grandpa's approaching steps. "We were all giggling and trying to pretend we were asleep."

But when the door flew open, it was not Grandpa. A stranger stood in the doorway. The man looked as if he had been caught in a downpour. "He was so wet that his hair was matted to his forehead," said Marilyn. He wore a plaid shirt like a lumberjack, and his eyes were bloodshot. "They were so bloodshot that they were completely red."

As he stood there, the stranger made a sound that is hard for Marilyn to describe yet impossible for her to forget. "It was as if he were laughing and crying at the same time." The children were dumbstruck by the image of the wild man with the maniacal cry. They watched in horror as he suddenly bolted toward them. When he reached the beds, he did not stop. He ran right *through* the beds. "We could feel him," said Marilyn, describing the sensation as a rush of cold wind. The man dove for the window, and as he broke through the glass, they heard it shattering around them. And then, the only sound was the steady patter of rain.

Was the crazy man outside, broken and dead on the ground, far below the attic window? The kids were too scared to get out of bed and look. They huddled beneath the blankets, waiting for what seemed like hours. "Then we heard footsteps on the stairs again." The children were petrified and barely able to breathe as heavy feet thundered up the stairs toward them. Again, the door flew open. This time it was Grandpa. "We jumped out of bed and ran to him. We were all crying."

Their grandfather listened as they clung to him and told their wild story. "It was just your imagination," he said, consoling them as he patted their heads. He led them to the window. "See," he said patiently. "The glass isn't broken. And it's not raining." It was true. The window was intact, and the night was dry. Grandpa must be right, six-year-old Marilyn decided. There was no man. No shattered glass. No one had jumped through the window. They had imagined the whole thing.

Decades later, she had not forgotten the crazed man who dove through the attic window. She was reminiscing with her cousin, Tony, at a family gathering when he mentioned the ghost in the attic. She gasped. "I thought I imagined that!"

"Oh, no!" he assured her. "It really happened." Tony recalled the scene exactly as she had, and he told her that he and Reuben had discussed the bizarre occurrence many times over the years. Marilyn had accepted her grandfather's explanation without question when she was a child. Now, she realized that his reasoning was wrong. It wasn't possible that all the kids would imagine the same thing.

She tried to make sense of what had happened and asked her mother if she'd ever noticed anything odd about the house. Her mother confided that she, too, had seen something peculiar there. On one memorable afternoon, she had been napping on the couch in the living room when she awoke to see a woman with a dog, walking across the room. "My mother told me that the dog stopped and licked her hand," said Marilyn. As the woman strolled by, the canine followed, and then, suddenly, they both vanished.

Who were the ghosts? Had they lived and died in the house? Had the clothing found in the wall belonged to former tenants who met tragic endings? And what about the madman in the attic? Had he killed himself by leaping through the window? If so, why did he do it? Had something awful happened to him? Or had he done something so bad to someone else that it drove him to suicide from guilt?

Despite my digging, I have yet to find a historical account of a man leaping through the window in the grandparents' attic. I've found nothing to explain the paranormal activity in the spooky, old house. While this mystery may never be solved, I'm continuing to research. The source of the haunting in the next case, however, *has* been determined. Just like the children who witnessed the madman in the attic, the little boy in this story saw a ghost at his grandparents' house. He, too, was dismissed when they chalked the sightings up to a child's imagination. In this case, however, the boy was finally believed when his grandparents learned the shocking truth.

# Imaginary Friend

When the couple moved into their new home in Modesto, California, they did not inquire about its history. They knew only that the cute ranch-style house in the quiet neighborhood seemed perfect for them. After they moved in, their little grandson, who often stayed with them, made a new "imaginary friend." He called her Debi.

As the adults relaxed and enjoyed their dream home, the toddler played with his invisible buddy. The grown-ups just laughed and shook their heads. It did not occur to them that Debi was anything other than a figment of the child's imagination. And they had no idea that their dream house had turned into a *nightmare* house for someone else.

Deborah Ann Whitlock was a vivacious woman who loved life. At thirty-two, the Modesto wife and mother worked for Sears and was slated to be their youngest female store manager. She was hardworking and dedicated to her job, but most of all, she was devoted to her three-year-old daughter, C.J. It was the love for her daughter that allowed her to endure the worst that any human being can—without uttering a scream. On March 25, 1988, Debi was brutally attacked in her own bed as her toddler slept in the next room. "She was a hero," said Debi's mother, Jacque MacDonald. "If she had screamed, C.J. would have woken up. She kept quiet to save her daughter's life."

Scott Avery Fizzell was a teenage meth addict in the spring of 1988. He prowled the Whitlocks' neighborhood in camouflage clothing, looking for things to steal to fund his habit. He carried a burglary kit that included gloves and a Halloween mask as he crept through backyards, searching for unlocked doors and windows. It was close to midnight that Thursday when he discovered the Whitlocks' sliding glass door unlocked. He slipped into their home and found Debi's purse in the kitchen. He took the purse, containing seven dollars, and left.

*Why did he return?* Why didn't he just take the money and move on? Tragically, he had something more sinister than theft in mind. He returned to the house, went to Debi's room, and touched her as she slept. When she awoke in a panic, he killed and then sexually assaulted her.

Debi's husband, Howie Whitlock, was at a coworker's bachelor party on the night of the murder. He was out very late, and when he arrived home at quarter to six in the morning, he got the shock of his life. He discovered his wife, lifeless, in the hallway outside of their bedroom. Her throat had been slit, but their little daughter was unharmed. Miraculously, C.J. had slept through the night.

Debi's friends and family were devastated. Her mother was so overcome with grief that she could barely function. When she learned that detectives had no viable suspect, she was outraged. She knew that her son-in-law was a suspect because spouses are the first to be scrutinized in homicide investigations. There was a moment when Jacque, too, wondered if Howie could be guilty. But despite the fact their marriage had been troubled, Jacque realized that Howie did not kill Debi. He was a gentle man. Jacque defended him, and she was bothered by the gossip.

When neighbors were interviewed by reporters from the local newspaper, one was quoted saying that she hoped that the murder was the result of a domestic dispute, rather than a random occurrence. *She* would be safer, said the neighbor, if there were no random killer stalking their street. As it turned out, of course, the culprit *was* a random killer, and the neighbor who had made the thoughtless remark could have been a victim just as easily as poor Debi.

*After Debi Whitlock's shocking death, her spirit was seen in the home where she took her last breaths.*

But it was nine long years before Scott Fizzell was caught. Throughout that time, Jacque worked tirelessly to get justice for her daughter. In her campaign to keep Debi's memory alive, she plastered posters and fliers all over the city. She placed Debi's picture on pizza boxes and grocery carts, and she also appeared on dozens of television programs to tell Debi's story.

Her efforts finally paid off when a witness saw one of Jacque's billboards and came forward in 1997. He had been a casual acquaintance of Scott's. On the night of the murder, Scott had visited and confessed that he had just killed a woman. Thanks to the informant's tip, Fizzell was arrested, and the DNA evidence from the crime scene proved he was the killer. He pled guilty in 1999 and was sentenced to thirty-one years to life in prison.

Jacque MacDonald's quest for justice did not end with the conviction of Debi's killer. She was passionate about justice for *all* victims and launched *Victim's Voice*, a thirty-minute TV program that addressed the concerns of victims and their families. In one segment, with prior permission, she visited the crime scene where her daughter had drawn her last breath. The house's new owners were stunned to learn of the murder but graciously allowed the video cameras inside. Jacque swallowed hard and followed the woman to the room that had once been Debi's.

The homeowner was astonished to realize that her grandson's special friend, Debi, was not imaginary after all. *She was a ghost!* While only the little boy had actually seen the spirit, others had witnessed the door to Debi's room opening and closing on its own. The new lady of the house told Jacque that she had been startled to see the rocking chair suddenly begin to rock. It happened when no one was in the chair, and no one was near enough to touch it. As the chair swayed, her grandson had pointed at it and announced, "Debi's in the chair."

Stranger still was the visit to the grocery store. When his grandmother lifted him up to put him in the shopping cart, the preschooler had taken one look at the face printed on the seat and screamed, "No! I don't want to sit on Debi!" The child could not read, but he pointed to the photograph of the smiling young woman. It was a picture of Debi on one of the notices that Jacque had had placed on the cart seats! At the time, however, the grandmother had no idea who Debi was or that anyone had been murdered in her home. After Jacque MacDonald's visit, everything was chillingly clear.

Jacque was not surprised to hear that the little boy had interacted with Debi's ghost. The grieving mother believed with all her heart that her daughter's spirit was still around. "Debi loved children," she told me. It was just like her to befriend a little boy.

Paranormal investigators have long noted that earthbound spirits seem to be intrigued by people who remind them of those they knew in life. In Debi Whitlock's case, she was devoted to her young daughter. Debi's sudden and violent death may have been such a shock to her soul that she didn't realize she was dead. Possibly, she was searching for her daughter, and when she couldn't find her in their home, she gravitated toward the new homeowners' grandchild who was about the age of C.J. when Debi last saw her.

## — *Update* —

While living in Merced, California, Jacque MacDonald hosted *Victim's Voice* on TV and radio for eighteen years and placed a special emphasis on unsolved homicides. She was a recipient of the Justice Department's National Crime Victims' Service Award in 2007. Her health declined in recent years, and she died at age eighty-six in Grants Pass, Oregon, on March 11, 2020.

Stressed by the accusations against him, Howie Whitlock's life took a downward spiral, and he died in 2001. His daughter (Debi's stepdaughter), author Angela Dove, wrote a book about the murder and the toll it took on their family. *No Room for Doubt* is a powerful story, published by the Berkley Publishing Group in 2009.

Scott Fizzell is currently incarcerated at the Mule Creek State Prison in Ione, California. In July 2020, he was denied parole after a psychologist determined he still posed a high risk for violence.

\* \* \*

Hollywood screenwriters seem to relish frightening viewers with their fictitious films of horror-story hauntings, but in reality, most encounters involve benign spirits. Just as the child in the previous account befriended the ghost of Debi Whitlock, the little girl in the next case had a special bond with a friendly ghost that only she could see.

# Blissful Bond

When Cecelia Meurling was a little girl, she loved to visit her grandparents' farm on Gueme's Island. The small, secluded island is lesser known than the other popular tourist destination, San Juan Islands, that are scattered across Puget Sound like irregular puddles of pancake batter on the grill. Gueme's Island is just north across the channel from Anacortes, Washington, and was first settled by Cecelia's great-grandfather.

"My grandparents lived in a one-story house, painted white. It sat back some distance from the road, and it was about a half mile up the hill from the ferry," said Cecelia, who today is the mother of a grown son. The Burien, Washington, cat shelter volunteer can close her eyes and still see Dolly and Bonny, her grandfather's sturdy, white plow horses. "He had chickens, too, and it was my job to watch for hawks and tell him right away when I saw one."

The picturesque farm, surrounded by pastures and cornfields, had been in the family for generations. In fact, Cecelia's mother had been born in the house. Dozens of cousins and aunts and uncles had also grown up on the island. Her grandparents, Bob and Mary Merchant, knew everyone who lived there.

"I called my grandmother Sela. She was short and plump with curly, dark hair. She loved her flower garden, and when I stayed there, we would get up early with the chickens! And with our pajamas still on, we'd go out to see how her 'girls' were doing," she said, describing how they would admire the daffodils, roses, and pansies as the sun peeked over the horizon.

Cecelia remembers the swing on the old crabapple tree, and how her grandmother took time from cooking to push her on it. "She would stir a pot, and run out to give me a push, and then run back in and stir some more. We were very close. We could talk about anything." Yet there was a time when one topic was off-limits. Cecelia was four years old when she found herself unwilling to speak to anyone about someone very special to her.

One bright spring day, Cecelia told her grandmother that she was going out to play. She stepped outside into the fresh, salty air, and as she skipped toward the fields, she was met by a girl. "She was not familiar to me," Cecelia said. "Yet, it was like she was waiting for me." The little girls looked into each other's smiling eyes and clasped hands. It was an instant, blissful bond. "I was so happy to see her, and she was just as happy to see me. We ran into the field, holding hands and giggling."

The child was about Cecelia's size and clad in a pair of blue overalls. Her blond curls bounced, shining in the sunshine as they frolicked. "We never talked," said Cecelia. "We never said a word." The girls headed toward the barn and were playing behind it when Cecelia heard her grandmother calling. Grandma Sela's voice was strained with worry. Cecelia knew that her grandmother liked to keep an eye on her, so she let go of her little friend's hand and stepped out from behind the barn. "I waved to my grandmother to let her know where I was," she said. She turned back to her friend. The girl with the curly hair was gone.

When Grandma Sela approached to see what her grandchild was up to, Cecelia excitedly told her that she had been playing with her new friend. Her grandmother glanced around. "I would like to know who you are talking about," she said. Cecelia grabbed Grandma Sela's hand and pulled her along, saying, "Come and meet her!" She knew her friend could not have gone far. But the child had vanished as suddenly as she had appeared. They gazed about, their eyes searching the pastures and fields stretched out before them. The corn hadn't started to grow again, and there wasn't anywhere to hide. *Where* was she? "I want to play with her," Cecelia insisted.

"I wish I knew who you were talking about," said Grandma Sela and shook her head. "I can't imagine who she could be." The nearest neighbors lived far down the road. Grandma Sela knew everyone on the island and had never seen a child like the one Cecelia described. Yet at age four, Cecelia could not grasp the enormity of the mystery. She knew only that her friend had brought her joy, and she could not wait to see her again. She searched Grandma's barn and yard, peeking behind the apple trees. She circled the house, desperately hoping that the giggling girl would pop out from a hiding place. "I never saw her again," Cecelia said sadly. "I was overwhelmingly disappointed that I could not find her."

Later, when she overheard her grandmother telling her mother about the mystery girl, Cecelia felt an odd stirring in her belly. Her grandmother made it sound as if something was wrong. "To me it had been the most natural thing in the world," she confided. "But my grandmother made such a big issue of it, I decided not to talk about it anymore." She still missed her friend, but she kept it to herself.

Years later, when her grandmother mentioned the puzzling visit from the little girl, Cecelia told her that she still remembered it. Grandma Sela's eyes narrowed as she pondered the possibilities. "I don't know who she could have been," she said. "Unless she was an angel." It was then that Cecelia began to wonder. Perhaps the little girl had not been of this world. It was hard to imagine. Her hand had been warm and solid when she held it in her own. Where had the girl come from? How could she have appeared so quickly and then disappear again? Why didn't they see her running away across the fields?

If she was a spirit child, perhaps she was a relative. Cecelia's great-grandmother had given birth to seventeen children on the island, and not all had survived childhood. It seems that whoever she was, the gleeful child was indeed from another place. She had not arrived on the island by ferryboat, as Cecelia had, but had journeyed there from an unknown world in a mysterious fashion. Angel or ghost, Cecelia will never forget her. "The little girl brought me such a feeling of pure joy and bliss," said Cecelia. "I've never felt that happy since. I wonder if I will ever see her again."

When it comes to ghost encounters, the younger the child, the more accepting they are. Older kids tend to be spooked when they see apparitions, probably because they've internalized our culture's fearful attitude about the paranormal. Reactions are varied, and sometimes children are afraid because they sense the fear that the spirit felt in their last moment alive. Sometimes kids aren't really frightened but simply startled because the encounters take them by surprise. In the following case, two young girls had just such an encounter when they met in an unlikely place. One of them told me her story.

# Stranger in the Shower

It was early in the morning, and Kya Dunagan was getting ready for the first day of school. As her mother urged her to hurry, Kya stepped into the bathroom of their south Seattle apartment, flicked on the light, and reached for her hairbrush. The seven-year-old looked into the mirror, pulled the brush through her long blond hair, and froze. There, reflected in the glass, was an unfamiliar girl.

"She was in the shower behind me," Kya explained. The strange girl's lips were curved into a friendly smile. She wore a nightgown, and her auburn hair curled about her pretty face. Instinctively, Kya turned around to look at the shower.

*No one was there.* Kya glanced back at the mirror. The girl was still there, captured in the reflection and smiling expectantly. In a moment of confused silence, Kya could only stand there, holding her hairbrush, her arm paused in midair. Then the girl spoke. It was a single word, sweet yet piercing. "Hi." Kya dropped the brush and ran.

Her mom was waiting for her at the front door, and Kya tried to tell her about the girl in the mirror. Jennifer Dunagan was running late, trying to juggle coats and keys and money for school lunches. Though she appreciated her daughter's imagination, she was not in the mood to indulge her. "She didn't believe me," said Kya.

Three years later, ten-year-old Kya explained that she understood why her mother was skeptical. For at age seven, Kya had had an imaginary friend. "My imaginary friend's name was Olla, and she looked a little like the girl in the mirror, but Olla's hair was long and dark." With all of the wisdom of a fifth grader, Kya told me that she definitely knows the difference between an imaginary being and an apparition in the mirror. The mirror girl was real, she insisted, and she remembers her with detailed clarity.

Jennifer no longer doubts her daughter. Kya, like all of the females in her family, is psychic. "She can sense something is wrong when we pass a bad person on the street," said Jennifer, describing how Kya's thin shoulders sometimes shudder when they encounter a seemingly benign stranger. The Dunagans have moved from the apartment complex where the mirror girl appeared. And after that one exciting morning, the apparition was not seen again.

In retrospect, Jennifer remembers other odd things that occurred in the apartment. "The TV turned itself on and off," she said. "I still have the TV, and it doesn't do that anymore." That makes Jennifer wonder if the apartment was haunted. I wondered the same thing, so I went to the apartment complex and

*Kya Dunagan will never forget the stranger she met in her family's Seattle apartment. (Leslie Rule)*

spoke to the managers. They had no information for me. If they were aware of paranormal activity occurring in their buildings, they did not admit it to me.

Who was the girl in the mirror? Was she attached to the apartment, and if so, could she have been a former tenant who died there? I've searched newspaper archives but have yet to find an account of a girl who died near the spot.

The hillside apartments where the Dunagans lived are fairly new. A century before they were built, a few cabins were sprinkled upon the sloping terrain, homesteaded by pioneers without permits, and demolished before most of us living today were born.

The memory of the long-gone homes is buried beneath asphalt, concrete, and four-story buildings. The ghost of a little girl who had once lived, and perhaps *died* there, may be the only one who remembers.

Paranormal researchers have noted that spirit activity often escalates on anniversaries and holidays. Perhaps the mirror girl was enticed by the excitement of the first day of school. It's possible she was one of the many children of early Seattle, stricken with a deadly disease, maybe just before school began.

It doesn't seem to matter *when* a death occurred, because it's *emotions*—not clocks and calendars—that influence earthbound spirits. A leading theory suggests that time as we know it does not exist on the Other Side. A century in the life of a live human being might feel like a blink of an instant to a spirit. The child in the next story lived and died decades before her new roommates were born, but that didn't stop her from trying to join in their fun.

# The Joke Is on You

Elizabeth Wilson was sixteen in 1972 when she, her mother, and her four siblings moved into a rental house in Skykomish, Washington. "It was a shabby, brown two-story house," she said, shuddering with the memory. "It was haunted. You can ask my brothers and sister, and they'll tell you the same thing! I get goose bumps just talking about it."

Skykomish has a rich history as a mining and logging town, with a railroad established there in the 1890s. Elizabeth's home had played a significant role in the area's history. Built around the turn of the twentieth century, it had once been the headquarters for the Apex Gold Mining Company. Elizabeth's family was just one of many who had occupied the house over the years. But she wasn't thinking about those who might have lived and died there as she helped her mother unpack their boxes. It was not until odd things began to occur that she wondered about those who came before her.

Her three brothers shared an open space on the second floor of the drafty, old house, and Elizabeth and her eleven-year-old sister each got their own rooms. The girls were not thrilled with the arrangement because of the disturbing things that happened. Each night, Elizabeth turned off her light and crawled into bed and felt a cold whoosh of wind. "It rushed right over me, lifting my hair. It was the most eerie feeling!"

Alyce, too, was spooked and told the others that a strange girl appeared in her room at night. Not only that, but the ethereal child *spoke* to her. They soon learned from neighbors that they were not the first tenants to be afraid. The prior renters had a little boy who insisted that his bedroom door always remain open when he was in his room. "He would cry and tell his parents that there was someone in the room with him."

While Elizabeth and her siblings didn't like to be scared, they enjoyed scaring others. In fact, they loved to play practical jokes. "We bought a mannequin head at a thrift shop," said Elizabeth. "It looked real." It was a woman's head with rooted blond hair and "wicked staring eyes." The pranksters stuck the head on the antenna of their car and drove around town. "We almost caused a few accidents," Elizabeth sheepishly admitted.

The kids thought they were pretty clever, but the joke was on *them*. For one evening, all five of the siblings were downstairs when they heard a hollow thud. *Thud. Thud. Thud.* Baffled, the kids stared at each other, wide eyed. *What in the world could be making that noise?* "It sounded like something was rolling down the stairs. And then it rolled back *up!*"

When the noise stopped, they crept upstairs to investigate. "We found the mannequin head had been moved. And it was not the last time it happened," said Elizabeth. On several other occasions, the kids were downstairs when they heard the mannequin head rolling around. Finally, they had had enough and "got rid of it."

Alyce had a favorite prank she liked to play on her sister's friends. It involved the old player piano that sat in the corner of Elizabeth's room. The insides of the piano were long gone, and there was just enough room for Alyce to climb inside and hide. She'd figured out that she could pluck the keys from inside the piano, and she relished doing this when no one was expecting it. She would wait until the older girls were lost in conversation, and then she'd pluck the keys. "It made a 'dink, dink, dink' sound," said Elizabeth. "She always made the exact same sound." Elizabeth would laugh when she heard the familiar pattern because she knew it was just her mischievous little sister, but the sudden playing of the piano startled her friends.

Then one evening, as the family was eating at the dinner table, they all heard it. *Dink, dink, dink.* Alyce up to her old tricks? *Not exactly!* All eyes went to Alyce, who sat with them at the table. Realization sunk in. "We were all there," Elizabeth remembered. "And we were stunned when we saw she was there too! We got up to investigate." Was someone hiding in the piano? They lifted the lid and peered inside. It was empty! Once again, the joke was on them!

Alyce was so rattled that she "never played that trick again." Who was the mysterious prankster who seemed to join in on the kids' jokes? Was it the girl who had materialized in the night beside Alyce's bed? Those encounters were not only spooky but also sad. On several occasions, Alyce had heard the spirit's anguished voice crying, "Mommy! Mommy!"

Elizabeth wondered if the pitiful little soul belonged to a child who had died in the house. Determined to get to the bottom of the mystery, she struck up a conversation with old-timers in the neighborhood. Elizabeth hoped they would know something about the house's history. They certainly did. A neighbor remembered something significant that had occurred there in the early 1900s. A little girl had once lived and *died* there. She got very sick with pneumonia and passed away, probably in the room that now belonged to Alyce.

Though the child had been dead for decades by the time Elizabeth's family lived there, she was stuck, frozen in time. The poor, confused little spirit was apparently unaware of the passing years, for she was still looking for her mommy. Had she had siblings? If so, she may have stirred whenever a child moved into the room that had once been hers. She may have thought the newcomers were her long-lost sisters or brothers. When she saw the fun that the kids had with the mannequin head and the practical jokes with the piano keys, she, too, became drawn to those things.

Elizabeth suspects that the little girl was not the only ghost residing there, because some of the episodes were too menacing to be attributed to an innocent child. The incident in the kitchen was especially disturbing. "We had one of those old wringer-washing machines," she said. "One day, my sister was standing in the kitchen when the washing machine lifted five inches off the floor." Several family members watched in horror as the machine levitated, then tilted toward young Alyce as if it were going to dump water on her.

For one unreal moment, reality was turned inside out. Then the appliance returned to the floor, and the incident was over. It was hard to believe such a thing could have happened, but they'd seen it with their own eyes. No one was harmed, but everyone was thoroughly rattled. Was it just another prank, played by a mischievous ghost? Or was something more sinister in the home?

A few years after the family moved out, the house was burned down as a practice exercise for local firefighters. The histories of all who lived and died in the home are lost to the ages, and we'll likely never know the details of the drama that played out there. Perhaps the only untimely death was that of the sick child. Beyond that, the secrets of the past might as well have been incinerated when the house was burned down. The answers are ashes in the wind.

The next story also involves an unsettling encounter. It happened years ago, but the witness recalls it vividly. The grown-ups told her it was only a nightmare, but she knew she wasn't dreaming.

# Eye to Eye

When Dhebi Siconolfi was a child, she did not have to travel far to visit her best friend. Their families shared a duplex in Southbridge, Massachusetts. Dhebi's family lived on the floor above Nona's family, and it was not unusual for the girls to spend the night with each other. Yet one night was so unusual that Dhebi cannot forget it, despite the fact that four decades have passed. After an evening of watching television, giggling, and snacking on popcorn, the eight-year-olds fell asleep, side by side in Nona's bed.

"Sometime during the night, I woke up," said Dhebi. A figure darted across the room, deliberately moving toward her. The lights were out, and Dhebi could not see who it was. "I wasn't alarmed," she said. "I figured it was Wayne, Nona's big brother." He was several years older than the girls and liked to tease them and play pranks. So Dhebi was not worried when she saw someone stoop over and scoot beneath the bed.

*I wonder what he is up to*, she thought. She ignored him and rolled over to lie face down on the bed. Her eyes were wide open, but she should not have been able to see a single thing. Yet, suddenly, she could see right *through* the mattress and was horrified to see a pair of eyes staring back at her. The disembodied eyes were not cloaked in darkness but as clear and vivid as if she were viewing them in daylight.

When Dhebi screamed, her shrieks roused the household. As Nona sat up in bed beside her, the lights in the room came on, and Nona's parents were huddled in the doorway, peering in at them. "There's someone under the bed!" Dhebi cried. "It was just a nightmare," they told her. Nona's father dutifully peeked beneath the bed and reassured her, "There's no one there."

"I *saw* it!" Dhebi protested. "I saw eyes!" She tried to tell them about what she had witnessed. She knew it sounded impossible, yet she had seen it. The eyes were topped by brows and spaced like a normal pair of eyes. She had also seen the bridge of the nose in between, but the rest of the face was invisible. Nona's mom shook her head. "We told you girls not to watch that scary movie," she scolded. "See what happens? You had a nightmare."

"I was awake, and it was real," Dhebi protested as the adults patiently tucked them back into bed. Today, Dhebi is the mother of three grown children, and she is still adamant that she was awake and alert when a phantom being crept across the room and slid beneath her bed. She remembers the eyes, unblinking as they stared back at her, burning through the mattress.

The vision was not from a nightmare inspired by the scary movie, though she remembers that the film *did* frighten them. "It was *The House of Wax*, an old horror flick with Vincent Price. We weren't supposed to watch it, but we left the bedroom door open, so we could see across the hall into the living room where the adults had the TV on," Dhebi remembered. The details of the movie have faded, but the eyes have seared a permanent place in her memory.

When they describe their ghost sightings, many people report seeing partial apparitions. The following case is another example.

# Edward's Punishment

Over half a century has passed since Louise Inman Strother witnessed something peculiar that both frightened and pleased her. The Oakdale, Louisiana, mother of two has always lived in the South. She grew up in Mermentau, Louisiana, near her cousin Edward and her aunt Carrie. "My older cousin almost died when he was born because he was so tiny," Louise told me. "I remember the adults saying that he was so little that he could fit on a dinner plate. They worried about him so much that they ended up spoiling him."

The sickly infant grew into a strong, husky boy who was used to getting his way. And when he *didn't*, he bullied his widowed mother until she gave in.

While her cousin had grown strong, Louise's aunt had developed health problems, and Louise felt sorry for her. "My aunt was precious," she emphasized. "She didn't deserve to be treated like that." By the time Louise was eight years old, her cousin towered over her.

One day when she visited her aunt, she heard her cousin speaking harshly to his mother. "He cussed at her, and I hated it," she said. "He was so ugly to her." But there was nothing she could do but stand by helplessly and watch as Edward mouthed off.

Suddenly, as he was spewing obscenities, Louise heard a loud smack. Her cousin grabbed the side of his face and staggered backward. The boy's mother raised her eyebrows. "What's the matter?" she asked him.

"Someone slapped me!" cried the stunned boy. His mother shook her finger at him and said, "That was your dead daddy!"

"It scared me," Louise confided. "But I was so happy it happened." Recently, she asked her cousin if he remembered the ghostly slap. "Sure," he replied. "How could I forget?" In fact, Edward told her that it was not the last time it happened. Shortly after the first incident, he was in his room when he saw a disembodied hand fly through the air and smack him. "I wish I could say that it straightened him out," said Louise. "But it didn't."

Today her cousin is over seventy and suffers from the same ailments that plagued his mother. Louise doesn't know if he feels any guilt over his spoiled behavior. She often finds herself wondering who the punishing hand belonged to. Was it her deceased uncle's hand, as her aunt said, or was it the hand of an unknown spirit attached to the property? The mystery, she said, sparked a lifelong fascination with ghosts.

Maybe it is not kind of me, but I can't help the smile of satisfaction when I picture the hand smacking the rude boy. The following cases, however, cause me to quickly lose that smile. They reverberate with the kind of creepiness that sparks nightmares.

# Restless Nights

Traci Bartolone never felt safe when she went to sleep in her bed in her childhood home in Hammonton, New Jersey. "When I was about nine years old, I used to wake to someone touching my feet under the covers."

She knew, of course, that she was alone in the bed and hoped that the sensation was just the blankets tangled about her feet. Still, it scared her, and whenever she felt the fingers on her feet, she called to her older sister, Michelle, who snoozed in the bed next to hers. "I could never get her to wake up," Traci told me, as she described how she would scrunch up in the bed with her knees to her chest, wishing the light from her nightlight burned brighter. "One night I felt something pull real hard on my big toe," she told me. "I was tired of being scared. I got mad." Traci lifted the covers and peered down at her feet. "That's when I saw a hand quickly retreating to wherever it had come from." Traci shrieked for her sister, but Michelle would not wake up.

The image of the withdrawing hand has stayed with her, and she is positive it was not a dream. "I saw a whole hand and wrist," she said. "It was masculine, solid, and pale. I actually saw it snap back when it let go of my toe and quickly went straight down, almost as if it was scared that I saw it."

Michelle also experienced odd things in the room. The television and radio would constantly turn themselves on, but this was nowhere near as frightening as her sister's episodes. Today Traci is a grown woman and the mother of a toddler. Yet she cannot shake the image of the phantom hand. "I still sleep with the lights on," she admitted.

Jason Perrone, Traci's fiancé, does not provide much reassurance. For he, too, is haunted by a childhood specter, and he cannot sleep with the bedroom door open. While Traci needs the light on to sleep, Jason insists that the bedroom door must be closed. It's the only way they get any rest.

Jason is a twenty-five-year-old frozen food clerk at an upscale grocery store near his home in Medford, New Jersey. While handling frozen food all day may give him the chills, nothing makes him shiver like the memory of a nighttime visitor. He was a small boy, living in an apartment complex in Edgewood Park, New Jersey, when the haunting began.

"The first time I saw her I was six years old," he told me. He shared a room with his older brother, Tom, who had a much later bedtime. Their mother tucked Jason into bed early and then left his bedroom door ajar, so he would have light from the hallway. As the little boy lay in bed, he was startled to see an elderly woman walk past the open door. When the shriveled being ambled by, he saw that she had curly white hair that fell past her shoulders. She wore a silky, white nightgown and carried a large wicker basket clutched to her chest. "She walked past my door a couple of times, and then she looked in at me," Jason said.

Her eyes frightened him the most. The white orbs contained no pupils, yet they seemed to bore into him. "It was as if she stared into my soul," he said. Jason was immobilized by fear, unable to dive beneath the covers or call out. Later, he tried to tell his mother about what he had seen. "She thought I was making it up," he said.

Over the years, the spirit appeared frequently, always following the same pattern and always carrying the basket. No one else in the family ever saw the old woman, though he sometimes tried to wake his brother when she appeared. "I wanted someone else to see her so that they would believe me," Jason said. "But I could never wake up my brother. He was always in a deep sleep, almost like a trance."

The Perrone family moved twice, and Jason was dismayed to find that he could not escape his night visitor, for the old woman moved with them and continued to appear outside of the frightened boy's bedroom. Jason continued to tell his family that the entity was real, and eventually, his mother began to entertain the idea that he was actually witnessing something, but she did not grasp the full horror of the encounter.

"She said it was my great aunt Bess looking out for me," he told me, still sounding somewhat bitter as he explained that the apparition did resemble his deceased aunt. He did not know who the being was, but he did not believe she had his best interests in mind.

She was a creepy phantom, a nightmare image that he could not shake. He never got over his fear and wished his brothers would remember to keep the bedroom door shut. But inevitably, someone would leave the door ajar, and he would find himself terror struck with the empty eyes fixed upon him. "The last time I saw her, I was fourteen," Jason said. He believes that as he grew older he lost his ability to see those who lurk on the Other Side.

I was intrigued by Jason's and Traci's encounters. Each had experienced something odd that was unlike anything I have previously come across. I researched the backgrounds of their childhood homes where the encounters occurred, in an effort to make sense of cases so spooky that they gave *me* nightmares. In Jason's case, the apparition's eyes puzzled me. No one before him had ever described such eyes to me. Usually, the description of a ghost matches the appearance of the live human being it represents—though it sometimes is missing feet or manifests as colorless or pale. This made me wonder if Jason had seen the ghost of a blind woman.

Could unseeing eyes appear as the blank, white orbs that Jason described? Some quick research verified that blind eyes can indeed appear as white orbs. The condition can occur as a result of a severe infection of the cornea, an accident, or, in rarer instances, as an inherited defect. What about the basket? Although Jason was unable to see the contents, he assumed it was a laundry basket. He described it as wicker, with the circumference larger at the top.

More research revealed that basket weaving has long been a common trade among the sight impaired in the general area. For instance, in the neighboring state, the New York School for the Blind in Batavia opened in 1868 and is dedicated to teaching students skills, so they can become independent. Basket weaving was one of the early trades taught there.

The ghost of an elderly blind woman may have been wandering the grounds for some time—quite possibly for centuries—before Jason saw her. He may have been the first person to see her, and as a result she felt a connection with him and followed him to his new homes. Though the apparition's eyes appeared blind, she most likely could see as well as any other ghost, though a ghost's way of seeing is beyond our understanding.

Sometimes ghosts are seen with props, such as the basket in the old woman's arms. These props, somewhat like the clothing apparitions wear, become part of the manifestation. If a basket was ever-present in the woman's arms in life, it is not surprising it should materialize with her in death.

Who was the frightening entity who tormented Traci Bartolone? The land in Hammonton was surrounded by marshes and woods, with the Wharton State Forest beyond. Traci's grandfather had had a house on the land. And Traci's father had later cleared a spot in the woods to build their home. "My neighbors once told me that their children had found arrowheads in the woods behind our house," said Traci. "That was in the 1950s and 1960s."

My research revealed that the Lenni-Lenape tribe had roamed the area long before the first Europeans settled there. They had generously welcomed pioneers and taught them how to build temporary housing and how to farm the land. It was a fatal mistake. While the tribe showed the newcomers how to live, the pioneers showed them how to *die*. The Lenni-Lenape had no natural immunities, and more than half of their population succumbed to diseases such as smallpox and measles.

"My family is part Sioux, and we're from the Rosebud tribe," said Traci, explaining that she wondered if the spirit of a Native American who died on the land was drawn to her long black hair and chiseled cheekbones, perhaps mistaking her for someone else.

Of all the paranormal experiences shared with me, I think Traci's is the scariest. Almost every child has indulged the fear that something could emerge from beneath our beds and grab us! Traci's description of the creeping, pale hand grabbing her toes is something I try not to think about when I'm falling asleep! While we share common fears, each of us is unique when it comes to the things that frighten us most. When the following story was included in my book *Coast to Coast Ghosts*, my editor told me that it scared her more than any of my other cases.

It's not my intention to scare readers (or my editors!) with these accounts, because too many writers and filmmakers are working overtime to make the paranormal far more frightening than necessary. I am fascinated by people's spirit encounters, and I report what they tell me without fabrication. It has not escaped me, however, that some of the incidents I report on are downright spooky—and the spookiest encounters seem to be the ones experienced by children! What is it about "The Man with the Blue Hand" that chilled my editor? Read on and decide for yourself!

# The Man with the Blue Hand

Peggy Bailey woke to a terrified shriek. A devoted mother, she leapt out of bed and rushed toward her children's bedrooms. Little Caleb sat in his bed, tears coursing down his chubby cheeks. "What's the matter, honey?" Peggy cried, as she ran to him. She held the trembling two-year-old in her arms. "Everything is okay. Mommy's here," she soothed. *A nightmare.* What else could it be? Caleb was probably upset about sleeping in a new place, she told herself. The single mom and her mother had recently moved to the rented house in Chilton, Wisconsin. Five-year-old Caitlin was excited about the adventure, but Caleb seemed frightened. The old five-bedroom farmhouse was close to her work, and she was happy to have found it. The children each had their own rooms, with plenty of space for their toys.

Peggy had figured her little boy might be uneasy about sleeping alone for the first time, so she tried to make it as special as possible. She tucked him in with his favorite stuffed animals and told him he was a big boy with his own room now. But night after night, the family awoke to Caleb's cries. "He began to talk about a man," confided Peggy. "He talked about the man in his room or the man on his bed. Most often, he talked about the man with the blue hand. It got to the point where he would not even go in his own bedroom!"

Meanwhile, Caitlin was happy about the new place and cheerfully lined her dolls up on a shelf in her room. No one else seemed to sense anything—*except for the Baileys' two dogs!* "They frequently ran through the house, growling and barking for no reason," said Peggy. "And they refused to enter Caleb's room too." Perdie, the smart poodle-terrier mix, was especially disturbed by the unknown presence. Peggy watched, concerned, as the little dog bared her teeth and snarled at thin air. She had read that animals are sensitive to haunted places, and she found herself wondering if her little boy could be seeing something from the Other Side, something that the protective Perdie also sensed. "One day my mother went upstairs to get Caleb some clothes from his room," said Peggy. "He followed her up and stood outside the door and pointed to the corner."

The little boy asked his grandmother, "Do you see him?" His eyes were huge and frightened, pleading with his grandma to see and understand. "He did the same thing with me," Peggy added, describing how the toddler would stand and point a trembling finger. The adults could only stare at the empty corner. Was there really a man there? If so, who was he? Why was his hand blue?

Peggy did her best to listen to Caleb when he talked about the man. Even as she reassured him, she did not want to dismiss his fears. What if there *was* someone there? She did not want to make her child feel worse by alienating him. She tried to strike a fine balance between not feeding the fear and supporting her belief in Caleb.

Things got worse. Barely a night passed when the family slept without interruptions. The toddler's midnight screams became part of the routine. Peggy did her best to comfort her child, but it scared her to see him so frightened that his little body shook. Finally, Caleb refused to enter the house when they returned from the grocery store, and Peggy knew she had to act. "I phoned the minister from the church I attended when I was twelve," she said. "I thought of him because he was an enormous man, six foot five. I was scared, and I wanted someone big."

Her minister put her in touch with another minister who lived in her area. "His name was Leon. He and a deacon from his church met with us. We went through every room of the house together and prayed that it be cleansed of the spirit. We left Caleb's room for last."

When they approached the little boy's room, Caleb stood hesitantly in the hallway and latched onto Peggy. He watched solemnly as the men prayed. Halfway through the prayer, Caleb looked up at his mom and announced, "He's gone now."

"It was slow going," Peggy confided, "but he *will* walk into the room now. I switched bedrooms with him, and he's doing fine." Though Caleb does not want his old room back, he is a happy little boy again. Peggy is still curious about the identity of the mysterious stranger with the blue hand, but she has not researched the history of the house because, as she explained, "I'm too afraid of what I might find out."

It's not just houses that are haunted! Anything or anyplace that was important to a person in life could attract them after death. Researchers have gathered evidence supporting the theory that haunted places are most often associated with deaths that occurred there. In many instances, however, ghosts appear in places that were not the sites of their deaths but were meaningful to them in life. In the following case, a pair of sad little spirits have a puzzling attachment to something that may or may not be connected to their deaths.

### Ghost or Night Terror?

While experts agree that sightings by children should not be dismissed, parents should consider all possibilities. For instance, a scream in the night may signal a night terror. A night terror is an abrupt arousal from slow-wave sleep (stage three or four), most often early in the night. It is most common in young children and is frequently marked by a terrified scream. The child can appear to be awake and may be violent, but later will usually have no recollection of the experience. Parents who suspect their children are suffering from this sleep disorder should consult a physician, as the episodes can be harmful for kids—or adults—who unknowingly put themselves in dangerous situations.

# The Lonely Ride

It was the early 1980s when Mike Ball took his four young daughters to ride the carousel in Portland, Oregon, at the Jantzen Beach Mall. Ages two through ten, his girls were well behaved as they waited in line for their turn to mount a majestic animal aboard the historic carousel. Two other children, however, were *not* so well behaved. In fact, they were so naughty that Mike found himself getting annoyed as he watched them playing on the merry-go-round.

"I thought they were the children of the operator," remembered the letter carrier, who lives in Portland with his wife, Pat. "They were unruly, but she didn't pay any attention to them. They were running around in the middle of the carousel, in the machinery," he said, explaining that the mechanical workings were housed in a cylinder in the center of the merry-go-round. It looked like a dangerous place to play. An open door allowed visitors to peer inside, and from his place in line Mike could see the naughty children playing in there.

The boy appeared to be about ten and the girl around eight. Mike was struck by their odd clothing. "I thought they were foreign," he said. "Their clothes looked like they were from the 1920s. The boy wore knickers, and the girl wore a dress." It did not occur to Mike that the two were ethereal beings. Over fifteen years passed, and he did not give the encounter much thought until he began exploring a favorite hobby—*ghost hunting*. He set up a website, devoted to haunted places in Portland. And then one day, he opened an email that sent a chill skipping down his spine.

"*. . . I was wondering if you've ever heard of any sightings at the carousel up at Jantzen Beach,*" wrote Sarah Robinson. She explained that she had been researching, trying to learn if there had ever been an accident on the carousel, as she had seen the ghosts of two children playing on it. "*. . . When I was a small child, I saw two children, a boy and a girl, playing in the center of it through an open door . . .*" She went on to say that they were dressed in 1920s attire, and she had seen them several times, but only when the door to the machinery was open.

"It wasn't until I got that letter from Sarah that I *knew*," Mike Ball told me. He cast his memory back and tried to recall details as I grilled him. After so many years, he could not remember the color of the children's hair or exactly what he'd heard them say. He remembered that they whispered to each other. "Every once in a while, they'd stop and gaze off to the right, as if they were looking for someone," said Mike. I asked him if his daughters had seen the mysterious children too. "I don't think they did," he said. His girls are grown now, the youngest twenty-two. "They've seen my website and know the story, but they don't remember seeing the children."

While Mike's children are now adults, the two otherworldly children will never grow up. According to Sarah, the little ghosts were recently seen by her young son. "*. . . When I moved back to North Portland, my husband and I took my oldest boy on the carousel a few times,*" read her posting on Mike's website. "*He was about one and a half. He liked it when the doors were closed and screamed if they were open, so we stopped taking him there. I didn't tell my husband a thing until last week when I took my son, alone, on a ride. He just turned three and he talks a LOT. While we were waiting for the ride to begin, I noticed that we were* *directly in front of the open door. I got a shiver, and my son looked up at me and said, 'There's kids under there, Mama.' I said I knew, and he said very seriously with some fear in his eyes, 'I don't want to go under there . . .'"*

When I spoke with Sarah, she described the scenario she'd witnessed as a child in the exact way that Mike had. Unaware of his description, she, too, remembered that the boy wore knickers. "Mike said the boy wore knickers when he saw the children twenty years ago!" I told her.

"It's funny that he saw them twenty years ago," she said. "That was around the last time I saw them—when I was eight. I saw them about three times—but only when the door to the machinery was open. The first time I saw them, I was three or four, and I didn't like it. When I was eight, they wanted me to join them. That's what I felt. They would stare me down. I always picked the outside horse because I didn't like to be close to them." Each time the carousel horse glided past the open door, Sarah glanced down and saw the solemn faces of the two odd children peering up at her.

She first visited the carousel with her mother and her little brother. When she tried to tell her mother about what she'd seen, her mother said, "You're pipe dreaming." But Sarah knew she wasn't dreaming. The children were as real and solid-looking as everyone else she had seen at the mall that day, but there was something disturbing about them. She somehow sensed they were not of this world.

"The girl had long brown hair, and she may have been wearing a big, white bow," she said, as she tried to recall details from the long-ago sighting. "I think the boy was wearing suspenders and a white shirt and a flat hat. They were always huddled together and turned away from me when I first saw them. And then they would look at me."

When her young son, Benjamin, said he saw the children, Sarah looked for them. "I could feel them, but I couldn't see them," she said. She knows the exact day—February 28, 2001. "It was the last free thing Benjamin would get to do because he was turning three the next day," she remembered. "He was really upset when we got home and wanted to talk about the kids. He felt really sad for them." Sarah questioned him carefully to see if he would describe the same thing she had seen years before. "How many children did you see?" she asked.

"Two."

"Two boys?"

"No," said Benjamin. "A boy and a girl. They wanted me to play with them."

"Did they say anything to you?" asked Sarah. His little voice quivered as he answered sadly, "They got hurt, and they can't leave. They're stuck in there. The girl said, 'Don't throw him!'"

I asked Sarah what it was that had bothered her and Benjamin so much about the sighting. "What did you feel that was so upsetting?"

"Maybe it's the loneliness," she answered carefully, pointing out that she felt the two little souls are very alone. "It is a heavy, *heavy* feeling—a trapped feeling."

Who are the ghosts who haunt the old carousel? It was built in 1921 at the factory of the C. W. Parker Amusement Company in Leavenworth, Kansas. At least one historian insists that the exquisite machine operated at the Venice Beach, California, Pier from 1921 to 1924. If indeed the carousel was there, my research indicates it would have operated adjacent to the roller coaster. Interestingly, old newspaper articles report numerous fatalities on the coaster, some which occurred while the carousel was there.

Most of the people killed during this time appear to have been teenage boys who stood up during the ride and were thrown to their deaths. *Thrown.* That is the word articles usually use to describe what happens to victims when they are catapulted from a coaster car. It brings to mind the thing that Benjamin had heard the spirit child say, *"Don't throw him!"*

Is there a connection between the people killed on the coaster and the ghosts of the Jantzen Beach carousel? Possibly. I do not have all the history of the accidents on the Venice Beach Pier. Confused souls who died there could very likely have attached themselves to the merry-go-round. Or is it possible that the two children were thrown from the pier? Could they have been drowned by a suicidal parent who joined them in the ocean? Was the girl speaking to her mother or father when she said, "Don't throw him"?

One report says that the carousel was in a major fire there in 1924. The notorious 1924 fire, however, occurred not on the Venice Pier but on the Ocean Park Pier, less than a mile away. Was anyone harmed in the fire? Perhaps a boy and a girl? After the fire, the merry-go-round spent several years in storage before it was moved to the Jantzen Beach Amusement Park in Portland in 1928.

The 123-acre park was a focal point of fun for folks from miles around. With ballrooms and swimming pools and a funhouse and rides, the park entertained the crowds until 1970, when it was shut down and razed to make way for the Jantzen Beach Mall.

A death on the Big Dipper roller coaster reportedly contributed to the demise of the park. After the park closed, the carousel was set up in the mall, where it operated until 1995, when it underwent a half-million-dollar renovation. It is now the pride and joy of the new Jantzen Beach Supercenter. Some visit for nostalgic rides on painted ponies of the past, while others scrutinize it, hoping for a glimpse of the spectral children.

At least one carousel operator is unhappy with the idea of ghosts. When Mike posted Sarah's story on his website, he got an email from an angry woman who said that the reports were nonsense and that she is annoyed when visitors ask her about the ghosts. "She said she's worked there for years and has never seen anything," said Mike, who did not bother to respond to her *or* to tell her that he himself had witnessed two very unusual children playing on the merry-go-round. Somehow, he didn't think she'd be convinced.

We can only speculate on why some people see ghosts and others don't. Children and sensitive adults tend to see ghosts more than others. A leading theory is that these perceptive people have an ability to see into the Other Side in the same way that a musically talented person can identify a note or an artist can draw an accurate sketch. As so few people can actually see the ghosts on the Parker carousel, it must indeed feel lonely for the little stuck spirits, as Sarah Robinson sensed. It's no wonder that they ask those who *can* see them to come and play!

## — *Update* —

The case of the sad little ghosts on the Parker Carousel first appeared in my book, *Ghosts Among Us*, in 2004 and is one of the most intriguing I've come across. It initially fascinated me because I couldn't imagine anything disastrous occurring on a merry-go-round that could result in a fatality to explain earthbound spirits. In my mind, carousels were charming relics from the past, beautiful and romantic, but not dangerous. They were *kiddie rides*, suitable for small children.

I've continued to research, however, and realize my perspective was naive. It's now possible to find billions of historical newspaper articles online, and

*The forlorn spirits of two children have been spotted on the historical Jantzen Beach carousel. Only those with a keen sixth sense seem to be able to see them. (Leslie Rule)*

when a researcher enters the right combination of search terms, they can find eye-opening information. I recently spent weeks combing archives, learning everything I could about the history of merry-go-rounds, their manufacturers, and the C. W. Parker Amusement Company in particular.

I was shocked to learn that horrific accidents on carousels have occurred all over the world, the worst in the late 1800s and early 1900s before safety was a priority. Some of the most gruesome deaths involved maintenance workers. In one incident that was so ghastly it would make horror writer Stephen King shudder, an electrician was working on a carousel engine at the Steeplechase Pier in Atlantic City while the ride was in motion.

It was June of 1918, and Matthew Hand, age twenty, was out of view of the operator and riders when his clothing got caught in the cogs, and he was pulled into the machinery. His shouts for help were drowned out by children's laughter and the cheerful music of the pipe organ.

Passengers got on and off, and the carousel continued to revolve for quite some time before the operator noticed it was becoming sluggish. He investigated and discovered the dead man. Carousels were a lucrative business, however, and unsavory incidents were swept under the rug.

The big names in merry-go-round manufacturing included Herschell, Spillman, Dentzel, Looff, and, of course, Charles Wallace Parker. The circling menageries were extremely popular a century ago, with Coney Island boasting over twenty different machines operating simultaneously.

Charles Parker went into business in the late 1800s and was so successful that the media crowned him "Carnival King." In addition to producing hundreds of carousels, his Kansas factory manufactured all kinds of amusement park equipment, including Ferris wheels and shooting galleries. His creations were used by both traveling carnivals and permanent parks all over the world.

Historians have noted that it's sometimes difficult to determine whether early machines were manufactured by Parker because he signed his name to each carousel he did repair work on. When he made his own merry-go-rounds, he instructed his carvers to create "flying horses," designed with their legs in an outstretched position, so that they were easy to pack up and move for travel.

While Parker carousels dominated the Midwest, they can be found throughout America. Sometimes he recycled parts, including carved horses from broken-down merry-go-rounds.

As for the haunted carousel in "The Lonely Ride," while it was built in 1921, some pieces could have come from machines that met disaster. In some cases, these recycled parts may originate from merry-go-rounds created by his competitors.

I suspect that the spirits attached to the haunted Parker carousel didn't result from accidents when the ride was on the California piers or during its decades at Jantzen Beach but instead were connected to trauma on *other* machines. When the ill-fated machines were discarded, parts were reused for repairs, and haunted pieces may have ended up on the Jantzen Beach carousel.

While scrutinizing dozens of news accounts of fatal accidents on merry-go-rounds, I looked for incidents that could fit the scenario of the haunting of "The Lonely Ride." I searched for accidents in the Midwest where the Carnival King ruled, accidents involving children, and accidents that occurred in the early 1900s. In addition, I had my eyes peeled for anything involving victims "thrown" from the ride because of the words spoken by the little ghost to the toddler on the Jantzen Beach ride.

I found several incidents that fit, including one that occurred in Evansville, Indiana, in June 1903. A short circuit caused a carousel at an amusement park to pick up speed, and it began churning so fast that in order to rescue the children, the operator plucked them off the wooden horses and threw them off the ride. The whole carousel spun so fast that the horses flew off. Some kids were severely injured, and one news account reported fatalities. I can't say for certain that the Evansville incident is connected to "The Lonely Ride" haunting, but it's something to consider.

In 2012, Jantzen Beach's Parker carousel was dismantled and put into storage. It was donated a few years later to Restore Oregon, a nonprofit preservation group. Plans are currently in the works to find a new location for the treasured relic. Whether or not the ghosts are still attached, time will tell.

# 2

## IT'S A SCREAM!

What is it that is so especially creepy about a haunted amusement park? Perhaps it is the fact that these places are supposed to be about fun and laughter—places where young romance blossoms in the "tunnel of love" and where families enjoy caramel apples and big wads of pink cotton candy and make happy memories on the merry-go-round. The thrills at amusement parks are supposed to be just that. Thrills. Yes, youngsters like to be scared silly on rides, but they don't expect to actually *die*.

The International Association of Amusement Parks and Attractions recently reported that the chances of being killed on a ride are 1 in 760 million. Statistically, folks are safer on a roller coaster than driving on the freeway. Yet with the millions of people who indulge in thrill rides, the rare mishaps do occur.

Disaster eventually strikes almost every amusement park. Odds are, you will have a great time and leave intact. But not everyone does. Accidents happen, and some thrill seekers *never* leave. Oh, their bodies may be ferried away and laid to rest, but their spirits remain behind where they sometimes give unexpected thrills and chills to others who are just like they used to be. *Alive*.

The longer an amusement park is in business, the greater the chance it will see tragedy. In the following story, a destination designed for fun has had 130 years to experience both good times and bad. The dark days were rare and happened so long ago that most of those who remember are long dead, leaving only the restless spirits to remind us.

# Ghosts on the Lake

It was dusk on a cold October evening in the year 2000 in Conneaut Lake, Pennsylvania, as Bonnie and Regis Easler waited for the last guest of the season. As managers of Conneaut Lake Park's historic Hotel Conneaut, it was their job to tuck the rustic old building in for the frigid winter ahead. A chill wind blew off the lake, and dark clouds smoldered in the sky. A storm was coming.

The nearby rides had stopped twirling, churning, and rolling. The excited shrieks of the passengers had faded with the summer, and the scent of cotton candy was now a sweet memory. The amusement park was empty, and the icy fingers of winter were creeping in. Bonnie shivered and stepped inside. She was in the lobby when she heard music. "We don't have TVs or radios in the rooms," she told me. "So I figured the guest must have arrived and brought his own radio."

She headed down the hall toward the music. As she got closer, she recognized the tune as an old-time waltz, and it was coming from the ballroom. The huge sliding door to the ballroom was slightly ajar, so Bonnie peered in. She was stunned to see a couple dancing. "They wore old-fashioned clothes," she said. "The man's suit had tails, and the woman wore a gown, and her hair flew out behind her." The apparitions' profiles were sharp and clear, yet they were as colorless as an autumn mist.

Curious, Bonnie slid open the door for a better look. "The door made a big clunking noise," she said. And with the shock of the sound, the scene ended. The couple dissipated like two puffs of smoke in a breeze. Bonnie was both shaken and excited. In her many years at the hotel, she had heard stories about the ghosts there, but until now had never seen one. Moments later, she had yet *another* paranormal experience. "I was outside with my husband and a friend, and I noticed that a second-floor window was open."

As raindrops started to spatter around them, Bonnie said, "The bed will get soaked!" Her friend had never seen the rooms, so the three trooped upstairs. Bonnie slid the window down and locked it. Back outside, they looked up and saw that the window was wide open, its curtain flapping in the wind. "Our friend left and refused to come back!"

*Restless spirits roam the grounds of the Hotel Conneaut. (Leslie Rule)*

*The Hotel Conneaut deck looks out over the lake. If you visit, enjoy the view, but beware—someone could be looking over your shoulder. (Leslie Rule)*

Western Pennsylvania's Conneaut Lake Park opened in 1892 as Exposition Park and was once *the* destination for excitement-seeking travelers. Forty-five miles south of Erie, it was *more* than a park—it was a *city*. Visitors could arrive by train from a number of places and had their choice of over a dozen hotels within the park.

In the 1930s and 1940s, big stars such as Doris Day and Perry Como started their careers with nightclub performances there. (Before he was famous, Como worked cutting hair at his uncle's barbershop in the Hotel Conneaut!) Today the park is rich with charm but poor on the funds needed to run it. It is owned by the community, and volunteers are scrambling to save it from demolition. Conneaut Lake Park and its remaining hotel are favorite places of those who visit for the nostalgia and some who visit for the *ghosts*!

Bonnie is just one of many who have experienced ghosts at Conneaut Lake Park. In fact, others have described the exact scenario of the dancing couple in the ballroom. In addition to seeing apparitions at the hotel, people have witnessed objects floating in midair and heard phantom footsteps and crying. Dozens say they have seen the specter of Elizabeth, and area people are aware of her legend. The story goes that she was a lovely woman whose wedding took place at the hotel. On her wedding night (or sometimes on the night *before* the wedding, depending on who is telling the story) a fire ravaged the hotel, and poor Elizabeth was trapped. Her husband escaped harm, but his bride perished.

Archive searches have yet to validate this, though the park has suffered fires, including one in 1908 that gutted a major part of the midway and destroyed four hotels within the park. The Hotel Conneaut lost 150 rooms in an April 1943 fire. Was there a bride killed in that fire? Or was that story born out of imagination? Perhaps concocted to explain the many sightings of the ghostly woman who wanders the hotel's halls?

Hotel management points to countless reports from guests and employees who have spotted the ethereal lady. Some say she steps out of the wall that once opened to a hallway in the part of the hotel that burned. Clad in dated clothing, she glances around as if lost before she vanishes. Perhaps there really *was* an Elizabeth. No matter her name, witnesses insist a ghostly lady haunts the halls of the Hotel Conneaut.

## — *Update* —

Through my continuing research, I discovered that a woman *did* die in a fire in one of the hotels inside of the Conneaut Lake Park, but she was elderly, and the hotel was on the other side of the park. If the ghost who stalks the halls of the Hotel Conneaut is not that of a honeymooner killed in a fire there, then who is she? Witnesses often describe the apparition's long white dress, and because of that, many assume she was a bride. In the year 1912, however, the typical warm-season apparel for ladies often consisted of long, summery dresses made of flowing, white fabric. It was just the sort of dress that Miss Lillian Gustafson would have chosen for a romantic ride in a boat on a July night.

The Conneaut Lake Park was home to Lillian, twenty-one, and her friend, Alda Robinson, twenty-four, that tragic July in 1912. A Pittsburg employment agency arranged for the ladies to waitress at the Hotel Virginia, the little sister hotel to Hotel Conneaut. The Virginia was directly behind the lakefront Conneaut and under the same ownership. In newspaper advertisements, the hotels were promoted together as the largest in the park, with Conneaut accommodating five hundred guests and Virginia with enough space for three hundred. The buildings resembled each other, with squared cupolas gracing the corners of their roofs. Guests and employees of the Virginia could take a shortcut to the lake by walking through the lobby of the Hotel Conneaut.

One evening, Lillian and Alda were invited to go on a boat ride after work with two young men. It sounded deliciously refreshing after waiting on guests all night in the stiflingly hot restaurant. Mckinney Ouffutt and William King were members of the Knights of Pythian Camping Club and were staying nearby. A cool breeze blew across the lake as the small boat left the shore under the rowing power of William, who had control of the single pair of oars.

It was about 9:00 p.m. when they set out, and the group of four must have been enjoying themselves because they were still on the lake at 1:00 a.m. when they noticed their feet were getting wet. A leak had sprung in the rented skiff, and cold water was seeping in. The men used their caps to scoop out the water, but the boat filled faster than they could bail. Panicked, the ladies shrieked and leapt to their feet. It was the wrong thing to do. The boat overturned, dumping everyone into the lake.

Only McKinney knew how to swim. He swam toward shore, desperate to get help in time to save his friends. But he became exhausted and wasn't sure if he could make it. He was just about to give up when his feet touched the lake floor. He was cold and wet, but alive.

The others were not so lucky. William must have been terrified as he clung to the side of the boat in the darkness. He couldn't see the ladies, and they didn't answer when he called out to them. McKinney would later comment that the women hadn't tried to save themselves, but they were at a disadvantage because of their outfits. Their long skirts became waterlogged, and the weight dragged them down to their deaths. It looked as if only the men would survive the boat ride.

Matt Keck, a nearby resident, heard King yelling for help. He jumped into his boat and rushed to the rescue. As he drew near, he saw the silhouette of William, clinging to the overturned skiff. "Hold on!" Keck called to him. But William panicked and lunged toward Keck's boat before his rescuer was close enough to grab him. William sank like a stone. At 8:30 the next morning, a recovery team with grappling hooks discovered the three bodies within thirty feet of shore.

Over the years, many have described the apparition of the lady in the long, white dress. Sometimes she manifests in the mirrors, and sometimes she is seen headed down a hallway, her feet not quite touching the floor as she floats along. Either Lillian or her pal, Alda, could be the lady in white seen in the halls of the hotel they had once used as a shortcut to the lake. They worked together, they played together, and they died together. Yet, the ghost is always alone.

If the spirit belongs to one of the drowned waitresses, she may be trying to find her way back to her quarters at the Hotel Virginia. She perhaps takes the same shortcut she did in life, moving through the lobby of the Hotel Conneaut. When she reaches the back door, however, she must be very confused, for her hotel is long gone. It burned down many years ago.

Where did the story of a fatal fire at Hotel Conneaut originate? The legend may have started to take shape in the spring of 1936 when a hotel manager lost his father in a fire in the park. When Maurice Duncan Bigelow, thirty-two, was appointed managing director of the Hotel Conneaut in the winter of 1935, newspapers reported that the Pittsburgher was the youngest hotel manager in Pennsylvania. Any joy he felt over the honor went up in smoke a few months later on May 1, when he woke in the middle of the night to a horrific scene.

Maurice and the other resort managers were staying in summer cottages in the park as they prepared for the busy season ahead. In a cottage next to Maurice's, Conneaut Lake Park auditor Donald J. Macdonald, thirty, was wrenched from a sound sleep by the noise of a crackling fire. He smelled smoke and realized the place was on fire. His first thought was for his roommates, William Adam Kleeb, fifty, vice president and general manager of the resort and Arthur Herbert Bigelow, sixty-six. Arthur was the resort's assistant manager and father of Maurice.

Macdonald told a reporter, "I shouted to the other two men and tried to get into Bigelow's room but was cut off by the flames. Then I groped my way to the stairway, plunged down, and found the first floor all ablaze. I ran outside and spread the alarm."

Park superintendent Clyde McAdoo, thirty-six, heard the cries for help and made a heroic effort to rescue the men. He placed a ladder against the cottage, wrapped a coat around his head, and entered via a second-floor window. McAdoo struggled to fight his way through thick smoke and flames as he searched for the men but was overcome by heat and forced to retreat.

The fire was blazing so brightly it lit up the room where Maurice slept in the cottage next door. The light woke him, and he rushed outside, stunned to see his father's place on fire. Maurice broke down a door and knocked the glass from a window, desperately looking for a way into the burning house. "The cottage seemed to be a mass of flames, and it was futile to attempt to enter," he told a reporter. "I thought perhaps my father had escaped, but after a search of the place, we decided they were lost."

Authorities determined that the fire was sparked when a woodstove over-heated in the kitchen of the nine-room house. At first it was believed that the two men perished in their sleep, but when the bodies were found, firemen realized that Bigelow had tried to escape. One account said that his body was found leaning on the windowsill of an open window in his upstairs room.

Did the spirits of William Kleeb and Arthur Bigelow linger in the park where they worked and died? *Maybe.* Other deaths that occurred there that might account for earthbound spirits include the case of Dr. Cornelius Edward Van Horn. He was a well-known physician from Pittsburg, staying at Hotel Conneaut in June of 1907 when he died suddenly and mysteriously. One night, he retired to his room, only to be found dead the next morning. His lifeless body was discovered outside in his robe, with rain pouring down upon him.

While he was only thirty-nine, Van Horn had been in poor health and had sought a restful vacation at the hotel because of that. The investigators theorized that he became restless during the night, stepped out of his window onto the porch, and tripped over the low railing. Dazed from the twelve-foot fall, he wandered aimlessly and ended up about three hundred feet south of the hotel. An autopsy revealed that he had suffered a concussion and cerebral hemorrhage, injuries that likely resulted from a fall.

Is Van Horn the ghost found rummaging through dresser drawers in the middle of the night? He may still be in a daze and confused about where he is.

Another candidate is sixty-nine-year-old Dan Williams. He, too, had been in poor health but seemed to be doing better. It was mid-August of 1919 when he dropped dead right in front of the hotel. This type of sudden and unexpected death sometimes leads to paranormal activity.

# Friction in the Kitchen

The Hotel Conneaut's downstairs restaurant, Steak on the Lake, is home to the ghosts of two chefs who have been seen frequently over the years. Witnesses have reported a spooky scenario played out in the kitchen. The scene, they say, materializes before their eyes as two men in chef uniforms fight, tossing pots and pans and knives at each other.

During my visit, I was walking up the stairs when I met a group of young women who were coming down, and we began talking. When the conversation turned to ghosts, they shared a startling encounter that they had had weeks earlier on one of their frequent stays at the hotel. Liza Shaftic, seventeen, Jennifer Hamett, twenty, Larissa Stefano, nineteen, and Nikki Jo Piccirillo, eighteen, all from New Castle, Pennsylvania, had been out late on a July night in 2003.

They returned at about three o'clock in the morning and entered through the hotel's backdoor, which took them past the closed restaurant. They glanced through the window and saw a chef. "We all stood there and just stared at him as he stared back," said Liza, shivering at the memory. "He was sitting at a table next to the hostess stand right through the main doors of the dining room. He looked as if he was writing on a piece of paper."

There was something about his penetrating stare that chilled them. His eyes seemed to bore into them. "After a moment, we realized what we were actually seeing," said Liza. The four stood frozen until, all at once, it hit them that he was not of this world. "We all ran up the steps toward the front desk of the hotel and straight to our room. The next night, we told the desk clerk and two security guards about what we had seen."

The girls were startled to learn they were not the first to see the ghost of a chef. "We knew the hotel was haunted, but it was the first we heard about a chef," said Larissa. On the night they saw the chef, the restaurant had been closed since 9:00 p.m. Employees had locked up hours before. "The security guards told us that they found a broken window in the restaurant the night we saw the ghost," said Jennifer.

Was the mysterious man simply an intruder? That, of course, would be the most logical explanation, if not for the fact the man they had seen was dressed in a vintage chef uniform—complete with a bow tied up at his neck. The girls were insistent about that fact. As I loaded up a plate in the buffet line during dinner the next night, I noticed the restaurant manager rushing by and stopped him to tell him about the girls' sighting. "Do your chefs wear uniforms like that?" I asked.

"No, our chefs don't wear ties," he replied. "And no one is *ever* here that late." Hotel security validated the girls' story. They had indeed reported seeing a man in the restaurant the same night the window was broken. What was the phantom chef writing on that piece of paper? His secret recipe? A suicide note? Since the frightened girls were in too much of a hurry to stop and read, it will remain a mystery.

*Left to right: Liza Shaftic, Larissa Stefano, and Jen Hamett on the pier outside the Hotel Conneaut. They were terrified when they encountered a ghost at the hotel. (Leslie Rule)*

## — *Update* —

I've always thought that the bizarre chef battle witnessed in the Hotel Conneaut's kitchen sounds very much like a "place memory," also called a "residual haunting," rather than an actual spirit sighting. A dramatic event can be imprinted upon the environment and replayed, like a loop of film. In a residual haunting, the "ghosts" seen can be alive and well, living elsewhere, but have left behind a visual of their dramatic moment. This type of apparition can't interact with the living any more than movie actor Clark Gable could interact with a viewer watching *Gone with the Wind* on TV.

When I first researched the Hotel Conneaut, nearly twenty years ago, newspaper archives from the area weren't available to me. The world has changed tremendously since then, and thanks to technology, countless newspapers can now be found online. Though I subscribe to numerous databases, I can't always find what I need to validate a ghost sighting. Through persistent research, I recently discovered something to validate the "Friction in the Kitchen" sightings.

I was astonished to discover the obscure 1908 newspaper article about a fight between two chefs that actually took place in the kitchen at Hotel Conneaut. The men threw cleavers at each other, and it was such a violent fight that it was mentioned in a newspaper—a two-inch column on page two of the *Evening Republican* on July 27, 1908. No one was killed, but the guy who stepped in to try to stop the fight was injured The article read in part, "There was a little excitement at the Hotel Conneaut at Exposition Park" when two chefs "connected to the hotel went after each other with cleavers."

As for the ghostly chef at the table, seen by the four startled young ladies, he, too, could be part of the "residual haunting" and left over from that same dramatic event. My feeling is that he is an earthbound spirit and not related to the chef fight. I'm still searching for news accounts to explain his presence.

# Ups and Downs

Click, click, click, click, click. It makes a sound like a stick running over a picket fence. The rhythm is slow at first and then so fast that it vanishes beneath the shrieks and screams. It is the "song" of the Blue Streak roller coaster. Since 1938, the rhythmic click of the coaster cars rolling over the wooden slats has been "music" as familiar to Conneaut Lake Park visitors as the sweet scent of cotton candy permeating the air.

The Blue Streak roller coaster, a vintage wooden relic that thrills today just as it did in years past, may give riders more than they bargained for. This writer normally avoids fast and furious white-knuckle rides, but for the sake of research I huddled into a car, held on tight, and managed to live through the sharp climbs and terrifying plunges. Though *I* managed to live, not everyone has.

A park historian, who was born and raised nearby, remembered the tragedy on the Blue Streak in the 1940s. "It was during the war," he recalled. "A drunken sailor stood up during a hairpin turn and was thrown out and killed." The sharp turn, he explained, was later softened into a gentler curve to prevent future accidents. Does the sailor haunt the Blue Streak? Maybe so, but I've found no one who has seen his ghost. A Blue Streak ride operator, however, confided he *has* seen a ghost there. A ride was just ending, and the empty coaster cars were shooting toward him, so he could load them up with eager passengers. "The

*A huge clown face grins above the entry to Kiddieland at Conneaut Lake Park. Phantom horses are heard galloping through this section of the park. (Leslie Rule)*

roller coaster malfunctioned," he told me, describing how instead of stopping, an empty car shot past him and disappeared into the "Skunk Tunnel."

The young man went to retrieve it, and the moment he entered the dark tunnel he felt his heart leap into his throat. There, in the middle of the tracks, was a little glowing girl. "She was in front of the car," he said. "She had a long dress on that came to here." He touched his midcalf and added, "I've never gone back into the tunnel since." He shuddered. "I refuse to do it."

*This Blue Streak Roller Coaster operator was shocked to see something unexpected in the tunnel. (Leslie Rule)*

Who was the ghostly child? Did she die on the roller coaster? No records of her have been found. Is she a child who died nearby? She could have lived in one of the homes inside the amusement park. Maybe she was drawn to the roller coaster by the excited energy of passengers.

If you visit Conneaut Lake Park and ride the Blue Streak, make sure you keep your eyes open in the tunnel. Perhaps you, too, will see the Skunk Tunnel girl ghost.

## — *Update* —

Despite the fact that historic Conneaut Lake Park was beloved by the community, and volunteer efforts kept it alive long past its prime, all good things must come to pass. When the COVID-19 pandemic struck in 2020, the park suffered financially. In March 2021, *The Meadville Tribune* reported that a judge approved the cash sale of the bankrupted park, including the hotel and rides, for 1.2 million to Keldon Holdings, LLC.

As of this writing, the Hotel Conneaut is still open for business, but some of the park's rides have been dismantled. The Blue Streak was demolished in January 2022. While the coaster is gone, spirits may linger.

The old roller coaster may have been haunted by those killed in accidents, though I'm still searching for a case of a girl dying on the ride—or any other ride at the park, for that matter. Other roller coasters operated there, including the Scenic Railway that occupied the same space prior to the Blue Streak.

Accidents occurred on the Scenic Railway, but I've found no record of fatalities on that ride. In one close call at Conneaut Lake in July of 1909, *The Pittsburgh Press* reported that "A peculiar accident occurred on the Scenic Railway" when one of the cars "was being drawn up the incline" and it suddenly "turned turtle." The car "raised up and turned over backward, enclosing the passengers and at the same time probably saving them from a dangerous fall." The four passengers, three young women and a man, escaped with their lives but suffered cuts and bruises on their heads and faces.

Scenic railways were common at amusement parks in the early twentieth century until they were replaced by more exciting rides. The Blue Streak was a creation of the Vettel family, famous for the many roller coasters they designed. Their thrill rides were fast, often dangerous, and always popular. The Vettel masterpieces included the Cyclone at Lakeside Amusement Park in Denver, Colorado, the Racing Whippet at West View Park, near Pittsburgh, and the Leap the Dips at Cedar Point in Sandusky, Ohio.

Historians reported that an original Vettel train was restored and used on Conneaut Lake's Blue Streak from about 2002 to 2010. I've yet to determine if that refurbished train originated from another park's roller coaster, perhaps one where a young girl lost her life. If so, Conneaut Lake may have inherited their Skunk Tunnel ghost from another city.

The Blue Streak, however, did not escape the grim reaper's wrath. Newspapers have reported on several deaths on the ride. John Charles Hyde, twenty, stood up on the coaster in June of 1942, in an attempt to grab a package that had fallen out. He was catapulted from the car and landed on tracks below. A Good Samaritan pulled him from the tracks before the approaching coaster could run over him. Hyde never regained consciousness and died three days later.

On a Saturday night in July of 1949, Reed Chester Cramer, forty-three, apparently removed his seatbelt and stood during the ride. He then hit his head on a post and was thrown from the car. His death was instant. Reed was a widower and the father of a fifteen-year-old son. He worked as an automobile painter and was at the park for the annual employee picnic of the Greenville Steel Car Company. Not only did Reed recklessly stand up, but he also released the safety strap, leaving the woman beside him vulnerable. The passengers in the car behind the terrified lady held onto her to keep her from flying out.

While evidence clearly showed that Reed was at fault, another case was controversial. On the Fourth of July in 1946, Harold Oran Thompson, twenty-one, boarded the Blue Streak, fully expecting to exit in the same way. He was wrong. He sat in a car with his friend, fifteen-year-old Neil Fox, who later described what happened. "The car gave a thump and Harold disappeared." He insisted that Harold had *not* unfastened the safety strap and had followed the rules. He was certain that Harold was seated when the accident occurred. Neil swore that when the ride was over, the safety belt was still in place, stretched across the empty spot where his friend had been. The ride operator supported Neil's statement, testifying that he had made certain that every safety strap was in place before the ride started.

Harold's death was especially sad for Neil's sister, Alice Fox. Alice was young, barely eighteen, but she and Harold were engaged to be married. She had been waiting for Harold, seated on a bench next to the Blue Streak. Alice and the friends in their group had enjoyed other rides but were so afraid of the roller coaster that they refused to get on it.

Was this the incident the historian had referred to when he said a drunken sailor was killed when he stood up on the Blue Streak? While Harold was a sailor, and the accident did occur on a hairpin turn, there is no mention of him being drunk in the news reports. The historian I spoke to had probably been confused and blended the details from two different incidents.

# More Conneaut Ghost Stories

Front desk clerk and college student Carrie Pavlik was so fascinated with the ghosts of Conneaut Lake Park that she compiled anecdotes from guests and fellow employees and published them in a seventy-one-page book. The chilling stories she collected include the following ghostly encounters:

- An employee unlocked the kitchen in the Steak on the Lake restaurant one morning and discovered all the brooms and garbage cans lined up in the center of the room.
- A soldier sitting in a tree beside the hotel has been seen countless times.
- A guest was tripped on the hotel stairs by a little girl on a tricycle. Legend has it the child had a fatal accident on those steps while riding her tricycle.
- Guests have awoken to find a "man" rummaging through their things. Before they can confront him, he vanishes before their eyes.
- The phantom trotting of horses' hooves is frequently heard in the park's Kiddieland.
- A gold wedding band once materialized in the change slot of the hotel pay phone. Some say the ring belonged to the ghost of Elizabeth, who died there on her wedding night.

## — *Update* —

Many have claimed to see an apparition in a tree, and I did, in fact, find a case of a fatal fall from a tree on the grounds. In April 1915, Ross Breese, age thirty, an employee of the park, was trimming a tree when he lost his balance. He fell forty feet and was knocked unconscious. His injuries were serious and resulted in his death, though he survived for a few months. He was partially paralyzed, and his feelings of regret were intense. His spirit may have returned to the tree as he tried to relive the moment that destroyed his life.

The sightings of the man in the tree often described a soldier. I could find nothing to verify that Ross was in the military. His father, however, was a police officer, wore a uniform, and passed away around the same time that Ross did.

In addition to writing a book about the haunting of Hotel Conneaut, Carrie Pavlik has also led ghost tours there and continues to collect accounts of spirit encounters from credible witnesses. When we spoke on the phone recently, she updated me on the hotel ghost sightings.

I was most intrigued by the case of a mysterious little boy, a forlorn little ghost, seen by several guests. Carrie learned of him years ago when she worked the front desk, her summer job when she was going to school. On three separate occasions, guests confided in her that they'd met a crying boy in the TV lounge, a room near the hotel entryway.

The boy seems to be about five or six, has dark hair, pale skin, and circles beneath his eyes. At first glance, there is nothing to suggest he's not a live human being, nothing to suggest he's not of this world. One couple noticed the boy weeping as he stood behind a couch where a woman was seated. They assumed she was his mother, and it struck them as odd when she ignored the crying child. They wondered why she didn't offer him a kind word or hug.

When the woman got up and left the room without looking back, they realized that she was not his mother. Even so, it seemed cold for anyone to ignore a sobbing child. It didn't occur to them that she couldn't see him.

The couple had children of their own, and their hearts went out to the sad little boy. They wanted to help when the child said, "I can't find my mommy." The father reached out his hand and said gently, "Come on. We'll help you find your mother." But instead of taking the man's hand, the boy did something strange. He disappeared before their eyes. It was only then that they realized he was no ordinary boy. *He was a ghost.*

Two summers in a row, shaken guests told Carrie about meeting the disappearing waif. One year, it happened twice, days apart. A woman was at the front desk, right in the middle of telling Carrie about the ghost boy as another woman came down the stairs, and when she overheard their conversation, she blurted, "You saw him too?"

The two guests had never met, and the stories of the ghost boy were not yet public. Both women had seen the crying boy, and Carrie observed how stunned they were as they compared notes about their encounters. She knew the sightings were valid because multiple witnesses had told her about the ethereal child, and their descriptions were consistent.

In one case, a guest watched as the boy crossed the room and crawled over a chair toward a window as if he planned to climb out of it. It was not dangerous because it was a first-floor window that opened out onto the balcony, but it wasn't designed as a passageway, so the guest attempted to stop him. Once again, the boy vanished.

Who was he? Carrie has two possible names. In one of the ghostly encounters, a guest reported that the child had told her his name was Cody. Had she heard him correctly? If so, had a boy named Cody died in or near the hotel?

Carrie learned about the other possible name for the boy via a psychic medium who visited the hotel. *Michael.* In my search for records of deaths

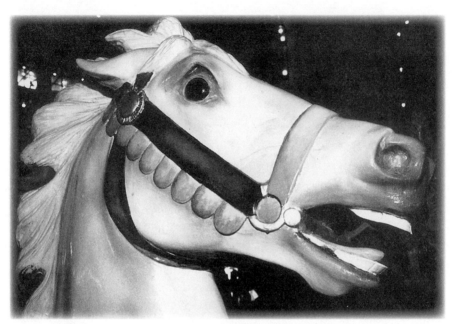

*This carousel horse at Conneaut Lake Park mirrors the spooked expression of some visitors when they encounter something strange there. (Leslie Rule)*

that could connect to the ghost, I have yet to find anything related to the name Cody, but I did find something that connects to a name similar to Michael. The name is actually *McMichael*, and it belonged not to the boy, but to his mother. She was born Mae McMichael in Conneaut Lake in 1904 and spent part of her childhood living on Water Street, near the south end of the lake. She became Mae McMichael Gibbs when she married Murray Gibbs. They had many children, including three who did not survive childhood and a fourth, Rose Marie, who was tragically killed at age 19 in 1949 while riding in a car that collided with a train.

Rose Marie was just a little girl of seven on March 8, 1938, when her family lost one of their own at Conneaut Lake Park. The parents weren't in sight as Rose Marie and her little brother, Frank, frolicked with a group of children. Frank had turned five just four days earlier, and he probably thought he was big enough to look after himself. The grown-ups had warned them to stay away from the water, but somehow, the kids ended up playing on the boat dock outside The Beach Club, a few hundred feet from Hotel Conneaut.

At about 3 p.m., Frank lost his cap. It fell off of his head and into the lake, so he knelt on the dock and tried to reach for it as it bobbed on the waves. Suddenly, he lost his balance, tumbled into the cold water, and disappeared beneath the surface. The frightened children cried for help, and adults came running.

Soon both the Conneaut Lake and Meadville Fire Departments were on the scene. The only sign of the boy was his cap, still floating on the surface of the lake. Rescuers used grappling hooks, and the body was finally located by park superintendent John Hackman. The boy had drifted twenty feet from the dock and had been underwater for over forty minutes. Firefighters administered artificial respiration as a physician injected adrenalin into Frank's heart, but it was too late.

Could Frank be the little ghost seen at the hotel, a child so confused by his shocking death that he's unaware of the passing years? The age matches, but I don't know if the hair color does. Witnesses say that the ghost boy has dark hair, and I'm still searching for a photo of Frank to determine his hair color. I did, however, discover that at least two of his brothers and father had dark hair, so there's a good chance that Frank did too.

If Franklin Donald Gibbs is the ghost seen at the hotel, he did not have to wander far to find sympathetic parents, but unfortunately, *his* parents are long gone. He may be drawn to the historic hotel because it's the last of the big buildings still standing in the park, and it's also a place where families gather. When he sees mothers cuddling their children there, it might spark a longing in the lonely little ghost.

Where was Mae when her son drowned? The news articles didn't say, so we can only speculate. We know she wasn't near enough to grab him when he fell into the lake because the children were alone on the dock. Records indicate that Mae worked as a housekeeper, and I wonder if she was employed as a maid at Hotel Conneaut. Many people in the community found work there, and I would not be surprised to learn that Mae did too. If so, it could have been the last place Frank saw her and the reason he's stuck there. Mae, of course, is no longer there. She died after a long illness at age fifty-one in the summer of 1955.

**Hotel Conneaut**
12241 Lake Street, Conneaut Lake, Pennsylvania 16316
(814) 573-7747
newconneautlakepark.com

---

# More Thrill Rides

### Cedar Point Ghost

Opened in 1870 on Lake Erie in Sandusky, Ohio, Cedar Point is the second-oldest amusement park in America. The seasonal 364-acre park also boasts the biggest collection of rides and roller coasters in the world and was once the site of a legendary haunted carousel. The 1921 Dentzel Carousel traveled from park to park and was moved to Cedar Point in 1971, where it stayed for over two decades. It was there that employees whispered about the ghostly lady who rode it at night.

Artist Shelley Gorny Schoenherr was unaware of the ghost stories when she visited Cedar Point. She was simply fascinated by historic carousels—so fascinated that she made them her favorite subject. Her life-sized renderings in pastels and oils depict carved animals from famous carousels.

Yet as drawn as she is to the marvelous menageries, she cannot explain why one "plain old brownish horse" captivated her two decades ago. "I spent several days in a row, one summer, going back and photographing it," confided the Detroit resident. She had no idea that the one horse that she was so inexplicably mesmerized by was haunted.

*This antique postcard depicts the Midway at Cedar Point where the ghost of a woman in white has been seen at night. She resembles the lady in the forefront.*

"I'd like to say it haunted me," said Shelley with a smile, "but the carving and the stature of the animal simply captivated me. Is this an example of the strange power it has over people? Without knowing a thing about the horse's history, I chose it above all the other magical animals on that carousel. Or did it choose *me*?"

During its time at Cedar Point, the Dentzel Carousel charmed children during the day and frightened employees at night. For it was then, when the lights were turning off and workers were sweeping up, that a ghost mounted the carousel horse. Witnesses swore that the carousel glowed as the specter rode around. The ghost always chose the same horse that Shelley had. It was carved in 1924 by Carl Muller. Witnesses said the ghost was a woman in a long white dress.

The identity of the ethereal lady remains a mystery, though some speculate she may be the wife of the carver. The carousel was eventually moved to Dorney Park. The haunted horse has a place of honor in the carousel museum at Cedar Point. Is it still haunted? If anyone has seen the ghost of a woman in white in the carousel museum, perhaps they will write and let me know!

**Cedar Point**
1 Cedar Point Drive, Sandusky, Ohio 44870
(419) 627-2350
cedarpoint.com

---

## Old Man in the River

The Six Flags over Texas in Arlington is said to be home to many earthbound spirits. Rob Lockhart, who worked there in the 1970s, has never forgotten the excitement among the employees about the ghost sightings. Riders of the LaSalle Riverboat Ride got a thrill they hadn't bargained for when they spotted the specter of a nude old man swimming in the river. He was seen so frequently he was dubbed "the Madman of the Lavacca."

"Every time a swamp rat—that's what we called the river ride employees—would report seeing the old man in the water, security investigated," Rob remembered. "They never found anything. The ride was located in the center of the park, and it would have been very hard for anyone to sneak in and take a dip in the water." According to Rob, another haunting at the park is connected to a man who fell to his death while doing roofing work on the Southern Palace, which was once an amphitheater. "He haunts the theater," said Rob. Doors open and shut by themselves, and toilets flush when no one has touched them.

### Six Flags Over Texas
2201 E Road to Six Flags St, Arlington, Texas 76011
(817) 640-8900
sixflags.com/overtexas

---

## Shattered Grave
Largo, Maryland, is legendary as the site of the haunted Six Flags America, previously known as Adventure World. Some say that the apparition of a child in white has spooked employees there for years. She is rumored to be buried in an old family graveyard on the site. The grave of "Elinor" was marked with a stone that was broken when a bulldozer ran over it, and some think she has been restless ever since.

### Six Flags America
13710 Central Ave, Bowie, Maryland, 20721
sixflags.com/america

---

## Peek-a-Boo
Paramount's Kings Island in Cincinnati, Ohio, has had just a little over three decades to gather ghosts, but it has managed to muster up a few, according to local legend. A blonde girl wearing a blue dress is said to play in the Waterworks, where she startles employees after closing. Just like Elinor in Largo, this ghost is rumored to be that of a child buried there. Her graveyard is supposedly between the parking lot and the campground. Other ghosts there are believed to be people who allegedly died on the Beast and the Octopus.

## Kings Island
6300 Kings Island Dr, Mason, Ohio, 45040
(513) 754-5700
visitkingsisland.com

---

When it comes to haunted amusement parks, the concept is particularly macabre because these places are designed for fun. The deceased are often earthbound because they purchased tickets for rides on gigantic, shiny contraptions that promised *thrills*, not devastating accidents resulting in death.

Accidents, of course, are *always* unexpected. Whether the victims were indulging in entertainment or hard at work at their jobs when disaster struck them dead, their souls are shocked by the trauma. As a result, their ghosts could wander indefinitely.

In the following pages, we'll explore two of America's most astounding accidents to result in earthbound spirits. Each broke records for the number of victims, and while these heartbreaking events occurred a long time ago, the trauma was so intense that restless spirits remain.

# 3

## ACCIDENTS HAPPEN

What happens when another's carelessness causes a death? Are the dead less insulted when their killers didn't mean to hurt them? Probably. Still, fatal accidents seem to account for many earthbound spirits. Reports of hauntings around this sort of tragedy are countless. The popular theory among paranormal investigators suggests that some spirits are so shocked by sudden deaths that they're unable to move on.

While natural disasters can be blamed on no one but a higher power, almost every other type of accident is the fault of someone. Often it is the victim themself. Other times it is a well-meaning person who made an unforgettable mistake. I grew up beside one big, beautiful accident waiting to happen. Puget Sound was so near my home that on stormy days when the waves grew wild, the salty water splattered our windows. When the sky churned, the waves turned a smoldering green as they rushed to crash upon the rocky beach.

On the days when Puget Sound shimmered blue, each white-ruffled wave glinted in the sunshine. Still, it was cold. At fifty-five degrees in the summer, the chill can cause a person to succumb to fatal hypothermia in five minutes. As a teenager, I saw that as a challenge and was determined to swim to the lighthouse on Maury Island, two and a half miles across the sound from my home. I thought of myself as a tough girl who could walk barefooted across barnacle-covered rocks without flinching. I'd done it so often that I had hardened the soles of my feet until they were thick and leathery.

Just as my feet could learn to take the sharp barnacles, my body could adapt to the cold. At age twenty, I acclimatized myself to the icy water by swimming in it daily, adding a few minutes each session until I could remain immersed for over two hours. I planned my swim for the afternoon of a new moon when the tide was the calmest. I coated myself with vegetable shortening to seal in body heat, and with two boats by my side, swam across the sound. Not a fast swimmer, it took me two hours and twenty minutes. Though I was prepared, the average person is not. While many people who live on Puget Sound wade into the waves on hot summer days, only the hardiest fully immerse themselves in the frigid water.

One poor soul took an unexpected dunk many decades ago and now lives on as a ghost of Puget Sound. I learned about him while my mother and I were signing books. A woman came through the line and told us of an eerie encounter. Years before, she and her husband had ventured out in a rowboat, and as they neared the shore of Maury Island, a storm hit, and the water grew wild. They were tossed about as they tried to avoid the big, jagged rocks. Cold water splashed into their boat, and they feared they would sink.

Suddenly, a fisherman appeared, wading toward them. "He grabbed the boat and pulled us in," the woman confided. Once ashore, the man left so hurriedly that they did not see him go. Puzzled, the couple headed up a path to a small store. When they told the cashier about the man who had saved them, she was skeptical. "She told us that that part of the beach was deserted and she had never known anyone like the old man we described."

They mulled over their experience. It had had a surreal quality to it. Their rescuer had appeared and disappeared so quickly it was as if he was a ghost. *A ghost!* They were not prone to fanciful notions, yet they felt in their bones that they had met a ghost. After the woman finished her account, I turned to my mother and said, "I wonder who he was. I don't remember a fisherman dying out there."

"Don't you remember?" she exclaimed. "It was one of your Grandma Doris's favorite stories!" Doris Rule, my father's mother, had lived on the beach many years before. I didn't recall the story, but my mother did. Sometime back in the 1940s, a fisherman had regularly fished in the waters between our beach and Maury Island. An obese woman began to pester him for a ride in his rowboat. He politely turned her down, but she kept asking, until one day he gave in.

Unfortunately, the woman was so big that she tipped over the boat. The fisherman and his passenger were suddenly bobbing in the chill water. The woman's fat saved her life. It provided extra insulation and protected her from the cold. But the fisherman quickly turned blue and was in the fatal grips of hypothermia before rescuers could reach him. While I cannot be certain that the helpful mystery man who saved the couple was the spirit of the dead fisherman, it makes sense that he was. It was as if he were on a mission to save others from his icy fate.

I could not find the name of the lone fisherman lost to the cold, salty water on that long ago day. History has forgotten him. If my mother had not repeated my grandmother's recollection, I would never have known of the nameless man's fate. There is no plaque commemorating his last moments. That is often the case when one or two people die in an accident. When a large number die, however, they earn memorial plaques, planted firmly near the accident sites to remind passersby that tragedies occurred there. In our country's most devastating disasters, there are too many names to list unless the plaques are of gargantuan proportions.

A small plaque on Chicago's LaSalle Bridge acknowledges the tragedy that occurred there over a century ago. It's probably just as well that the hundreds of victims' names aren't listed on the plaque because thieves have been known to steal it, a rather dark souvenir. Those who died in the Chicago River had something in common with the fisherman and the fat lady. One moment, they were comfortable in a boat, and in the next, they were in the water.

# Last Picnic

In a bustling Starbucks coffee shop in downtown Chicago, Illinois, courteous baristas in green aprons served lattes to throngs of businesspeople. As I sipped an espresso, I asked the servers what they knew about the SS *Eastland*.

"The *what*?" they asked. "Never heard of it." The two people I chatted with had lived in Chicago the entire twenty-something years of their lives. They were aware of Al Capone and the gangster wars that made their hometown infamous. Yet they appeared baffled by the mention of one of our nation's largest maritime disasters—a tragedy that took about half as many lives as the *Titanic*. "It happened just a block from here," I explained, but they had turned away to wait on customers.

Saturday, July 24, 1915, dawned as a gloomy day. But the early morning drizzle could not dampen the spirits of the nine thousand folks who swarmed the banks of the Chicago River, waiting to board boats for a much-anticipated picnic. The Western Electric Company had hired four ships to take employees and their families for a day-long cruise to Michigan City. Girls giggled and whispered to each other as they eyed the handsome young men. Mothers pushed sleeping babies in buggies, and boys raced excitedly along the shore as the ships docked beside the Clark Street Bridge.

Jack Billow, fifteen, a deckhand on the *Roosevelt*, glanced up at 7:23 a.m. as the *Eastland* was about to cast off. "My God!" he cried. "The *Eastland* is lurching!" Aboard the lower deck of the *Eastland*, Hubert Boettcher, twenty-one, was visiting with friends when he felt the floor tip. "Move to the other side of the boat!" someone shouted. The young women Hubert had been chatting with laughed, ignoring the command. But as cold water crept over the floor, the giggles turned to shrieks. In the next instant the ship "turned turtle," keeling over on its portside.

As the river flooded the steamer's cabin, several girls clung to Hubert. He grabbed onto a chain of people who were bobbing in the water as they thrust their faces into an air pocket. As he kicked his legs, he felt people struggling beneath him. Hubert gallantly helped several men save panicked females. They pushed them through a porthole where rescuers waited outside. Finally, Hubert climbed through the porthole, saving himself. In all, he had rescued twenty but watched helplessly as many others drowned.

Meanwhile, Jack Billow, too, had joined rescue efforts, at first from a rowboat and then by leaping into the river. Despite the many heroes, there were simply too many people to save them all. The next day's edition of the *Chicago American* reported that the river was "thick with the bobbing heads of passengers." One survivor exclaimed, "I heard the sound of five hundred women and children screaming at once."

It was especially difficult for the women, who were dragged down by their heavy skirts and cumbersome shoes. Some clung to the sides of the boat, tearing off their clothing. Hundreds were trapped *inside* the cabin. Police rushed to find steel saws and electric drills to pierce the steel plates of the ship.

Meanwhile, the river was writhing with hundreds of drowning people. One woman recalled how she was forced to the muddy bottom of the river by the layers of struggling victims above her. As she sank, she was horrified at the eerie sight of baby buggies littering the river floor. With a rush of adrenaline, she managed to fight her way to the surface and survive. Many people escaped the ship by popping out of portholes. One man, too fat to pass all the way through, refused to budge as he gulped precious air. In the death trap beneath him, victims screamed for their lives. Rescuers had no choice. They beat the man until he slid back into the ship, allowing others to escape.

Bodies were laid out in a seemingly endless row along the Clark Street Bridge. Amid the chaos, thieves took advantage of the situation and picked the pockets of the dead. An outraged mob beat up the robbers, and citizens volunteered their automobiles to carry the dead to a makeshift morgue. In the end, 835 lost their lives. The ensuing investigation turned into months of reports of negligence on the part of the ship's captain and crew for overloading the ship and ignoring those who tried to report the problem. These men were arrested but later acquitted.

The July 1915 Chicago newspaper listed the unidentified dead only by number, as they waited for loved ones to claim them:

> *745—Girl, twenty years old, dark brown hair, white waist, yellow skirt, three large bone buttons on front, white gloves, black tie, white stockings, slippers. 53—Woman, thirty years old, 5 feet 5 inches tall, lavender dress, lavender silk hose, black pumps. 396—Boy, eight years old, 4 feet 6 inches tall, brown hair, full face, broad nose, brown suit.*

It took days for some of those numbers to become names. The city mourned when it became clear that *entire* families were lost. *A picnic!* What could be more festive than a picnic on a summer day? Who could have guessed that ladies in lavender who were primping in front of the mirror at six would be laid out in a morgue by nine?

Parapsychologists agree that sudden violent death confuses the soul, that those who pass in such a way are often too confounded to "go to the light."

*A photo of the aftermath of Chicago's most heartbreaking accident appears on a 1915 postcard.*

They become trapped, unaware of passing years, oblivious to changing times. It is no wonder, then, that that long-ago morgue is still swarming with ghosts.

The *Eastland* passengers died before television was invented. If they *are* aware of their surroundings, they surely can't comprehend the nature of the business bustling around them, for the building where volunteers once solemnly brushed out the long hair of drowned women and sorrowfully wrapped children in blankets is now part of Harpo Studios, where Oprah Winfrey produces her TV show.

Harpo security guard Robin Hocott, who worked the overnight watch for three years, told a reporter, "I can say for sure that there are spirits walking the halls." She first suspected something was amiss the night she got an urgent call from a producer working late in her office. "There are people outside my door!" the panicked woman cried. "I can hear them laughing!" When Robin arrived to help, the woman admitted that she had opened the door to see *nothing*, yet the laughter and chatter continued. Others at the studio have reported hearing mournful sobbing, whispering, old-time music, and the marching footsteps of a large crowd.

And then there is the Gray Lady. This mysterious woman has been spotted by several people, once even appearing on a security camera monitor. Some claim that she floats rather than walks. Smartly dressed in a long gown and an old-fashioned hat, she looks as if she is indeed on her way to the picnic.

Time, they say, heals all wounds. It is an empty cliché. If you think about it, it is not really true. Those who were wounded the worst in the disaster—by hearts broken from grief—are almost all deceased. The tiniest babies to survive are now over eighty-six. One unidentified baby boy was found alive in an air pocket of the *Eastland*'s hull eight hours after the tragedy. Is he still alive? If so, he surely still carries the pain of losing his family before he could even know them. As for the other broken hearts, they were not actually mended. They simply, *eventually*, stopped beating.

Time, they should say, *forgets* all wounds! For that is what has seemed to happen, if my poll of the Starbucks baristas is any indication. But if the citizens of Chicago set down their lattes and pry their eyes from their laptop computers and their cell phones from their ears, they may find the past is not really gone—especially if they take a stroll over the Clark Street Bridge on a quiet night.

*Chicago's Clark Street Bridge where the Eastland capsized, killing hundreds. (Leslie Rule)*

Many have been startled there by banshee-like shrieks coming from the river. Luminous figures have been spotted bobbing in the black waters. Richard Crowe, a Chicago ghost hunter for over three decades, told me, "It happens so frequently that the police have become accustomed to the reports." The drowning ghosts appear so real that onlookers rush to call 9-1-1. Rescuers are skeptical because there have been so many false alarms but are obligated to respond. They are, of course, too late.

## — *Update* —

Richard Crowe died at age sixty-four in June of 2012. He was a beloved Chicago celebrity and one of the most requested guests on a long-running WGN-720 Radio show. Richard led ghost tours for over forty years and is missed by many.

Chicago ghost hunter and tour guide Tony Szabelski reports that apparitions of drowning passengers are still seen in the river, often witnessed from the windows of a restaurant near the bridge. Szabelski also noted that paranormal investigators placed recorders near the water on the one-hundredth anniversary of the disaster and captured voices that they at first dismissed as gibberish. After running the recording through linguistics software, however, they realized that the mysterious voices were speaking Czek. Considering that over two hundred of the *Eastland* victims were Czek immigrants employed by the Western Electric Company, the voices captured are astonishing.

* * *

While Chicago claims the *Eastland* as its most devastating accident, Boston's worst was the Cocoanut Grove fire. The tragedies occurred three decades and a thousand miles apart, and each left ghosts in its wake.

# Night on the Town

It was a quiet night at the Radisson Hotel in Boston, Massachusetts. As the security guard performed his routine check of the sixth floor, he paused and looked around. Everything was as it should be. The floor reserved for conferences was still. The doors were all locked. The smiling people with their notebooks and name badges had all gone back to their rooms on other floors. He glanced at the wall, where his own shadow had paused with him. Suddenly, a chill swept through him. *The shadow was walking away without him.*

He spun around to see who had crept up behind him. There was no one there. Who had cast the mysterious shadow? It may have been a confused soul, endlessly wandering the hallways of the Radisson, perhaps looking for the exit. For the hotel now occupies the spot where a popular nightclub once stood and where customers desperately searched for a way out many years ago.

November 28, 1942, was a cold night, but that didn't stop Bostonians from stepping out on the town. Crowds gravitated toward the Cocoanut Grove on Piedmont Street in the city's theater district. The nightclub was the closest thing to a tropical oasis in the middle of a Massachusetts winter. The ceiling was painted to look like a starry sky, and fake coconut trees "grew" between the tables where customers sipped cocktails. With the rattan-covered walls and island-themed drinks, a bit of liquor-fueled imagination could almost make it feel like an exotic place.

That evening it felt balmy. Maybe it was the body heat because the place was so crowded. Customers were jammed close together, good-naturedly jockeying for tables. To some, it was stifling. Many latecomers took one step inside and decided it was too hot and too crowded to stay. They went back into the icy air to find another place to celebrate Saturday night. Those who stayed looked forward to the entertainment. Comedians, singers, and dancers all performed at the Cocoanut Grove.

Entertainers that evening included Buck Jones and Dotty Myles. Cowboy Buck Jones, fifty-three, was a movie star and a veteran of World War I. In town on a war bond-selling tour to aid soldiers in World War II, he was busy doing good deeds. Just hours earlier, he had visited a children's hospital to cheer up his young fans. Dotty Myles was a seventeen-year-old singer. She hoped that her gig at the Grove was the start of an exciting career. Lovely and talented, everyone said she would become a big star.

The club boasted three bars. The Caricature Bar and the Broadway Lounge were on the main floor, while the Melody Lounge and the kitchen were tucked into the basement. At a little after 10:00 p.m., bartender John Bradley called to sixteen-year-old bar boy Stanley Tomaszewski and pointed to one of the palm trees in the Melody Lounge. The lights were out beneath the palm fronds there. The customers seated at the table beneath it had apparently unscrewed the bulbs so that they could sit in the shadows.

Following the bartender's orders, the teenager went to fix the light. As he stood on a chair and peered up at the light bulb, the couple at the table laughed and asked him to leave it dim. That decision, however, was not up to him. He could not see well enough in the dark to tighten the bulb. In the next

instant, he did something that many believe dramatically and irrevocably altered the lives of too many people to count. He lit a match.

It took a moment for the world to turn inside out. Stanley tightened the bulb and left the customers in a pool of cold light. He walked away and looked back to see sparks on the fronds of the tree. He

*An advertisement for the Cocoanut Grove's Melody Lounge depicts the tropical oasis that many unlucky Bostonians sought on a cold winter night.*

figured he could easily extinguish them, but the tree suddenly burst into flames. People laughed as the boy tried to beat the fire out with his hands. Someone threw water on the fire, but it was too late. In a flash, the ceiling was ablaze. Before anyone could react, a ball of fire rolled through the nightclub.

Moments earlier, Dotty had been studying her algebra book as she waited for her turn to sing. When the fire raged, the girl tried to flee, but she was knocked down by a herd of screaming people. Meanwhile, some folks who knew they should leave the burning building figured that there was time to get their hats and coats, and they headed for the cloakroom instead of the exits. It was a deadly detour.

Some people ran toward the kitchen, searching for a way out. A few huddled in the walk-in freezer, a decision that would save their lives. Others managed to squeeze out of the tiny kitchen windows. Cashier Katherine Swett refused to leave her moneybox and stayed put to guard the cash. She was later found dead. A coworker who survived told reporters that he'd begged Katherine to follow him outside, but she was afraid her boss would be angry if she lost track of the money.

As luck would have it, firefighters were nearby extinguishing a car fire and arrived on the scene quickly. They went to work, trying not to think of the charred victims piled up outside the nightclub. When rescuers entered the building, they were startled by the sight of customers sitting calmly at their tables, their hands still curled around their drinks.

What were they waiting for? Why hadn't they fled the club as the others had? But as their eyes adjusted, the firefighters realized that the people were lifeless. Poisonous gases had killed them so swiftly they had had no time to react. They didn't know what hit them.

Theirs were merciful deaths compared to some of the others. Witnesses described beautifully dressed women, shrieking as their evening gowns went up in flames. While many were burned to death, others were trampled by the stampede of panicked people. Some choked on the black smoke.

The Cocoanut Grove was a death trap. Terrified victims funneled toward the doorway, but the revolving doors allowed few to escape. That exit soon became jammed with bodies. The last man out looked back to see the person behind him go up in flames.

The other exits were locked from the outside. Stacks of human beings were found just inside these doors, a sight that made firefighters cry. Rescuers pulled countless people from the building. While some were shuttled to the hospital, the deceased were tossed into piles. In the confusion, a few live folks were thrown into the carnage, only to awaken later to a nightmare.

Within twelve minutes of the time the sparks were noticed, more than 490 people were dead or dying. It was the worst death toll a fire had ever visited upon Boston. Dotty Myles was found crumpled on the floor and carried to safety by a fireman. Her burns required years of medical treatment, including seventeen operations to restore her face. But she inspired many when she continued with her singing career and eventually went back to performing in clubs. Cowboy Buck Jones made it out of the club but was burned so badly that he later died in the hospital, his name added to the growing list of the mortally wounded.

With the public crying for justice, the stern finger of the law was soon leveled at the greedy club owners who had put profit before safety. Each of the accused seemed to have an excuse or someone else to blame. One boy told the truth. With the weight of the grief and anger of an entire city on his young shoulders, Stanley Tomaszewski told authorities that his match may have sparked the fire. Outraged relatives of the dead wanted revenge, and it was feared the teenager could be the next victim of the Cocoanut Grove tragedy. Stanley was put into protective custody.

The cause of the fire has been a great source of debate. Some believed that it was not the match but a problem with the wiring installed by an unlicensed electrician. Others think that methyl chloride gas, used in the club's refrigerator, was a factor in the inferno. Whatever the cause, Stanley carried the burden of the tragedy with him until the day he died at age sixty-eight in October 1994. Though Stanley was never held legally responsible for the fire, at least one bitter person would not let him forget. The cruel anonymous phone calls never ceased.

Club owner Barnett Welansky did not escape unscathed. He was found guilty of involuntary manslaughter and was sentenced to twelve to fifteen years in prison. He later suffered from cancer and was released early to die in peace. Barnett's prosecution was an empty victory for the relatives of the victims. And the new safety laws and medical discoveries in the wake of the fire were not much comfort.

They had no idea how many lives their hapless family members saved. Thanks to the 1942 tragedy, exits in public places are today clearly marked and unlocked from the inside. Doctors used innovative treatments on the burn victims that greatly advanced medical procedures. The information gleaned from the Cocoanut Grove fire has had a positive effect on future generations. Are those who died in the long-ago fire aware that their sacrifice saved others?

Perhaps many of them are aware. Maybe they're in a peaceful place and are glad that they could help other victims. But a few stragglers remain. Shocked and confused, still trying to find their way to safety, they endlessly roam the site of the tragedy. Despite the fact that a luxury hotel, complete with its own theater, has been built on the deadly spot, energy from the horror may remain.

Wendi Clarke, human resources manager at the Radisson Hotel Boston, is well aware of the hotel's haunted reputation. While she has yet to encounter a ghost there, she has heard from those who have. "An employee saw the ghost of a woman on the sixth floor," she told me. The man had been cleaning up after a conference when he saw the apparition. He assumed she was a guest but could not understand where she had come from. The conference floor was locked, and only the cleaning crew was there. "He was really confused," remembered Wendi. The woman disappeared as swiftly as she had appeared, leaving the cleaner with a story he could tell his grandchildren.

Wendi steered me toward the hotel's theater, the Stuart Street Playhouse, which sits in an adjacent building. "Employees have seen the ghost of a man there," she told me. Those working in the ticket booths on the day I visited confirmed that the theater was haunted. Much of the paranormal activity there centered on water, they pointed out. There have been inexplicable floods in the building. And they once found a sopping wet seat. The theater had been vacant, and no one could figure out where the water had come from.

A water faucet on the second floor of the theater is notorious for turning itself on. Why is so much of the paranormal activity focused on

*A plaque marks the site of Boston's deadliest fire. (Leslie Rule)*

water? It's as if panicked fire victims are still trying to extinguish the flames. Other activity includes a disembodied voice, calling out the names of employees who work alone in the theater at night.

Jacques Cabaret, a longtime bar that today features drag performances, served as a makeshift morgue on the night of the deadly Cocoanut Grove fire. A stone's toss from the back doors of the theater, the bar has long had a reputation for being plagued by the ghosts of the victims of the 1942 blaze. Though the employees openly admitted that the bar was haunted, they were tight lipped when it came to sharing their own ghostly encounters. Most of the fire's victims have probably moved on, but the paranormal events indicate that a few ghosts remain.

In the Radisson's restaurant, the Theatre Café, bartender Edward Gormely has sensed their presence. Odd noises, he told me, emanate from the kitchen. One night as he was carrying dirty dishes into the kitchen, he was startled by a sudden pop, accompanied by a flash of light. "It was right in front of my face," he said. He turned to the chef and asked, "Are you messing with me?" But the chef also looked startled. "I don't know what that was!" he exclaimed. The noise had sounded like a balloon popping, and the light was as bright as fire.

The ghostly woman who walks the halls of the Radisson could be any one of the women who died in the Cocoanut Grove. I wonder if she is the spirit of Katherine Swett, the cashier who steadfastly guarded the nightclub's money even as the walls around her went up in flames. Those who knew her said

that she feared her boss, Barnett Welansky, who worried over every nickel. His temper apparently frightened her more than fire. Is she still looking for the cashbox? Is she afraid she'll be fired for losing the money?

*Ghosts have been seen at Jacque's, and some believe that they are left over from a sad night in 1942 when the building became a makeshift morgue. (Leslie Rule)*

— *Update* —

The Radisson Hotel, at 200 Stuart Street, has been replaced by the Revere Hotel Boston Common. The Stuart Street Playhouse is closed. Jacque's Cabaret is still in business, and employees still report paranormal activity.

\* \* \*

In both the *Eastland* and Cocoanut Grove disasters, the trauma gave the recovery teams nightmares for the rest of their lives. In the next account, those trying to help saw things that they wished they could forget. They also witnessed things they could not explain.

# Ghosts of Galaxy Flight 203

It was about 1:00 a.m., January 21, 1985, when Galaxy Flight 203 took off from what is today known as the Reno-Tahoe International Airport. The chartered flight held sixty-five passengers who were headed to Minnesota. Many of them had enjoyed a weekend of gambling in Lake Tahoe during the Super Bowl Sunday weekend. Tragically, the plane crashed in a field shortly after take-off. Seventy passengers and crew members lost their lives.

The lone survivor was a seventeen-year-old Minnesota boy who was thrown free of the burning crash. He was still conscious when he found himself strapped in his seat, on the ground. He unbuckled his seatbelt, got up, and ran away from the plane. Today, the area is covered by retail stores and parking lots. Let's hope that the spirits of the accident victims have been able to move on. That was not the case in the hours following the crash.

Paranormal investigator Debby Constantino spoke with a member of the recovery crew, who was on the site immediately after the crash. As he worked on the grisly task, ghosts of the dead wandered aimlessly through the wreckage. "He wasn't the only one who saw them," said Debby. "He said nearly everyone there witnessed apparitions."

## — *Update* —

I've heard no more reports of sightings of the victims of Galaxy Flight 203. The spirits of the dead have most likely crossed over. As I revisited this story, I was reminded of just how fragile life is. I didn't know any of those lost in the plane crash, but I was friends with the investigator who provided me the details of the paranormal activity, and she, too, died in an abrupt and shocking manner. After Debby Constantino was killed, news reporters noted that she often said, "The veil is getting thinner."

I think that Debby spoke the truth—*her truth*. When we're approaching death, the veil *does* get thinner. In my book *Where Angels Tread—Real Stories of Miracles and Angelic Intervention*, I included cases of dying people who could clearly see angels and spirits around them in the days leading up to the end. This is a common occurrence, and it happens when death is near. (If you are seeing apparitions, however, it does *not* mean you will die soon. Your third eye could pop open for reasons other than pending death.)

Debby was more aware of the Other Side than most people because of her paranormal research. In the last decade of her life, she attempted to communicate with ghosts via electronic devices, and she was amazingly successful with her results.

In the next chapter, we'll explore the art of recording the words of ghosts, commonly referred to as electronic voice phenomena (EVP). I'll also reintroduce Debby Constantino, the EVP specialist featured in stories in two of my previous books. I wish her life had not ended in a scandalous tragedy, and I debated on whether or not to include the cases that she and I investigated together. How could I mention Debby without mentioning her fate? And how could I mention that without upsetting some readers?

While the hauntings I cover often involve tragic deaths, in most of the cases I select the deaths happened a long time ago. I deliberately choose hauntings connected to long-ago deaths, and I tread very lightly when it comes to writing about recent tragedies because I want to be sensitive to those who are grieving. At times, I've decided against including fascinating cases of hauntings because the tragedies connected to them were too recent, and the grief of those mourning was still raw.

While my first inclination was to simply skip over the stories where Debby was mentioned, I realized that she was an integral part of several cases that belong in this book. It would be more disrespectful to her memory to delete her contribution than to just openly reveal what has transpired. Read on to learn about EVP expert Debby Constantino and the various ways spirits speak to us. It might surprise you to learn that ghosts communicate via a device so common that almost everyone in America owns one.

## Proving the Existence of Ghosts

Do we have concrete evidence that spirits survive past the death of the physical body? Do we have definitive proof that ghosts exist? No, according to Dr. Sally Rhine Feather, Director of Development at the Rhine Research Center in Durham, North Carolina. In fact, it was this type of evidence that her famous parents, Dr. Joseph Banks Rhine, and Dr. Louisa E. Rhine, were seeking when they began their landmark research on psychic ability.

"My folks got into their work via wanting to study the survival question but were stymied because no one had done the basic work on psi [psychic] ability on the living," said Dr. Rhine Feather, coauthor of *The Extraordinary Experiences of Ordinary Americans* (St. Martin's Press, August 2004).

J. B. Rhine coined the term "extrasensory perception" (ESP) when he authored the book *Extra-Sensory Perception* in 1934. The Rhines' laboratory studies included testing subjects' ability to sense shapes on cards. The cards, which show a star, a plus sign, a circle, wavy lines, and a square, were created by the Rhines.

Though Dr. Sally Rhine Feather is still "very, very interested" in the ghost question, she stresses that their existence has not been scientifically proven. As her parents before her did, Dr. Rhine Feather collects stories sent to her by people who say they have seen ghosts.

When it comes to proving the survival of the spirit, Dr. Rhine Feather said, "I think it is the most important question we could ask. Even the most skeptical people stop and listen when they hear you are contemplating research in that area."

*Dr. Sally Rhine Feather at the Rhine Research Center in Durham, North Carolina, with a bust of her famous father, Dr. J. B. Rhine, who was known as "the Father of Parapsychology." (Leslie Rule)*

# 4

CAN YOU HEAR
ME NOW?

As I write these words in January of 2022, most of the people I know communicate by cell phone and have all experienced the frustration that comes when a signal is lost, particularly when we're in the middle of an important conversation. When the voice on the other end of a phone call fades, or the person we're talking to suddenly can't hear us, we find ourselves shouting, "Can you hear me now?"

That question is spoken so frequently that a major carrier made it the catchphrase on their TV commercials, advertising their claim that fewer of their calls were dropped. If it's frustrating for us to face these communication challenges, imagine how frustrating it must be for those on the Other Side when they fail at their attempts to be heard. I've collected countless examples of the dead attempting to talk to the living, using the same communication device that we do. *The telephone!*

Readers of my books might recall that my childhood home on Puget Sound was haunted. It was built atop an old graveyard in Des Moines, Washington. My father had grown up in the house, and when my parents purchased it from my grandparents in the early 1960s, our family moved there. My parents remodeled the place before we moved in, and as they worked, they often heard the phone ring. They never answered, but not because they didn't *want* to. They didn't answer because they *couldn't.*

They followed the sound of the ringing to the wall, where the old-fashioned phone had once been mounted. All that remained were a few wires sticking out of the wall. Bell mechanisms are *inside* of phones, not embedded in walls and certainly not inside of wires. My parents were well aware that it was not "possible" for the telephone to ring, because it no longer existed. The old phone had been disconnected, discarded, and was long gone. Bill and Ann Rule knew that the persistent calls came from the Other Side. They weren't frightened but fascinated. If it had been possible, they would have answered the calls.

*Who was calling?* They concluded it was the Reverend William John Rule. He was my father's grandfather, and he had lived in the home when my dad was growing up. My great-grandfather was a kind Methodist minister, and my parents felt he was a benign presence. The novelty of living in a haunted house tickled them, and they relished telling the story of the ghostly ringing to visitors.

While paranormal phone calls were a new phenomenon to my parents, they are not an unusual occurrence. In fact, many people insist that they have received calls from the dead. Most often, the ghostly calls are made by deceased loved ones reaching out from beyond. While an actual *conversation* with a ghost via the telephone is rare, cases of calls made from the phones of the dead are commonplace. This usually happens within days after a death when the recipients of the calls are grieving.

The calls originate from the cell phone of the deceased, yet no living person has access to that phone. The phone in question is usually tucked into a drawer or in a purse, and there is no "logical" explanation

*Reverend William Rule was a kind man, and his benign spirit watched over the author's childhood home.*

for how the call was made. The person receiving the call might answer but usually hears nothing. Sometimes the grieving will receive texts or find voice mail messages from their deceased loved ones. Most recipients of spirit calls are comforted because they perceive this as evidence that their loved ones have survived death of the physical body and that their souls live on.

The dead have been dialing the living since the invention of the telephone, but it was not until caller ID became available that most of us realized that. In June of 2021, the *Washington Post* was among the newspapers reporting on the inexplicable phone calls received by a family with loved ones lost in the horrific collapse of the Surfside, Florida, condominiums. Ninety-eight people died when the Champlain Towers fell in the middle of the night without warning. It took weeks for rescuers to find some of the victims in the rubble. Meanwhile, their anxious families prayed for miracles.

Because I don't know how the family in question feels about spirits and paranormal activity, I'll respect their privacy and not mention their names here. I'll say only that the victims were an extremely beloved and charismatic couple in their eighties and that they lived on the third floor of the twelve-story building. Most likely, they died immediately and did not suffer, but their family didn't know what to think when they received sixteen calls from the couple's landline in the days following the collapse. Each time they answered the phone, they heard only static.

Authorities grasped for logical explanations for the mysterious phone calls but admitted to reporters that they were stumped because the elderly couple's telephone was a landline. The calls could not be explained away as an electronic glitch. The inexplicable calls not only gave the family hope that their loved ones had survived the collapse but also filled them with horror at the thought the grandparents might be trapped, injured, and unable to speak.

The tragedy was devastating, and many died. I was one of the millions of people throughout the world who followed the story of the disaster on the news, praying for the victims and their families. Each day, I woke up hoping that a survivor would be found but became depressed as the death count grew. Days turned into weeks, and rescuers found no living people.

Eventually, it was announced that the rescue efforts had been reclassified as a recovery mission. I felt sad for all involved but was reminded that there *is* life after death when I read the news stories about the phantom phone calls. I don't think there is a "logical explanation" for the calls because I've collected too many cases about this type of occurrence. The calls from the rubble very likely originated with the spirits of the elderly couple, reaching out from the Other Side.

The telephone is not the only electronic device that spirits use to communicate. Paranormal researchers have been collecting electronic voice phenomena (EVP) for decades—long before ghost hunting became a popular hobby in recent years. EVP collectors don't wait around for random conversations with ghosts. They *initiate* communication, and some have gotten amazing results.

I first saw EVP specialists in action when fellow ghost author, Janice Oberding, invited me to Reno, Nevada, to accompany her and paranormal researchers, Mark and Debby Constantino, to haunted sites. At that time, the Constantinos were just beginning to develop an expertise in the collection of EVP. They had met Janice when they attended a ghost-hunting class she taught. Janice liked them and took them under her wing. She went out of her way to introduce them to people in the field who might be able to help them achieve their dream of becoming professional ghost hunters.

When I met the Constantinos in 2006, they were a very attractive couple in their forties with two teenage daughters. Mark was tall and rugged. Debby turned heads with her trim figure, shiny black hair, and eyes that appeared larger than most because of the great care she took applying makeup. Debby confided that she became interested in the paranormal because they'd lost a baby daughter. It was the most painful episode in their past. Confirming the existence of spirits gave Debby hope that life continues on the Other Side and that she would one day see her daughter again.

I found both Mark and Debby to be kind and sincere. We bonded over our mutual love for animals and devotion to our pets. I was so impressed with the Constantinos that I featured them in my book *When the Ghost Screams—True Stories of Victims Who Haunt.* Here is excerpt:

> *When they visit haunted locations, the husband-and-wife team turn on a voice-activated tape recorder and take turns asking questions, posed to whatever entity is within earshot. They then wait for a full ten seconds to give ghosts plenty of time to respond. Sometimes, one of the team will generate white noise, such as that created by a small hand-held, battery-operated fan. They wait, the fan whirring softly as ten seconds drift by.*
>
> *As Debby explains it, the white noise is a sort of raw material, akin to a sculptor's slab of clay. While the sculptor can turn an indefinable lump of clay into a magnificent bust, the ghosts can take the noise of a whir of a fan and mold the sound into words, complete with distinctive voices, inflections, and accents. Though the voices are rarely heard during the actual recording, they are inexplicably on the tape when it is rewound and played.*

The Constantinos and I took trips to several haunted locations, some of which are mentioned throughout this book. They became celebrities, starring on the Travel Channel's reality show *Ghost Adventurers* with hosts Zak Bagans and Aaron Goodwin. Debby and Mark were my friends, but we didn't keep in close touch. One day, it occurred to me that I had not heard from them for quite some time. I figured they were still involved in paranormal research, so I checked YouTube to see if they had posted recent videos. I entered two search terms: Constantino and EVP. A video immediately popped up, and I clicked on it. I expected to see Debby and Mark at work, recording ghostly voices.

I was stunned to realize that the person attempting to obtain the EVP was neither Debby nor Mark. He was a stranger to me, and he was trying to reach the *spirit* of Debby. It was a shock to realize she was dead and more shocking to learn that Mark, too, was gone.

It happened on the last day of the summer of 2015. No one knows exactly how the scenario unfolded, but it started either very late on the night of September 21 or very early on the morning of September 22. A man was killed, apparently because he tried to protect Debby from her husband. James "Jimmy" Charles Anderson was fifty-five and one of two roommates who allowed their friend Debby to sleep on the couch in their Reno apartment after she filed for divorce. The other roommate came home to find Jimmy dead from a gunshot wound to his head. Debby was missing.

It didn't take long to put the puzzle together. It was obvious that Mark had abducted his estranged wife. He'd recently attacked her, and she was afraid of him. Police pinged the Constantinos' phones, tracking them to a relative's apartment in Sparks, Nevada. It was about 11:00 a.m. when they found Mark's car parked outside of that apartment.

Teams from the Sparks and Reno police departments joined forces to evacuate the entire apartment complex and put it on lockdown. SWAT teams were ready for anything and very aware that the wrong move could end a human life. Mark was barricaded inside of the apartment, and hostage negotiators spoke to him on the phone. But it didn't change the devastating fate of the Constantinos.

At one point, police heard gunfire. That was probably the moment Debby's life ended. But no one could be certain what was going on inside that apartment. There was hope that Debby was alive when Mark shouted through the door, "Give me fifteen minutes to gather my thoughts, or I'll kill her!"

At about 1:30 p.m., they heard a single gunshot and stormed the apartment. Mark and Debby were dead. Mark had killed his wife and taken his own life.

How could this couple who had seemed so devoted to each other end up like this? I've heard through the grapevine that Mark became addicted to pain meds after injuring his back. Opioids disrupt the brain circuits vital to impulse control, and this can lead to aggression.

I don't know whether Mark was addicted to opioids, but I prefer to think that the man I knew was not a monster. I prefer to think that the violence originated not with *Mark* but with his *malfunctioning brain*, damaged by the drugs. I'm clinging to the idea that while Mark did an evil thing, he was *not* an evil man.

Because of Debby's interest in life after death, I can't help but wonder what it was like for her when her soul left her body. Was she fascinated to find herself in spirit form? Or was she so distressed by what had transpired that she was consumed by grief for all that was lost? I ask this question with the utmost respect. I'm well aware of the fact that a day will come when *I'm* on the Other Side and that some who crack this book will wonder what *my* ghost is up to.

As for Debby, I hope her spirit is free and that she's been reunited with the sweet soul of her baby. It's possible, however, that Debby is earthbound. The Constantinos were familiar with the theory that brutal deaths result in the most earthbound spirits. They may be lingering in the apartment where they died, so overwhelmed by the violence that they're rooted there. But before we get too upset worrying over souls stuck for decades in the dismal apartment where they died, we should consider that it might feel like a brief moment for them. Time, as we know it, probably does not exist on the Other Side. For a spirit, a century may seem like a fleeting instant.

Whenever we learn that tragedy has struck someone we know, our minds tend to go around in circles as we try to make sense of what happened. When I think about Debby Constantino, a troubling memory continues to surface. I remember her being *afraid*. She became frightened while we were staying in the haunted Oxford Hotel in Denver. Debby not only collected "class A" recordings of spirits speaking but she also *heard* the ghosts in our room with her own ears, without any assistance from electronics. She heard them, and it scared her.

When I remember how afraid she was, I imagine the fear she must have felt when her husband held a gun to her head. In those last panicked moments of her life, she was terrorized by someone she loved.

When Debby heard the spooky, disembodied voices, we couldn't have known that she would one day have something in common with those who had died there. The victims who haunted our hotel room had been shot to death by scorned lovers. Those killers then turned the guns on themselves, just as Debby's husband would do.

In the next chapter, we'll explore haunted hotels, starting with the Oxford where Debby not only recorded the voices of ghosts but also heard them in the night when she wanted nothing more than for them to shut up.

# 5

# OVERNIGHT WITH GHOSTS

# The Oxford Hotel

*Author's note: The following story appears as it did when it was published in my book,* Ghost in the Mirror, *in 2008, when Debby Constantino was still alive. It has not been altered to reflect the tragedy.*

When Denver's Oxford Hotel opened its doors in 1891, the public was amazed by the modern conveniences. Guests could check into rooms on the top floor of the five-story brick building without climbing stairs, because they could ride "the vertical railway." Though the first elevator was installed in a New York building in 1856, it was still a new concept to many Americans in the 1890s. It was a treat to ride to the top floor of the Oxford to view the city. Oxford Hotel guests were also impressed by the luxury of heated rooms and electric lights. By today's standards, the Oxford is clean and comfortable with a charming ambience.

My friends, Debby Constantino and Janice Oberding, and I stayed at the haunted Oxford for a paranormal investigation. When I made the arrangements, I emailed the hotel manager and requested the most haunted room. She quickly responded, securing reservations for us in room 320. She did not offer details of the room's haunting *or* its history. That was fine with me, for as a writer, I prefer to experience things without preconceived notions. Our trio checked into the Oxford with open minds.

*Denver's Oxford Hotel may be the city's most haunted. (Leslie Rule)*

Soon after we arrived, Janice, Debby, and I took a stroll. As we reached Wynkoop Street, Debby said, "It feels like there are tunnels under this street." It was her first time in Denver, and she knew little about the Mile High City, but she had just zeroed in on something significant. While researching archives at the Denver Public Library the following day, I learned that though historians have yet to verify it, they have long suspected a secret tunnel exists beneath Wynkoop Street. They believe it connected the Oxford to Union Station so that important guests could discreetly arrive at the hotel.

Debby is shy about presenting herself as psychic, but she has a keen sixth sense. This may be why she is so successful in recording phantom voices, something that reaps more impressive results when a sensitive is present.

While Debby and Janice were excited about researching the haunted Oxford, they were also afraid. Neither would spend one minute alone in our room. The suite consisted of two adjoining rooms. I slept in the bedroom, and Debby and Janice shared the front room. One day, as I snoozed, they went out, and when they returned, they slipped the key into the lock and were startled by the sound of retreating footsteps.

"That night I slept on the cot," Debby recalled. "Janice was on the couch. I clearly heard two men talking, but I could not make out what they said." She said that the voices seemed to come from two invisible men sitting on the couch. "It freaked me out!" She shuddered with the memory of the eerie mumbling. "A bit later that night, I felt something lightly touch me across my stomach. At that point, I asked Janice if she would sleep on the cot with me."

The spooked pair stuck together, and I explored by myself through most of our stay. My time was dominated by photographing haunted locations and searching library archives, while they concentrated on investigating the Oxford. Janice and Debby roamed the hotel at all hours of the day and night. They carried tape recorders and captured many phantom voices. After they learned that the basement men's room was especially haunted, they slipped downstairs where the lower floor was closed off to the public and entered the large, tiled room. Apparently, the ghost did not appreciate the ladies' intrusion in the men's room, for Debby taped an angry male voice, snarling, "Get the [expletive] out." Around midnight of our second night, my friends were standing at the top of the stairs, above the bell desk, when a shadowy figure darted past them.

Many guests and employees have had ghost encounters at the Oxford. A manager told me about a cleaning crew who reported to her immediately after an unsettling experience. They regularly cleaned the annexed addition to the hotel, where rooms are now used as offices. "As they approached the door to an office, a woman in a white dress floated *through* the closed door," the manager said, adding that the crew was visibly shaken.

I contacted historian Kevin Rucker of LoDo Historic Walking Tours to ask for his impressions. In addition to interviewing witnesses about their ghost encounters, he frequently studies the archives at the Denver Public Library. According to Kevin, a number of restless spirits wander the hotel, sometimes materializing in the mirrors. As guests wash up in the downstairs men's room, they sometimes glance in the mirror and see the reflection of a cowboy. The vestige of the Old West seems to be pacing behind them, but when they turn around, they realize they're alone.

Kevin also told me about the dancing teenager who employees have glimpsed in the ballroom mirror. "She looks to be about fourteen and is pirouetting," he said. On another occasion, the hotel suffered a power outage in the night. A guest staying in a room on the third floor got up to use the bathroom, holding a penlight to find her way. She pointed the thin stream of light into the bathroom and was shocked to see a child perched on the toilet, solemnly gazing up at her. "The girl was about seven years old and wore a lace nightgown."

Infamous Wild West character Bat Masterson lived in room 320 in the 1890s, said Kevin, adding, "He killed a man there." Single men rarely manage to spend an entire night in the room. "If a single man checks into room 320, he will show up downstairs at the front desk in the middle of the night, claiming someone is in his room. Single females and couples have no problems."

There's another story about room 320, though Kevin didn't refer to it. Many claim that an enraged man caught his wife with another man and shot them both dead in the third-floor suite. As a result, room 320 has been dubbed the "Murder Room." This may have really happened, but I've not seen the proof. I did find something that could be the key to the most impressive EVP that Debby Constantino got at the Oxford. It's a female voice, speaking so distinctly that there is no mistaking the words for static. "It is a class A recording," said Debby. She captured the voice in the hallway outside of our room, room 320. The woman's words are clear, and her message is chilling: "I'm sick."

What was the voice from beyond trying to tell us? When I found news of a long ago tragedy, I concluded that the lost soul may have been trying to convey that she was sick in the head. A two-inch column of blocky words, printed over a century ago in the *New York Times* told the story. On Friday, September 9, 1898, a distraught young woman pointed a gun at her lover and pulled the trigger. She then turned the gun on herself. A bullet pierced her broken heart, and she died instantly in her hotel room.

*Debby Constantino holds the voice-activated recording device she uses to communicate with ghosts. While normally excited about capturing the voices of spirits, her enthusiasm gave way to fear when she stayed at the Oxford Hotel. (Leslie Rule)*

They had checked into the Oxford, registering as husband and wife, and giving their names as H. Rockwell from Greeley, Colorado, and Florence Montague from Pittsburgh. The names were aliases. Rockwell was actually William Henry Lawrence, and while he *was* married, his female companion was not his wife. She was later identified as Florence Richardson. She was about twenty-four, and he was forty-five.

William died in St. Luke's Hospital, two days after he was shot. He had a family in Cleveland, Ohio, and owned an interest in Ohio Farmer Publishing, where his brother was president. That brother came to retrieve William's remains. Several brief newspaper pieces told the story. Florence had lived at the Oxford for several weeks and had been planning "an overland trip by wagon" with her "husband." One account described her as a woman "of dissolute character."

Paranormal researchers note a strong correlation between traumatic death and haunted locations. The emotion and violence associated with Florence's demise definitely make her a strong candidate for an Oxford ghost. She may be the ghost who spoke to Debby's recorder. "*I'm sick.*" If only we could hear the whole story that eight inches of fading newspaper print can't tell us.

Did Florence want more than her lover could give her? Did she know he was married? Had she just learned the truth? Was he leaving her? Was she pregnant and suffering from morning sickness? Is Florence aware she is dead? Maybe she feels so odd in spirit form that she assumes she is sick.

Florence's tragedy was not the only one that unfolded at the Oxford. My digging also unearthed another bit of dirt. In the summer of 1937, notorious German-born killer Anna Marie Hahn passed through Denver with her twelve-year-old son and her latest groaning victim in tow. George Obendoerfer, sixty-seven, had been fed an arsenic-laced sandwich by the murderess on the train to the city. She and her ailing victim checked into the Oxford for a brief stay before moving on.

While the poor man soon died elsewhere, he spent some of his last tormented hours in the grand hotel. Thirty-two-year-old "Arsenic Anna" became America's first woman serial killer to fry in the electric chair on December 7, 1938.

While documented accounts of violence at the Oxford Hotel are tough enough to find, odds are that most of the drama there was never recorded—except, perhaps, *by the walls*. If it weren't for the ethereal figures that float through the doors, dance in the mirrors, and wake up the guests, the people who lived and died there would be long forgotten.

**The Oxford Hotel**
1600 Seventeenth Street, Denver, Colorado 80202
1-833-524-0368
theoxfordhotel.com

---

The Oxford was just one of the haunted places I visited with Janice and Debby. We also went to a charming spot for artists, and I included the following story in my book *When the Ghost Screams—True Stories of Victims Who Haunt.*

# Secrets in the Attic

On a quiet summer day in 2002, ghost hunter Janice Oberding visited one of her favorite haunted places. She had brought her son, Brad, and daughter-in-law, Peggy, along for the adventure. As they drove up the hill to St. Mary's Art Center in Virginia City, Nevada, they noticed that the big old house looked deserted. "I don't think there is anyone here today," said Janice. Her son pointed to the center attic window. "No, there is someone here," Brad protested. "I just saw someone standing at the window."

Janice glanced at the window but saw no one. Perhaps whomever Brad had seen was now running down the stairs to let them in. They rapped on the door and waited for a long moment on the big porch. Finally, the caretaker came around the side of the house. He had been in a back room, he said. Asked about the figure in the attic, he shook his head. He was the only one there, and he had not been in the attic all day. Janice knew it was not the first time that ghostly eyes had watched visitors from the attic. "Many people have reported seeing a nun standing at that window," she told me.

Those familiar with the Art Center are not surprised to hear about ghost sightings there. The place is extremely haunted and is popular with ghost hunters. The entire house can be rented out for a weekend and is a favorite place for ghost investigators' paranormal slumber parties. Built as a hospital in 1876 by the Sisters of Charity, the site had previously been Van Bokklen's Beer Gardens. The mountainous land had once echoed with drunken laughter as the beer flowed. Owner Jacob Van Bokklen was killed in an explosion in 1873. Some folks wonder if his ghost is among those who wander the rooms of St. Mary's Art Center.

A variety of art classes are taught at the nonprofit center, and the creative people who frequent the place may be more open to the idea of ghosts than most. "The ghost of the nun is seen most often," said Janice, who explained that visitors to the center find the specter in white to be kind and gentle. "They usually see her in room 11. One student entered her room and was startled to see the nun sitting on her bed." As the stunned student stared, a sad smile touched the nun's lips, and then she vanished. But it was not the last she would see of her. That night, when the student was in bed, the nun again appeared and gently pulled the blankets up around the woman's chin. Others have encountered the ghost of a hefty woman in the kitchen. She materializes with the distinct scent of violets surrounding her.

What happened at the house to cause so much activity? Maybe the spirits are left over from the days the building was a hospital. Overnight visitors have

*A heavy snow falls upon the St. Mary's Art Center, where the ghost of a nun wanders. (Leslie Rule)*

been startled awake by someone trying to take their temperatures. And they have heard the squeaking wheels of a nonexistent gurney as it rolls past their rooms in the dead of night. But something *else* likely causes the ghostly activity, Janice said. "There was a terrible fire there," she explained. "Many people were killed, including a nun." The heroic nun helped many people out of the burning house and continued to go back in to rescue more. The last time she rushed back into the house, she did not come out.

St. Mary's Art Center has a welcoming aura. It's unpretentious and cozy, with a hodgepodge of funky furniture filling the main floors. The attic, however, is another story. When paranormal investigator Debby Constantino and I ventured into the attic, we felt uncomfortable. In one cramped storage area,

we each had the sense that something bad had been done to a child there. We later learned that others have sensed the same thing in that spot.

And in one of the larger attic rooms, we both felt so anxious that we could barely breathe. When we told Janice about our reaction, she said, "That's where the mental patients were. They kept them chained in the attic." At least one patient had been chained during the fire, she said. He perished there when he could not break free.

*Debby Constantino, an electronic voice phenomena expert, in the attic of St. Mary's Art Center, preparing to communicate with spirits. Most visitors report that the guest rooms have a wonderful aura, and that the spirits there do not frighten them. (Leslie Rule)*

*— Update —*

An October 2015 edition of the *Reno Gazette Journal* relayed a report by visitors to St. Mary's Art Center who say they've witnessed an unusual apparition. The ghost of a man, seated in a wheelchair, manifests in the corner of one of the rooms.

**St Mary's Art Center**
55 R Street, Virginia City, Nevada 89440
(775) 847-7774
stmarysartcenter.org

Just as the Art Center is housed in a building that was once a hospital, the hotel in the next story was a place where people came to heal. For many of them, it was their last hope. They had no idea that the miracle promised to them was nothing but lies.

# Something in the Water

The two middle-aged ladies giggled as Keith Winge walked by. He turned to smile at the women, who were huddled in the hallway of the second floor of the Elms Resort in Excelsior Springs, Missouri. "What's so funny?" he asked politely.

"Nothing," one said. "We're just waiting to see the little girl."

"Oh." He knew who they meant. "Enjoy your stay," he said as he headed back to his office, where he served as the resort's director of sales and marketing. *Word gets around fast*, he thought. For it was just a couple of weeks earlier that ten-year-old kids on a field trip had stood in that very hallway and seen the now-infamous girl. The entire class of fifth graders had claimed that they had seen the ghostly child race right past them and disappear into the wall.

In bygone days, Excelsior Springs was the last hope for many sick people. Doctors prescribed the "healing waters," and some very ill folks climbed out of their deathbeds to travel to the magical city in the northwest corner of Missouri.

Some were cured via the placebo effect because they believed the waters would cure them.

It all began in 1880 when farmer Travis Mellion saw his daughter healed of her skin disease after bathing in and drinking the rust-colored water that some called "pizen" (poison) because of its brownish appearance.

Word spread about the child's recovery, and within a year, the town overflowed with visitors who sought cures in the healing mineral waters. An industry was born. Factories bottled water and ginger ale there, and bathhouses were plentiful. Hotels were erected, and the best ones featured private baths and "hydrotherapy."

The Elms Hotel was designed to cater to the wealthy who came to town for the healing spring water. It opened in 1888 and burned down ten years later. The new Elms Hotel was built in 1908 and burned down a year later. The third time was the charm for the new hotel. It was erected in 1912, only a short distance from the original structure, and thanks to a steel skeleton and a facade of native stone, it still stands today. The Elms Resort and Spa, now owned by the city of Excelsior Springs, is a charming historical building surrounded by lightly forested acreage.

Excelsior Springs was once a booming town. A depot near the Elms saw droves of people arrive by train, and the streets bustled with tourists. During the 1930s, gangster Al Capone was a regular at the hotel. He had his own

*The sick and dying once hoped that the magical waters of the Elms Resort would heal them. (Leslie Rule)*

special quarters there, with a window facing the front so that he could watch for the police.

In the 1960s, however, business in Excelsior Springs went downhill after a national magazine published a story discrediting claims that the water had special healing powers. The Elms Resort suffered along with the rest of the enterprises in town. The building sat abandoned for a few years in the 1970s.

The neighborhood kids turned it into their private playground, climbing through the broken windows for games of hide-and-seek in the dark, dusty halls. One of those kids, now grown and living a few doors down from the hotel, told me his sister had encountered a glowing apparition in the dilapidated building. It was the ghost of a maid, pushing a cleaning cart through the shadows.

When the hotel was renovated and reopened in 1978, guests and employees reported paranormal activity. Waitress Cathy Zeller told me that the chandelier in the ballroom sometimes sways, as if unseen children are swinging from it. And she once saw a ball of light zip through the ballroom.

Could the ghosts be those who did not survive when they sought healing waters at the hotel? A former Minnesota congressman was among those who died at the Elms. James Albertus Tawney, age sixty-four, hoped for a miracle but passed away at the hotel on June 13, 1919. His story was not unique.

Though sick children also went to Excelsior Springs for the healing waters, and many died, records are sketchy, and it's difficult to determine exactly where they died. Most likely, some died at the Elms, but despite my research, I've not yet found a case of a little girl dying on the premises. The story behind the ghost child in the second-floor hall remains a mystery.

Though we find that the most paranormally active sites are tied to violent deaths, this is not a hard and fast rule. Ghosts can remain earthbound for a number of reasons. Most of those who passed away at the hotel succumbed to illness, but there were also sudden deaths. Almost fifty years ago, a guest died after falling from a balcony. And long before that, an Elms employee drowned, but it happened in a lake on his day off. Even so, it's not out of the question that his ghost could be among those haunting the hotel because spirits seem to be attached to places that were meaningful to them in life, including workplaces.

While the hotel has a heated outside pool and hot tubs, it also has an indoor pool in the basement of the building. Jay Manning, the nighttime maintenance

*Do unseen entities rock in these chairs outside of the historic Elms Resort? (Leslie Rule)*

manager, revealed that guests have reported seeing the apparition of a little boy swimming in the indoor pool, but no records of drownings at the hotel have been found. He might be the ghost of a sick child who spent time there at the end of his life because of the so-called healing waters.

*No one knows who may be hiding behind the trees on the grounds of the Elms Resort. (Leslie Rule)*

Jay took me to the basement pool and pointed out the spot where he had seen an unusual apparition late one night. In the fleeting moment he glimpsed the ghost, he thought the fellow was dressed like a mime, with dark clothing and his face painted white. The apparition sat in a deck chair beside the pool and stared at Jay intently before vanishing. "He looked as real and solid as any person," said Jay.

The lanes of the lap pool form a loop, like a track designed for joggers. Old-timers in town told me that the pool was once used to exercise racehorses. The trainers, they said, would stand outside the pool and lead the swimming horses. While the basement swimming pool

*Jay Fanning poses near the spot where he encountered an unusual apparition. (Leslie Rule)*

room is clean and in good repair, guests often avoid it. That may be because of an inexplicable eerie sense that an unseen presence is watching.

## — *Update* —

Ghostly activity at the Elms Hotel is as lively as ever, according to Jay Fanning. It's been fifteen years since he showed me the pool and the chair beside it where the pale-faced apparition had appeared. Jay now leads ghost tours at the Elms and has spent years collecting real-life stories from employees and guests about their ghostly encounters. He can point out every haunted nook and cranny of the historic building.

He has had more than his share of paranormal experiences because of the strong sixth sense he inherited from his mom. When she recently stayed at the Elms, Jay visited her room, delivering beverages. Shortly after he left, his mother noticed the doorknob twisting. She figured it was Jay, trying to open the door, so she opened it for him, and as she did so, she heard giggling in the hallway. It did *not* sound like Jay! Puzzled, she peered into the hall. There was not a soul in sight.

Elms front desk clerk Amanda Odaffer shared her peculiar experience with me. It was her friend Parker's fourteenth birthday in August 2018, and a group of five girls was celebrating by spending the night at the Elms. They checked into room 421 for a spooky slumber party. "We wanted to stay in room 422 because it's the hotel's most haunted room, but it was already booked," she explained.

Hoping for a spirit encounter, the teens played "a game" that they knew they shouldn't. When her friend brought out the Ouija board, Amanda was hesitant. "My mother had a bad experience, and she'd warned me that it was dangerous," she confided. Many years earlier, her mother's boyfriend had consulted a Ouija board, and the decision cast an icy shadow of evil over the home. He had unwittingly opened the door to an undesirable entity, and everyone sensed it. It was so disturbing that they threw the board into the trash, but it inexplicably returned. Determined to get rid of it, Amanda's mother had *burned* it, but it showed up again, intact.

That cautionary tale should have been enough to stop Amanda, but it's never easy for a teen to stand up to her peers. When she saw how enthusiastic her friends were, she bit her lip and went along. Not only had one of the girls brought her *own* Ouija board, but they also borrowed the hotel's board from the front desk so that they could play a prank on the noisy group from the bachelorette party in a room near theirs. "We slipped the board under their door and kicked it," said Amanda. The teens laughed with satisfaction when they heard the partiers shriek as the board shot into their room.

Amanda and her friends went back to their room, where they decided to attempt to contact the spirit of a deceased relative via the Ouija board. They asked that relative a question as they placed their fingers on the planchette. Normally, the planchette glides around the board as players unconsciously move it, sometimes guided by imagination and sometimes guided by entities. But the planchette would not budge. It seemed the experiment had been a failure.

They decided to go swimming and headed to the pool. The moment they stepped onto the elevator, they sensed something was off. "We all felt it," said Amanda. It seemed unnaturally still. They had been down in the lobby just minutes before, and there had been lots of people there, laughing and talking. Someone had been playing the piano, and the sound of murmuring voices and clinking dishes had drifted from the restaurant. Now it was quiet, and nobody was around. "There wasn't anyone at the front desk," she said.

*Where had everyone gone?* The girls tried to shrug off the sudden silence and went to the pool. Rowdy people had been there earlier, but they, too, were gone. It was as if everyone had vanished. "One of my friends was really scared," said Amanda. "She wanted to go back to the room." As they passed through the lobby, it was still quiet. No one had returned to the front desk. Reality had turned inside out, as if they were in an episode of *The Twilight Zone*. They hadn't seen another human being or even heard a voice since they had left their room. Even the bachelorette party was strangely silent.

Back in the room, they again got out the Ouija board and attempted to contact spirits. The spirits still had nothing to say, but the world shifted again. It was as if a spell had been broken. "After that, everything went back to normal," said Amanda.

What in the world had happened? Was this a case of youthful imaginations running wild? *Maybe.* But it is not the first time I've heard of this type of thing occurring. Others have told me about worlds gone strangely silent. This happens most often when they're in the grips of paranormal episodes. For example, in "Dead Man's Detour" in chapter thirteen, everything became unnaturally still when Angela Boley noticed the strange car on the road. All other traffic but her car and the ghost car had disappeared.

If, indeed, witnesses of this type of occurrence *really* find themselves in a place where all other people have vanished, it raises an interesting question. Have the other *people* disappeared, or have *they* disappeared? Have they somehow slipped into another dimension? Somewhere out of place and out of time? Did the Ouija board open a doorway to another realm that Amanda and her friends stepped through? If it's possible to step into another dimension, has anyone ever entered only to find they can't return?

While I find this fascinating to contemplate, I have no answers!

### The Elms Hotel & Spa
401 Regent Street, Excelsior Springs, Missouri 64024
(816) 630-5500
elmshotelandspa.com

I've spent the night at many haunted places in my quest for ghost stories. Two of my favorite places happen to be in Missouri, though they're nearly three hundred miles apart. While I enjoyed my stay at the Elms, I had no ghostly encounters there. Something odd *did* happen to me at the Lemp Mansion in St. Louis. I did not mention it when this story was first published in my book, *Ghosts Among Us,* nearly twenty years ago, but I've never forgotten it. It was a *good* thing, and one of the reasons I have such wonderful memories of my stay there.

I didn't include the incident the first time around because I couldn't get my mind around the fact it had actually occurred. After two decades of thinking about it, I've decided that it's finally time to say thank you to the spirit who helped me, so I will do so in my update!

# The Lemp Mansion and the Legend of the Monkey Boy

The day before I left for St. Louis, Missouri, I had learned just three things about the city's famous 1868 Lemp Mansion. It had once been the home of a family who made their fortune in the lager beer business. *Life* magazine had featured it as one of the ten most haunted places in the United States. *And it was haunted by the ghost of the Monkey Boy!*

The Monkey Boy was believed to be the spirit of a deformed child, trapped indefinitely in the attic of what is now a restaurant and bed-and-breakfast. Though I pride myself on never being frightened of ghosts, I must admit that my enthusiasm was somewhat dampened when I called to make reservations, and owner Patty Pointer told me that I would be the only person staying there. "The staff goes home at 3:00 p.m. on Wednesdays," she explained and cheerfully added, "and you'll be our only guest here that night. You'll have the mansion all to yourself to explore."

"All alone?" *All alone with the Monkey Boy!*

"Yes, but there is one problem," Patty said. "You'll need to get the key before we leave." My plane would not be arriving until after six, so I contacted fellow ghost author Troy Taylor for help. It was his invitation that had lured me to the area, as I would be speaking in his Alton, Illinois, bookstore the following Saturday. "You must know a reliable woman or two who would like to have a haunted slumber party," I suggested. He certainly did, and the arrangements were soon made.

Anita Dytuco and her daughter, twenty-two-year-old Amy, picked me up at the airport. We went out for dinner, and they told me they had picked up the key and later dropped their overnight bags off at the Lemp Mansion. "I turned on all the lights downstairs as a test," said Amy, explaining that many have reported that lights at the mansion turn off and on by themselves.

Sure enough, when we arrived at the big house, we found that the lights were off in two rooms. "Someone could be playing a trick on us," I said as I flipped the switches back on. But Amy was scared. She followed tentatively as

*A history of violent deaths at the Lemp Mansion may be the reason this B&B is the most haunted location in St. Louis. (Leslie Rule)*

we explored. The thirty-three-room mansion boasts high ceilings, impossibly tall doorways, ornate antique fixtures, and vintage decor.

It took some urging for us to convince Amy to explore the attic. Armed with flashlights, we crept up the narrow back staircase, once used by servants, past the attic's renovated area, down a long hallway, and into a dark, cramped space. It was in this hot, stuffy place that the help had lived. While the Lemp family occupied the opulent, spacious rooms below, the servants' quarters were divided into closet-sized spaces with tiny floor-level windows. This had been the quarters of the mysterious child.

The legend of the Monkey Boy began decades earlier when neighbors whispered that they had seen an apelike child peering at them from the small attic windows. A rumor spread that Billy Lemp, a married grandson of founder Adam Lemp, had romanced a maid and that the unfortunate child was a result of the forbidden union. The boy was exiled forever to the attic. It really wasn't a very scary idea. It was sad.

Our attic expedition yielded nothing exciting. The batteries in our flashlights went prematurely dead as we were exploring—a common phenomenon in haunted sites—and we fumbled our way out. Only one in our trio was to encounter a ghost before the adventure was over, but it would not be until

*This old postcard depicts the impressive Lemp Brewery when business was booming. Underground tunnels connect it to the Lemp Mansion. (Courtesy of the Ronald Snowden Collection)*

dawn's soft light embraced the mansion. As for the Monkey Boy, he did not appear. Was there such a child? Many have searched for documentation of his existence, but proof has yet to be found. The allegedly most haunted mansion in St. Louis, however, has no shortage of tragic stories to feed its ghost legends.

The story begins in the mid-nineteenth century when the city's natural underground caverns enticed German brewers who found them perfect for refrigeration. Adam Lemp built his empire above a long, rambling cave, which eventually connected the lager beer brewery to the family home. The beer business boomed, and the Lemps' fortune was made.

In 1876, Adam's son, William J. Lemp, moved his wife, Julia, and six children into the big Italianate structure. The kids were all under the age of ten, and the huge home's halls surely rang with laughter as Anna, William Jr., Louis, Charles, Frederick, and Hilda frolicked and played. When Edwin was born in 1880, and then Elsa in 1883, the family was complete.

During that era, wealthy children played with Steiff teddy bears, exquisite-faced porcelain dolls, wooden blocks, and marbles, and they rode straw-stuffed horses on wheels. The Lemp children's nursery, believed to have been located in the third-floor tower room at the top of the main staircase, had at one time been filled with the finest toys. I hope these were happy times for the children, for their lives were later marred by tragedy. Their father set a dark precedent when he took his own life in 1904, shooting himself in the mansion. His son William Jr. followed suit, killing himself in the same room eighteen years later, in 1922. His brother Charles committed suicide in a basement room in 1949.

Though there are four deaths in the Lemp family documented as suicide, one is particularly suspicious. Elsa, the littlest Lemp, born and raised in the mansion, died from a "self-inflicted" gunshot wound in 1920. When Thomas Wright proposed to her, she was the wealthiest single woman in St. Louis. On the tragic day, she was thirty-six years old and lived with him in a grand home on Hortense Place. She had been suffering from one of her mysterious bouts of stomach problems on the March morning she died. "She said she was feeling better," Thomas Wright told everyone after his wife died.

Was she simply depressed over her illness, as her husband had insisted? Or was the loss of her only child too much to bear? Baby Patricia had died six years earlier on the day she was born. Did someone else have a hand in Elsa's death?

Thomas had remarried the heiress to the Lemp fortune just eleven days before, after an earlier divorce that kept them separated for about a year.

The *St. Louis Dispatch* reported that on the morning of March 20, Elsa was in bed when Thomas headed for the shower. When he heard the blast of the gun, he rushed back to the bedroom and found Elsa wounded. He shouted for help, and the maid came running. Elsa died shortly after.

An inquest concluded that the death was suicide. Yet, the recent remarriage raises questions. Was the couple happy together? Why would Elsa kill herself when she was feeling better? And what was the cause of her stomach ailment? If this tragedy unfolded today, the coroner would have looked for signs she had been poisoned. Murder or suicide, it was a troubling death, the kind that often results in earthbound spirits. If anyone had an attachment to the Lemp Mansion, it would be Elsa, who was born and raised there. Witnesses have reported seeing both male and female apparitions there, so most likely, at least two members of the Lemp Mansion are earthbound.

A waitress was setting up one morning when she spotted an early customer, seated at one of the tables. "Would you like some coffee?" she asked as she approached him. The man stared into space, ignoring her. An awkward moment of dead silence passed. It seemed that he was either very rude, or he was so lost in thought that he hadn't heard her. She was about to repeat her offer when he suddenly vanished, and she found herself staring at an empty chair. She had just seen a ghost!

Was it one of the Williams, Charles, or Frederick, the favorite son who worked so hard on the family business that he dropped dead of heart failure in his late twenties? His daughter, Marion, was later denied a fair share of the Lemp fortune, despite the fact that Frederick had done more for the business than his siblings. A lawsuit was filed on behalf of twelve-year-old Marion, but most of her aunts and uncles fought her. They won, and young Marion was cheated out of all her father had worked for. If Frederick's spirit was aware that his siblings had cheated his daughter, it was a possible reason for him to be earthbound.

Many assume the female presence is Lillian Handlan, ex-wife of William "Billy" Lemp, Jr. She was affectionately known as the "Lavender Lady" because of her fondness for dressing in soft purple shades. The vivacious socialite was so adored by area residents that crowds met her train whenever she returned from a trip. Billy and Lillian split up in a contentious divorce with a public trial.

Reporters were present when Billy testified that his wife's love for the color lavender was one of the reasons for the divorce. Lillian, however, denied that. Newspapers quoted her saying, "I've never worn lavender in my life."

While the Lavender Lady may haunt the Lemp Mansion, Lillian had made it known that she was not fond of the place. She had never lived there, and when she died at age seventy-three, it was *not* at the mansion. She did, however, host parties there when she was married to Billy. It makes more sense to me that Elsa would attach herself to the grand old house. The youngest of the Lemp siblings, she had spent her entire childhood there.

*Elsa Lemp loved her childhood home. After her tragic death, she may have returned to the place of her happiest memories.*

Today, the Lemp Mansion is famous for its Murder Mystery Dinners, where actors add drama to mealtime with first-rate performances of fascinating characters involved in a crime. The actors use the Lemp nursery for their costume room, and many have reported odd things. One actress told me of a sighting that brings poor Elsa to mind. An old-fashioned baby buggy, apparently stored in the nursery, suddenly bolted out of the empty room and shot into the hallway as if invisible hands had pushed it. Was it Elsa, pushing the spirit of her baby daughter in the buggy?

The Pointer family bought the mansion in 1975, and in the years since they've owned it, many of their relatives have experienced paranormal activity. Bonnie Kleiss, Patty Pointer's college-age niece, will never forget her chilling experience there. "I was about six, and my grandma asked me to go upstairs and get some keys for her," she told me. "Right as I got to the top of the grand staircase, I heard a man's voice." He spoke just one word, "Bonnie." "I ran as fast as I could back downstairs and never gave an explanation as to why I didn't get the keys. I never told anyone in my family about what I had heard."

Bonnie showed up to stay at the Lemp Mansion on my second day there, and it was then that she confided in me about her experience with the disembodied voice. Later, when I was back home, I received an email from her. It had happened *again*! This time she was in bed in the Charles Lemp Suite. As she was drifting off to sleep, she heard a young man's voice. "The difference between this one and the one I heard years ago was that this time it was more playful, 'Bohh-nniee,' like it was calling out to me. When I first heard this, it was stated more matter-of-factly."

I wonder if the ghost had been listening when Bonnie confided in me about hearing her name called. Now, he was teasing her, calling out playfully. Though the ghosts of the Lemp Mansion didn't speak to *me,* they were in a talkative mode during my stay, for Bonnie wasn't the only one who heard them. Amy, the terrified member of our little slumber party, also heard from a Lemp ghost! She had gone to bed so frightened that she chose to sleep cuddled up to her mother in the big bed in the lovely Lavender Suite. "I couldn't sleep all night," she confessed. And then, just as the night was dissolving, a kind female voice whispered, "It's going to be all right." The words were gentle and loving and so soothing that Amy was swept into a peaceful sleep.

As I pored over the guest books, signed by past visitors who had written down their paranormal experiences, I was fascinated by the many descriptions of odd things that had occurred there. Some wrote about furniture that was inexplicably moved, lights turning on and off, and apparitions appearing. One guest wrote that "a toilet screamed." (That may have been more of a plumbing problem than a paranormal one!) One experience in particular caught my attention because it was so similar to Amy's encounter. A man wrote that he had spent the night in the Lavender Suite, and because of emotional turmoil, he could not sleep. Late into the night, a kind spirit spoke to him. "It's going

*Amy, with her mother Anita Dytuco, and Bonnie Kleiss, on the landing of a staircase at the Lemp Mansion. Before the end of their stay, two of these women would encounter ghosts. (Leslie Rule)*

*Nooks and crannies and secret tunnels are filled with ghosts at the spooky Lemp Mansion. (Leslie Rule)*

to be okay." And just as Amy had, the troubled man was enveloped by an instant peace and finally fell asleep.

Who soothed Amy and the troubled man? My guess is it was Elsa Lemp Wright. She still looks over her childhood home, a place that she loved, and she does what she can to make guests feel comfortable.

## — *Update* —

Ghosts of the Lemp Mansion are still very active. Visitors recently staying on the third floor, in a space that had once been servants' quarters, heard the persistent tinkling of a bell, as if someone were trying to get the attention of "the help" by ringing the call bell that had long ago beckoned servants to descend the stairs to see to the Lemp family's needs.

Some guests of late have been spooked to see doorknobs twisting when no living person is attempting to open the doors. And not long ago, a maid was on the third floor, engrossed in the task of cleaning a bathtub, when she heard a male voice call her name. She wasn't alarmed because she assumed it was her husband. She continued to scrub and yelled over her shoulder, "I'm in here!" She then heard footsteps walk up behind her. Naturally, she still assumed it was

her husband, but when she spoke to him, he did not respond. A chill crept over her as she turned around. She was alone. Her husband was downstairs, had not been upstairs, and had not called out to her.

When I stayed alone in my room at the Lemp Mansion two decades ago, I didn't feel the least bit frightened. But that is not unusual for me, because when I decided to research and write

*The Lemp Mansion in St. Louis, Missouri, has converted many ghost skeptics to believers. (Leslie Rule)*

about ghosts, I was not seeking scary things. My attitude was, *and still is*, that the world beyond ours is mysterious and magical. The spirits are mostly benign, and many of them feel so kindly toward us that they will actually assist us.

I understand that there are bad things in the spirit world, just as there is evil among live human beings, but I have rarely encountered anything that fills me with dread when I research haunted places. If something doesn't feel right, I leave. In fact, I don't go to places if I've heard they are associated with curses or evil. I'm not interested in studying *dark* things. For me, the confirmation of survival of the spirit is uplifting. It's exhilarating to document events that prove life goes on when our bodies stop.

While I admit the idea of the Monkey Boy was spooky, it was a *fun* kind of spooky. He is a legend, and we've seen no proof of his existence. As for Elsa, we know *she* existed, and I suspect that she is the kind spirit who soothes the worried guests as they toss and turn in their beds. Somebody helped me out with my worries when I stayed at the Lemp Mansion, and I think it was Elsa.

Each of my ghost books features at least fifty black-and-white photographs taken by me, and it was very important for me to get great images of the Lemp Mansion. I did not yet own a cell phone, and even if I had, they didn't double as cameras back then! I used an expensive, manual Nikon with a zoom lens.

As I prepared to go to sleep on my first night there, I unpacked the equipment I would need for the next day. I was dismayed to find that my Nikon was broken. The dial for the f-stop settings was loose, and it no longer worked. I fiddled with it, but the dial spun uselessly. I put the camera on top of the dresser and crawled into bed. I was very worried about my broken camera when I went to sleep that night.

The next morning, I picked up the camera, wondering how I was going to take photos with it broken. I touched the dial for the f-stop setting and was stunned to see that it was no longer loose. The camera worked perfectly! There is no scientific explanation for how the camera was repaired. I was grateful, and I have never forgotten it. Thank you, Elsa Lemp!

### The Lemp Mansion

3322 Demenil Place, St. Louis, Missouri 63118

(314) 644-8024

lempmansion.com

It's not unusual for the spirits of haunted places to lend a helping hand. In the next case, we'll visit Boston and meet the hospitable ghost of the man whose claim to fame is partly due to the mouthwatering Parker House rolls, named after him.

# A Ghost for a Host

James Smith stepped into the room across from the ballroom and froze. A shadowy figure had just rushed past him. He whirled around, trying to get a closer look, but the thing had vanished as quickly as it had appeared. He shuddered and went back to work. After working many years as a bartender at the Omni Parker House, he takes the unusual happenings in stride. "We have employees who are too afraid to go to the ballroom alone," he said, as he escorted me to the large room with the rounded ceiling. James is not afraid, but he normally does not talk about the ghosts. We took the crowded service elevator as he gave me a quick tour of the most haunted spots in the hotel. The male employees who shared the elevator appeared spooked when I asked them if they had ever encountered ghosts in the hotel. They all shook their heads no, but something in their eyes told me they were fibbing.

"People say they've seen ghosts on the sixth floor," said James. It's usually a fleeting glimpse, but full-figured apparitions have been spotted there. Years ago, an elderly woman saw a ghost outside of room 1078. He materialized as an indefinable cloud and gradually took the shape of a man. The heavy-set gentleman with the black mustache stared at her for a moment and then vanished. Everyone said that she had seen the ghost of Harvey Parker.

*The Omni Parker House, a short walk from the Common, is crawling with ghosts. (Leslie Rule)*

Harvey was a twenty-year-old farm boy with barely a dollar to his name when he arrived in Boston in 1825. Seven years later, he was a restaurant owner, but his ambitions did not end there. In 1855, he opened the grandest hotel the city had ever seen. Those he hired to create delectable meals for his guests included a German baker who apparently had a bit of temper.

Legend has it that the pastry chef had a confrontation with a customer, and still simmering with anger afterward, he didn't take his usual care with his baking. In a huff, he tossed some unfinished dough into the oven. He was surprised to find that his mistake

*James Smith is one of the few Omni Parker House employees brave enough to go to the ballroom alone. (Leslie Rule)*

was delicious. The rolls were soft on the inside with a crispy shell. The diners loved them, and Parker House rolls were soon in demand.

Though Harvey died at seventy-nine in 1884, many believe the perfectionist still tries to run the hotel and often helps out. But why would he throw teapots? Waitress Heather Alvarado was startled when she was in a storage room, and pots suddenly leapt off the shelf, as if invisible hands were tossing them at her. Apparently, Harvey is not the only ghost at the hotel because he certainly would *not* throw teapots or anything else at his employees.

Who are the other ghosts? The area is marked by violent death, and the Parker House is very close to the Boston Common, where many traumatic deaths have occurred.* Executions were routine there in the seventeenth century, with lynchings of Quakers, accused witches, pirates, and thieves. Do their ghosts visit the hotel? If they do, Harvey would surely make them feel welcome. He had a reputation for playing the consummate host to the wealthiest guests or the most ordinary of citizens.

*See Chapter Fourteen for information on the haunting and history of the Boston Common.

Hafeez Yassin agrees that Harvey is among the ghosts who wander the hotel. He was alone in the ballroom one day, cleaning up after a party and listening to reggae music on his radio. Suddenly, the station abruptly changed, skimming over a dozen channels until it settled on a classical station. "That's the kind of music that Harvey would have listened to," he said.

Another employee was exhausted after a long day but had not quite finished his work in the ballroom. He had one more table to set up. He left the room for a moment, and when he returned, the table had been magically set. He looked around, astonished. No one else had been in the area. It was probably Harvey, he figured, still helping out at the hotel where he'd made his fortune.

## — *Update* —

Omni Parker House management notes that ghostly encounters continue to be commonplace in the historic building. On more than one occasion, hotel security has responded to complaints of noisy guests in room 1040. Each time they investigate, they discover the room is empty. The elevator is another anomaly. It is frequently summoned to the third floor, despite the fact no one has called for it.

Room 1012 may be one of the more haunted rooms, and hotel staff is quick to point out that there is nothing scary about the friendly ghost who appears there. A guest woke at dawn, surprised to see a smiling man, in 1800s garb, standing beside her bed. "How are you enjoying your stay?" the fellow asked before he vanished. The guest later noticed a portrait on the wall in the hotel dining room, and she realized she had met Harvey Parker himself. Her morning visitor looked exactly like the painting.

**Omni Parker House**
60 School Street, Boston, Massachusetts 02108
(617) 227-8600
omnihotels.com/hotels/boston-parker-house

---

Harvey Parker isn't the only ghostly hotelkeeper working overtime. In Rapid City, South Dakota, a famously haunted hotel counts owner Alex Carlton Johnson among its many ghosts. The apparition of the distinguished AJ has been seen roaming all floors of the hotel, and he most often appears on the balcony overlooking the lobby.

The eleven-story Alex Johnson Hotel was erected in 1927, with the work beginning just one day before the construction of nearby Mount Rushmore. Alex Johnson created a unique building that was a blend of styles from two cultures that were important to him—that of the local Native Americans and the German immigrants who had settled in South Dakota.

In addition to the ghost of AJ, witnesses have reported encounters with the ghosts of children. Some say they have heard splashing and giggling as they walk by the hotel fountain, as if children are playing in the water. Kids are also heard running up and down the hotel corridors at all hours of the day and night.

The most talked about ghost is the Lady in White. Legend has it that she is the ghost of a bride, still wearing the wedding dress that she donned before leaping to her death from an eighth-floor window in the 1970s. This idea is fed by the many sightings of an apparition in white, most often seen on the infamous eighth floor. Some witnesses glimpse her from the corner of their eye, while others have seen the apparition walking toward them in the hall.

*From the eighth floor where witnesses have encountered the apparition of a lady in white, to the dismal basement where an employee lost his life, the Alex Johnson Hotel has no shortage of restless spirits.*

She appears so real that they assume she is a living person—until she vanishes before their eyes.

While it's certainly possible that a distraught bride in a white gown ended her life in the described scenario, my archive search produced no cases of brides leaping from the hotel windows. But I *did* find two cases of females who died after falling from the Alex Johnson Hotel's windows. Just as the legend dictates, the ladies were staying on the eighth floor and the deaths occurred in the 1970s. Whether the falls were intentional or accidental is uncertain, but reports noted that no foul play was suspected.

The first to fall was Shirlee Jean. She was a beautiful, blue-eyed girl with long red hair. She was just twenty years old, from Montana, and she gave the clerk an alias when she checked into the hotel on a summer day in 1973. When she was found crumpled on the ground next to the hotel, she was rushed to the hospital by ambulance. She died a few days after her fall.

Before she passed, authorities tried to figure out who she was, but she either couldn't or *wouldn't* reveal her name. Shirlee was finally identified, via her fingerprints, about two weeks after she died, and her devastated family was given the news. (Shirlee's last name is withheld here out of respect for her family who still mourns her loss.)

A few years later, on a winter night in 1978, tragedy struck again. "A New Year's Eve Gala Celebration" drew enthusiastic crowds to the Alex Johnson Hotel with promises of dancing, party favors, and free bottles of champagne with dinner. The atmosphere was festive, filled with fun and laughter, as party-goers rang out the old year.

But in a room on the eighth floor, there was no celebration. At age ninety, Chrysteen Christensen had rung in and out her share of years and was not looking forward to the future. It was a little after five in the evening when the elderly lady dropped from her window and died the instant she hit the frozen ground.

Chrysteen was from a well-known pioneer ranch family in Dawes County, Nebraska. Her parents were long dead, and her many siblings had also passed away. She had nieces and nephews, but she was the only survivor of her immediate family.

Did she intentionally take her own life, perhaps because she was lonely and sick? It's hard to imagine that her fall was accidental. It was cold outside—*too* cold to warrant opening a window for fresh air. In fact, temperatures were subzero that day, with a high of –3.8°F.

The deaths of Shirlee and Chrysteen were mentioned briefly in newspapers and eventually forgotten by almost everyone in Rapid City. While decades apart in age, the two women had things in common. In addition to the fact that both lives ended via the hotel's eighth-floor windows, they were also creative souls. Shirlee was musical and had been a member of her high school's band in the small Montana town where she'd grown up. Chrysteen was an artist who sewed, painted china, and designed hats for a swanky New York boutique.

Did either of these sensitive souls linger? Could they be responsible for the paranormal activity reported on the eighth floor of the Alex Johnson Hotel? Perhaps, but their fatal

## Chadron Woman Dies In Rapid City Hotel Fall

A member of a pioneer ranch family in Dawes County died New Year's-Eve as the result of a fall from the eighth floor of the Alex Johnson Hotel in Rapid City.

The victim was Chrysteen Christensen, who was believed to be about 90 years old.

Rapid City police said Miss Christensen either fell or jumped from the window of the room she was renting in the hotel. There were no witnesses to the event, which occurred shortly before 5 p.m. Sunday.

Miss Christensen was the final member of her immediate family to die. She still had ranching interests north of Chadron.

*While a crowd celebrated New Year's Eve at a festive party at the AJ Hotel, an eighth floor tenant made a grim decision to end her life, a tragedy that did not make front-page news.*

falls were not the only traumatic deaths there. Considering that the hotel has hosted over five million *live* folks in its illustrious history, it's no surprise that some of them died in or near the building. While most fatalities were due to natural causes, a few folks other than Chrysteen and Shirlee met their fates in shocking ways.

As researchers have noted, we see the most activity in places where sudden and devastating deaths have occurred, and the AJ Hotel has seen its share of shocking tragedy. Via my archive search, I found the case of Ray Bolton, a young Rapid City fellow who married his sweetheart, Zelda, in February 1924. He was twenty-one, and she was an older woman of twenty-three. The couple made their home on East Center Street, about two miles from downtown, and they soon started a family. A beautiful baby girl, Zola, was born nine months, to the *day*, after the couple wed.

Ray supported his new family by working as a heating engineer at the Alex Johnson Hotel. His job was to stoke the furnace in the cavernous basement so that the hundreds of guests in the floors above could stay warm and comfortable. Little Zola was just a month shy of her third birthday on the day her daddy went to work and never came home.

It was October 8, 1928, early in the morning, when the unexpected happened. As Ray lit the hotel's oil-burning furnace, a horrific blast sent waves of fire over him. Badly burned, the young man died within hours. He was twenty-five years old.

Zelda and Zola moved on without Ray because that's what the living do. Zelda eventually remarried, and Zola became the eldest of a number of half siblings. Zola grew up, got married, and had children and grandchildren of her own. She lived a full life.

Is Ray aware that many decades have passed and that his sweet little girl grew up, grew old, and died? Maybe not. In the timeless world that spirits occupy, Ray could still be trying to reconcile the fact that he is no longer made of flesh and bones—that he no longer has to work in the basement of the Alex Johnson Hotel to support his young family.

Ray might still believe he is on the job. As far as I know, I'm the first ghost researcher to discover his story, but many have sensed heavy energy in the hotel basement. One group of researchers brought their dog to the site. The dog, known for his ability to pick up on ghostly energy, barked as he zeroed in on something near the spot where Ray had lost his life.

Another tragic death occurred on October 17, nine days after the fatal furnace explosion. The second accident was also heating related. Archie Ibsen was at the wheel of his coal truck, right outside the hotel, and was unaware of the group of rambunctious little boys climbing on the back of his massive vehicle. Archie, age twenty-eight, was a longtime resident of the city, a stout, blue-eyed man who had no warning of the impending disaster.

The children were on their way to school and were oblivious to the danger. It was fun and games to nine-year-old Charlie Zabel. He and the other boys were enjoying a free ride on the back of the truck, but the laughter stopped in an instant as Charlie attempted to jump off the moving truck. His friends watched in horror as he fell beneath a rear wheel, and the tire rolled over his body. A Good Samaritan rushed him to the hospital, but nothing could be done for him.

Considering that Charlie was a mischievous lad who liked to get into trouble, I would not be surprised if he is one of the naughty ghostly children who race through the halls of the AJ.

**Hotel Alex Johnson**
523 6th Street, Rapid City, South Dakota 57701
(605) 342-1210
alexjohnson.com

---

# Room 611

San Antonio ghost hunter Martin Leal has been leading tours in one of the most haunted cities in the world for over twenty years. His interest in the paranormal was sparked decades ago when he was eight years old. He was visiting his grandmother's home when he saw an unfamiliar woman there. "Who is that?" he asked his mother, gesturing toward the lady.

His mother was confused. She could not see the lady and didn't know what to tell him. When he encountered the woman a second time, he pestered his relatives with questions until his grandfather finally sat him down and said, "That's my mother." As it turned out, his grandfather had also seen her and had long been interested in ghosts. He had a number of books on the topic and shared them with his grandson.

When Martin learned that the lady he'd seen was a ghost, he was surprised that she looked nothing like Casper. She was nothing like *any* ghost he'd seen depicted in movies. The movies always made them seem scary, but there was absolutely nothing frightening about the spirit of his great-grandmother.

As leader of the popular "Best San Antonio Ghost Tour," he tells fascinating stories, and while

*Entities sometimes materialize in the mirrors of this former San Antonio, Texas, hospital. (Leslie Rule)*

they're eerie by their very nature, they're not designed to terrify people. He agrees with me that we have more to fear from living people than dead ones! He shared the story of a woman who was terrified when she thought she'd encountered a *live* man, but she calmed down once she realized he was dead! It happened at the Emily Morgan Hotel. Once known as the Medical Arts Building, it housed a hospital on the fourteenth floor in 1926. The hospital eventually expanded to include other floors and served the San Antonio community for five decades.

Are some of the patients who died there earthbound? If so, they aren't discouraged by the fact the building no longer resembles a hospital, for apparitions have been seen wandering the halls. A few years back, a woman attended a conference at the hotel, and ghosts were the last thing on her mind when she checked in and accepted the key to room 611. At about 9:00 p.m. the hotel's front desk clerk received a phone call. It was the lady in 611, and she sounded frantic but was hard to understand. Her voice was muffled because she was trying to prevent someone else from hearing her—someone in the room with her! "Help me!" she cried. "*Save me! There is a man in my room!*"

The clerk immediately sent two security guards to the rescue. They were prepared for the worst as they opened the door with a passkey. Cautiously, they stepped into the room and glanced around. The place appeared empty. They saw no intruder, let alone the frightened guest. Then they noticed her peeking out from behind the curtains.

"There is a man over there!" she hissed and pointed to the bed. "*Get him!*"

The guards looked all around the bed. They searched the entire room, including the closet and bathroom. Finally, they told her it was okay to come out, assuring her, "There is no one here."

She was shaken as she emerged from her hiding place, her eyes darting around the room. "But he didn't leave!" she cried, bewildered. "I was watching, and I would have seen him leave." She explained that she had been applying makeup when she saw a man reflected in the mirror, standing behind her. She had whirled around, but he was too fast for her. She figured he had ducked behind something. Too afraid to walk past the bed where she feared he was hiding, she'd grabbed the phone and called for help.

The guards looked at each other. *Should they tell her?* It was not the first time something odd had occurred in that room. They knew why she had not

*The fourteenth floor of the Emily Morgan Hotel was the site of a hospital in 1926. (Leslie Rule)*

seen the man leave. He had not gone out the door. He had vanished into thin air because he was a *ghost*. But hotel managers had told employees that they must never mention ghosts. Management feared that guests would be afraid, and it would be bad for business. Unsure of how to comfort the woman, one of the guards suggested, "Maybe it was your imagination."

It was the wrong thing to say. The woman's face reddened as she cried, "I did *not* imagine it! I know what I saw!" As she argued with him, the other guard radioed for the manager, who arrived quickly and calmed her down with the truth. "We know it wasn't your imagination," he said, admitting that she had checked into one of the hotel's most haunted rooms. She had not seen a flesh-and-blood intruder . The intruder was a ghost, manifesting in the mirror for a shadow of a moment before slipping away.

"It was kind of funny," Martin remembered. "Because they did not doubt that she was looking in the mirror when she spotted the ghost. She had been applying lipstick when she saw his reflection, and she turned her head so fast that she left a lipstick mark from her mouth to her ear."

While many suspect the ghosts of the Emily Morgan are remnants from the era the building was a hospital, others suggest the source of the haunting is the Alamo. Famous for the violent battle that occurred there in 1836, the Alamo is also notoriously haunted and is less than two hundred feet from the hotel.

*The architectural detail on this one-time hospital is exquisite. While some visitors are drawn to the building's beauty, others are intrigued by its ghosts. (Leslie Rule)*

*The Emily Morgan Hotel peeks over the roof of the Alamo. (Leslie Rule)*

## — Update —

Ghost sightings continue at the hotel and the area surrounding it. Across the street from the Emily Morgan, the apparition of a fair-haired, little boy has been seen peering out of an upper window of the Alamo gift shop. Some believe that he is the ghost of a child evacuated before the savage attack and that he has returned to search for relatives who died there.

At the hotel, guests often report seeing the apparition of a woman in white in the hallways. Management no longer denies what they refer to as "mysterious occurrences," though they walk a fine line between trying not to frighten guests and boasting about their haunted status. Their website mentions that the Emily Morgan has been called "the third most haunted hotel in the world," but also insists that the hotel is "probably not haunted" and that the paranormal incidents have logical explanations.

I've found that haunted hotels tend to have areas with no ghostly activity and areas where spooky things happen regularly. I suggest that guests make their preference known when booking rooms in haunted hotels. You can often request a haunted or non-haunted room, just as you can request a smoking or nonsmoking room! The clerk will probably not raise an eyebrow because they've heard the request before. If they've worked at a place for a while, they'll have a sense of the level of activity in various rooms, but it's no guarantee you'll get what you asked for!

**Emily Morgan Hotel**
705 E. Houston Street, San Antonio, Texas 78205
(210) 225-5100
emilymorganhotel.com
bestsanantonioghosttours.com

---

# A Haunting in Bluegrass

Missi Nussbaum took a job at the Seelbach Hotel because she was bored. It was summertime 1992, and she was looking forward to her wedding day in the upcoming fall. But she had time on her hands, so she applied for a job as a maid at the historic hotel in downtown Louisville, Kentucky. She loved the rich elegance of the place. "I thought it would be fun to work in the building," she told me.

The beauty of the hotel and the palpable sense of history intrigued her, and soon Missi was employed there. It was routine work, vacuuming and scrubbing and changing sheets—until the day she was sent to the tenth floor by herself. Ballrooms and meeting areas dominate the tenth floor, with fewer rooms available for overnight guests, she explained. "The top-floor rooms were rarely booked. I had been sent up to do some freshening up before a big party arrived. Typically, roomkeepers work in pairs, but I was by myself that day. I was straightening the beds, spraying air freshener, and dusting."

Ever the multitasker, Missi decided to catch up on her favorite soap operas, so she turned on the television and watched while she worked. "My supervisor caught me," she admitted. When the woman admonished her, Missi sheepishly assured her that she would keep the television turned off. "I was on edge after that. I kept expecting my supervisor to sneak up on me and catch me doing something wrong. It felt like someone was watching me."

It was an uneasy feeling, and though Missi tried to focus on plumping pillows and polishing furniture, she could not shake the niggling sense of eyes upon her. The sensation continued as she worked in a corner room with a unique configuration. "In most of the rooms, the mirror hangs next to the door, but in the corner room the mirror is placed opposite the doorway," she explained. As she bent to straighten a wrinkle in the bedspread, the inkling that she was being watched intensified. She glanced up at the mirror and saw a woman.

She appeared to be standing in the doorway directly behind her, though Missi's own body blocked most of the image. "All I could see was her head," she said. In that instant, she took in the pale complexion, light hair, and bland expression. "There was no malice, yet the room became freezing cold, and I got an awful feeling."

Missi turned to the doorway, expecting to see a woman standing there. *No one was there!* "I looked back at the mirror, and she was *still* in the mirror doorway!" Missi ran. "I could not get out of there fast enough. My skin was crawling! It was weird because I'd always thought I'd be fascinated if I ever saw a ghost, but there was a physical sensation of having suddenly taken sick. It was dreadful. I did not go back up there that day. They had to get someone else to finish the rooms." Though Missi was not aware of it at the time, she was not the first or the *last* to encounter a ghost at the Seelbach Hotel.

Brothers Otto and Louis Seelbach celebrated the grand opening of their hotel on May 1, 1905, as a crowd of 25,000 people gathered. Inspired by French Renaissance architecture, the ten-story stone and brick structure was the tallest building in Louisville and the first fireproof hotel in the city, according to Larry Johnson, longtime Seelbach bell captain and author of *The Seelbach: A Centennial Salute to Louisville's Grand Hotel.*

Larry knows the hotel inside and out, and he can tell guests that the marbled walls were imported from Europe, that nine United States presidents have stayed there, and that F. Scott Fitzgerald was kicked out of the luxury hotel in 1918 after drinking too much bourbon. (Fitzgerald later used the Seelbach as the setting for the wedding of Tom and Daisy in his acclaimed 1925 novel, *The Great Gatsby.*)

In his three decades at the hotel, Larry has become aware of the ghosts. Though he and Missi Nussbaum have never spoken about her spirit encounter, the historian has talked with other employees who have seen apparitions materialize in the hotel mirrors. In December of 1983 an employee was alone in the hotel's first-floor Otto Café when he had a startling experience. It was after midnight, according to Larry, and the young man was busy cleaning the tables when he glanced up at the large mirror on the south wall. He saw the reflection of an elderly lady and assumed she was homeless. She wore tattered clothing and a floppy, orange hat. He felt a twinge of pity and decided to let her warm up a little before sending her back out into the frosty winter night.

As he busied himself cleaning, he casually noticed that the woman had made no move to leave. When it was time to ask her to go, he turned to speak to her but found himself alone. He turned back to see that the mirror image remained. Thoroughly shaken and unsure what to do, he called security, who soon discovered something strange. According to their records, exactly one year before, another employee had reported an identical sighting.

Larry is especially intrigued by another ghost at the Seelbach, known as the "Lady in Blue." The dark-haired woman in a blue dress has been seen on several occasions, always walking into the elevator. A woman boarding an elevator is not that unusual, *unless* the doors are shut as she enters. The Lady in Blue steps right *through* the closed elevator doors. Who is she, and why does she haunt the elevator?

Larry mentions the Seelbach's ghosts in his book and also includes information from a newspaper clipping about a 1936 tragedy that occurred at the hotel. Patricia Wilson was found atop the service elevator. By the time she was discovered, she had been dead for several hours. According to the account, the twenty-four-year-old woman had been planning a reunion with her estranged husband, but *he* had been killed just days earlier in a car accident.

Since the 1992 discovery of the old newspaper story, people have speculated that Patricia Wilson committed suicide because of her husband's death or was so distraught with grief that she was simply not paying attention and carelessly stepped into the empty elevator shaft. I, however, have found something that indicates Patricia's death may be the result of something far more sinister. After many hours of searching archives, I put my hands on an article that sent a chill skipping down

*Some believe Patricia Wilson died accidentally, while others insist she lost her life to a monster.*

the back of my neck. If the implications from the old newspaper are true, Patricia did not commit suicide. Nor did she have an accident. *Patricia Wilson was murdered!*

Finding all of the answers to the fatal elevator mystery is as challenging as putting together a jigsaw puzzle with pieces lost beneath the sofa cushions. Eyewitnesses have passed away, old records have been shredded, and only bits of the story remain in the form of neatly printed newspaper columns with scant details.

When the young woman's broken body was discovered on top of a linen elevator at the Seelbach Hotel on July 15, 1936, police were quoted in the newspapers, saying that she had been "a party girl." It was a dismissive label to slap on someone who had just been killed. And it invited a "blame the victim" mentality.

Patricia was supposedly at a "drinking party" at the hotel just prior to her disappearance. She had been missing for hours before the discovery of her lifeless body. A young woman with a troubled marriage who attended drinking parties did not garner much respect in the 1930s. Murder, *however*, is serious. And one would think that even the murder of a "party girl" would warrant some scrutiny. If they suspected foul play, surely the police would investigate. *Maybe not.*

Crime had previously gone unpunished at the Seelbach. The hotel's own website boasts that gangsters were welcomed there. Celebrity gangster Al Capone played cards there and, in fact, had a special mirror sent from Chicago and installed so that he could "watch his back." In addition, he had access to secret passageways and a tunnel beneath the hotel so that he could hide from police. The Seelbach website also notes that the hotel was "the center of Kentucky's bourbon and whiskey country" during prohibition in the 1920s.

Al Capone was in prison at the time of Patricia Wilson's death. So he, of course, was not her killer. But the notorious gangster was not the only unsavory character to swagger through Louisville. How much power would a man have to brandish in order to escape prosecution for the homicide of a young woman? What if he was a former prosecuting attorney, a general, a governor, *and* a publisher of a Kentucky newspaper?

It would be a year before just such a man was accused of beating Patricia and throwing her down the elevator shaft. It was not a criminal charge, however, but a civil suit that fingered him as an ice-blooded killer. When General Henry H. Denhardt learned of the suit against him, he dismissed it as "absurd and ridiculous." In a brief July 6, 1937, newspaper article, the sixty-year-old divorced Bowling Green, Kentucky, politician said, "I never heard of that girl. I was not in the hotel at that time."

General Denhardt scoffed at the $70,000 lawsuit leveled at him by Edward C. Langan, Jefferson County public administrator. The suit alleged that the six-foot-two, 230-pound "Denhardt had assaulted, beat, and bruised Miss Wilson, causing her to fall down the elevator shaft." The general soon retaliated by suing *Langan* for over double the amount for damages caused by the suit against him. He claimed his enemies were trying to destroy him and that the suit was "deliberate and maliciously filed" to harm him and rob him of his precious military rank.

The articles about Patricia Wilson's mysterious death were not much more than footnotes to front-page stories of Henry Denhardt's bigger troubles. For fifteen short weeks after Patricia's death, a bullet from his .45 revolver killed another Kentucky woman. Mrs. Verna Garr Taylor was a forty-three-year-old widow and the mother of two teenage daughters. The newspapers heralded her as a slender, dark-eyed beauty of high society. She owned a successful laundry business near her home in La Grange, Kentucky, and moved in the same social circles as the general. He was smitten with her, and they were engaged to be married.

What did Verna Garr Taylor see in Henry Denhardt? He was nearly twenty years her senior. The papers described him as portly and bald. But Henry Denhardt had an impressive résumé. He had served in three wars, been the governor of Kentucky, and held the rank of brigadier general in the Kentucky National Guard and lieutenant colonel in the army. He had been prosecuting attorney of Bowling Green for ten years and had also served two terms as county judge of Warren County. On top of all that, he had partnered with his brother as publisher of the *Bowling Green Times Journal*.

Maybe Verna was drawn to his status, wealth, and power. Or perhaps she really loved him. It didn't matter. She was dead in a ditch before they could be married.

On November 6, 1936, Verna and Henry went for a drive. As they headed along a lonely country road, the car stalled. Verna walked to a nearby gas station to get help. Oddly, Henry was quiet and sullen and remained seated in the car as Good Samaritans pushed it. Verna made excuses for him, saying he was sick.

Gunshots were heard within an hour, and Verna was found dead near the broken-down car. She had been killed by the general's service revolver. Henry claimed that they had taken a drive to alleviate Verna's headache and that she was distraught because her teenage daughter was opposed to their upcoming marriage. Verna, he insisted, had suggested a suicide pact. Later, however, he would testify that she was upset about his rival, a handsome twenty-six-year-old laundry truck driver, Chester Woolfolk. Chester and Verna had feelings for each other, and Henry suggested that Verna was suicidal because she was unhappy about the fact that Chester was pursuing her.

When Verna was killed, her three brothers were grief stricken and outraged. Roy Garr, Jack Garr, and veterinarian Dr. E. S. Garr urged the prosecutor to press charges. In April 1937, the general went on trial for Verna's murder. The State said that the general had killed her because she had rejected him. The two-week murder trial ended on May 6, 1937. The jury of eleven farmers and a filling-station attendant deadlocked with seven voting for his acquittal. "It's a great vindication," the general crowed to reporters, though he was well aware that a second trial would be scheduled.

On September 20, 1937, the eve of General Denhardt's new trial, he met with his three attorneys in his room at the Armstrong Hotel in Shelbyville. Around 10:00 p.m., the general and his attorney, Rode Myers, went out for beers. As they walked back to the hotel, they saw the Garr brothers. The three men got out of a parked car and strode deliberately toward the startled general. He took one look at their angry faces and ran toward the entrance of the hotel. He fumbled frantically for the knob, and when the door would not budge, he threw his bulk against it.

Two of the Garr brothers drew their guns, and seven bullets entered the big man's head and chest. Henry Denhardt rolled into the hotel entryway and died. The brothers turned themselves into the police, claiming that they had fired at the general in self-defense, though no weapon was found on him. Charges were filed against the brothers, and the courtroom was filled with spectators who cheered for them. Public sentiment was with the men who had avenged their sister's murder. Soon Roy and Jack were acquitted. Dr. Garr, shell-shocked from the war, was sent to a mental hospital for observation for a short time before all charges were dropped.

With two women and their suspected killer dead, the truth is as elusive as a piano note in a breeze. Yet some odd "coincidences" remain. Within a fifteen-week period, three people with connections to Henry Denhardt died in "accidents." According to the lawsuit filed on behalf of Patricia Wilson's estate, the general had some sort of a relationship with her—a relationship that was so emotionally charged it ended with her murder in the elevator shaft. If indeed Patricia *was* romantically involved with Henry, it's suspicious that both she and her husband should die violently just when they were about to reconcile and leave Henry out in the cold.

If Patricia had a connection to Henry, as the lawsuit alleged, what was the nature of the relationship? Were they dating? If so, was he enraged to learn she was going back to her husband? General Denhardt's detractors claimed that he had plenty of henchmen to do his dirty work, some suggesting that he had an accomplice in Verna's murder. Perhaps one of these helpers had staged Patricia's husband's car accident.

Many killers in recent years have been successfully prosecuted after staging car accidents to cover up homicides, but forensics in the 1930s was far less sophisticated than it is today, and myriad guilty people literally got away with murder. In the 1930s, "a good old boys' club" ruled the underbelly of the Seelbach. Patricia Wilson was probably not their only victim.

In the halcyon days of his romance with Verna, the bold Henry Denhardt likely returned to the scene of the crime to show off his new fiancée and to dine in the elegant Seelbach restaurant. After her violent death, Verna's restless soul may have been drawn to the tragic hotel to commiserate with Patricia. For all we know, Henry is there too.

## — *Update* —

In a case of sweet synchronicity, our family became friends with a relative of Verna Garr Taylor's, six years after I included the story of her murder in my book, *Ghost in the Mirror*. Ian Punnett is an author, a professor, and radio personality—perhaps best known as the weekend host of the nationally syndicated program, *Coast to Coast AM*, heard on more than 500 radio stations.

My mother, Ann Rule, authored three dozen bestselling true crime books. Ian reached out to us in the last year of her life when she was wheelchair bound, on oxygen and not her usual sharp self. Her memory for the past was incredible, however, and that was a good thing because Ian sought her insights about her early writing career when she reported for detective magazines half a century ago. I helped facilitate his interviews with my mom, and as I was on my way to coordinate their first meeting, I decided to bring him one of my books. I intuitively selected *Ghost in the Mirror*.

I gave Ian the book and then sat quietly as he recorded his first interview with my mom—until I interrupted. I could not contain myself when he mentioned that a relative of his was murdered. It was Verna Garr Taylor! I pointed at the book and exclaimed, "Her story is in my book!" As it turned out, Ian was writing a book about Verna. *A Black Night for the Bluegrass Belle*, published in 2016, is a beautifully written page turner.

Other revelations associated with the Seelbach include information I uncovered while researching. One article in particular is noteworthy because it may relate to the ghost of the homeless woman seeking warmth at the hotel on a cold night.

I learned that the homeless *did* warm themselves at the Seelbach and had been doing so since the 1930s. At about 8:15 on the night of October 27, 1937, engineer Ed King discovered a dead man on the catwalk above the boilers in the engine room. The stranger had apparently died in his sleep of natural causes about thirty-six hours before he was found. Authorities were unable to identify him but assumed he was homeless and trying to stay warm.

Did he make a habit of sleeping on that catwalk? Was he the only one, or was this a popular spot for transients to escape the cold? Was this man close to a homeless female, and if so, could her restless spirit be searching for him, appearing at the hotel café on frigid nights? The dead man on the catwalk is a mystery, and it's impossible to say if he had any connection to the ghostly homeless woman. It stands to reason, however, that the John Doe must have had someone who loved him—be it a mother, a sister, or a wife—and there is no doubt that they spent the rest of their days wondering what became of him.

With online access to billions of articles not available to researchers when I wrote about the Seelbach fifteen years ago, I now have more insights about the source of the paranormal activity there. One candidate is Claude Frederick Kimball, thirty-three, from Topeka, Kansas. His suicide was heard by everyone in the Seelbach Hotel at 3:30 on Monday afternoon, November 19, 1906. The newspaper noted that guests "were startled by the report of a revolver, which resounded with clearness through the halls and corridors of the entire building."

Records show that a number of other suicides occurred at the Seelbach, though it was not always clear if the deaths were accidental or intentional. For instance, in the case of Edward Peck, age fifty, there were no witnesses when he plunged from a fourth-story window at a little before 4:00 a.m. on February 19, 1906. Peck was from Saginaw, Michigan, and worked for Arthur Hild & Company, one of the largest lumber outfits in the country. His room faced Fourth Avenue, and he had been in town just a few hours when he dropped to his death, landing between the hotel's two entryways. Authorities could not determine whether he had jumped or fallen.

William Byrne, Sr.'s death, however, was *definitely* an accident. He was washing windows on the Seelbach's fifth floor in September of 1949 when he suffered a fatal fall. He worked for National Cleaning Company, and the accident occurred when his leather harness broke. Byrne, forty-eight, had worked for the company for eight years, and his harness had deteriorated from sweat and wear. The coroner was quoted saying that the accident "was inexcusable," but the company owner insisted that it was the responsibility of employees to notify management when their harnesses needed replacing. Byrne suffered multiple injuries and was rushed to the hospital, where he died two hours after his fall.

Alonzo George Fry, forty-seven, desperately tried to save himself in his last panicked moment of life. He was visiting his friend W. W. Hart in room 704 when the shocking accident occurred. Alonzo was a married father of five from Louisville. He and his friend were traveling salesmen and found themselves in town at the same time and decided to meet for dinner at about eight o'clock on October 24, 1907. While Hart filled out an order form for a sale he'd made, Fry took a seat on the windowsill and was preparing to pour himself a glass of water when he leaned back against the window. But there was no glass because the window was *open*.

Fry realized his mistake too late, and Hart would never forget the sound of his friend's anguished cry. Fry grabbed for the curtains, but they came with him, along with the brass curtain rod and the water pitcher he had been holding. It may have been the worst thing that Hart ever witnessed, and it was equally bad for John Morgan, a Seelbach employee who was in the basement storeroom when Alonzo fell. John was directly below the skylight where the victim landed with a thud. As glass shattered around him, John glanced up, stunned to see that a man had partially broken through the glass and was hanging above him.

In the hotel dining room, patrons were oblivious to the accident but grew curious when they saw through the window that a large crowd had gathered. Newspapers reported that the swarm of spectators was so dense "that it almost swept the policemen off their feet." When diners realized what had happened, they lost their appetites and left their meals unfinished. In the hotel's auditorium, an elegant banquet for the Retail Merchants' Association had just begun, with Otto Seelbach attending. When Otto was informed about the accident, he rushed to see if he could help. But there was nothing that Otto or anyone else could do for Alonzo Fry.

Almost every hotel with a century of guests has had its share of disasters. While the Seelbach has seen tragedy, it has also seen miracles. Peter Zanolari, eighteen, was an assistant cook at the Seelbach and was working in the hotel basement on July 20, 1905, when his skull was crushed in an elevator accident. The boy had called for the freight elevator and grew impatient when it took longer than expected. He opened the cage door, looked up, and was instantly struck by the descending elevator.

The fact he was not killed earned him the headline "Zanolari Mystery" in the July 23 issue of the *Courier-Journal*. The article reported that his survival astonished surgeons and that he was "a marvel to the local medical fraternity." Despite the fact his brain was exposed, Peter said he felt no pain, and he refused "to take an anesthetic" during the two-hour surgery and remained conscious throughout. He was so relaxed that he asked for a glass of water in the middle of the operation. The physicians were in awe as they told reporters, "His temperature has never risen above one hundred."

It was not all good news, however, because, as the *Courier-Journal* noted, Peter now had "a gruesome appearance, with one side of his head almost flat."

### The Seelbach Hilton
500 Fourth Street, Louisville, Kentucky 40202
(502) 585-3200
seelbachhilton.com

---

# Queen of the Sea

"Children should be seen and not heard." That old English proverb reflects intolerant views of kids who try to join in conversations with adults. The famously playful children in Long Beach, California, may have once obeyed those rules, but today, the opposite is true. These children are *heard* and not seen. They are heard giggling and running, their singsong voices piercing the silence. Sometimes they are heard splashing. But they are not seen.

They play in and around a swimming pool on the SS *Queen Mary*, something that startles the many witnesses who have heard them. They are the littlest ghosts of a ship so haunted that it's often listed among the spookiest places in America. Investigators say hundreds of restless spirits roam the ship that no longer sails but now serves as a hotel and museum.

Once a mighty vessel, the *Queen Mary* floats in a manmade lagoon in the salty waters of Queensway Bay. She is unable to break free because of the thick wire cables tethering her to shore. If it seems like an undignified ending for the last surviving prewar ocean liner, consider the alternative. The upkeep of the 87-year-old ship has been so costly that the city of Long Beach contemplated sinking her.

A July 2021 edition of the UK's *Daily Mail* reported that officials were deciding between dismantling and sinking her at a cost of 190 million dollars, or restoring her with a 500-million-dollar investment. The preservation effort would guarantee another century for the beloved ship and her ghosts to welcome aboard all who are fascinated by her history and intrigued by her mysteries.

What is to become of the ghosts of the *Queen Mary* if the vessel sinks to the bottom of the sea? Will the earthbound spirits finally crossover to the light, or will they wander aimlessly along Long Beach shores? Maybe they will stay aboard the sunken ship, unaware when air is replaced by water, and fish swim where humans once walked. We have, after all, seen evidence of ghosts oblivious to changing times. For instance, in some haunted places apparitions are spotted walking through walls, emerging from the exact locations of long-ago doorways that existed before remodeling was done on the buildings in question.

*Who haunts the Queen Mary?* Many researchers have speculated about their identities. I found a shocking case that I've not seen mentioned in any book, video, or documentary about the ship. The name of the victim is not included on the death-list plaques displayed on the boat. There are two plaques, one listing the names and dates of fatalities of crewmembers and the other listing passengers. Tour guides acknowledge that the lists are incomplete, but even they don't seem aware of what might be the first tragedy aboard the ship. That will change when *Haunted in America* is published.

Her name is Jane, and she's been forgotten by time. It took weeks of digging through newspaper archives to find her, but I sensed she was there somewhere deep in the files, so I kept looking. I will introduce you to Jane, a lovely young woman who took her last breath on the *Queen Mary*, but first I will introduce you to the ship herself.

She was built in 1935 in a Glasgow shipyard for the British-owned Cunard-White Star Line. Before White Star merged with the Cunard in 1934, it was notorious for its tragic *Titanic*, the ship launched as unsinkable in 1911 only to sink in April 1912. Over 1,500 people died in that disaster, something that could have been avoided if the ship had been equipped with an adequate number of lifeboats.

Cunard-White Star owners were determined to build something bigger, faster, and safer. At 1,018 feet long and 118 feet wide, the *Queen Mary's* dimensions are about 10 percent larger than the *Titanic's*. Management was well aware of the public's fear of shipwrecks and made sure to publicize their twenty-four "fireproof and unsinkable" lifeboats, each with a capacity to hold 145 passengers and each powered by a Diesel motor.

The steel lifeboats were unusually large, and safety features included a design that allowed for extra buoyancy. The buoyance chambers were made from copper, carefully fitted into each craft, and removable for maintenance. Articles about this began to appear months before the grand ship was launched in 1936.

Newspapers around the globe also reported on the new ocean-liner's luxurious accommodations. The steamer boasted twenty-one elevators, perfumed air, and a promenade deck for dogs. Dining areas stretched the width of the ship, with 10,000 meals served daily. Other offerings included air-conditioning, two heated swimming pools, therapeutic baths, and cabins with private toilets. Many rooms had telephones, and two passengers could simultaneously make long-distance calls from mid-ocean, each phoning a different country—technology that astounded many.

The vessel was engineered so that vibration was barely noticeable when motors were running. The foghorn was pitched two octaves below middle "A" and was imperceptible to passengers but still audible from ten miles away in stormy weather. Designers made sure that passengers would not be disturbed by the harsh clang of ship's bells when the crew changed shifts. The bells were "harmonically tuned" to sound like sweet, musical church bells.

Cabin-class passengers had the best accommodations, but those in tourist-class and third-class were also very comfortable. On May 27, 1936, approximately 2,500 passengers and 1,000 crewmembers boarded in Southampton, England, for the *Queen Mary's* maiden voyage to New York. Newspaper Headlines shouted sentiments such as "*Queen Mary* Combines Utmost Safety with Great Luxury" and "Stateliest Ship in Being Sails the Sea."

Flash forward to October 1988 when an *Unsolved Mysteries* episode, hosted by Robert Stack, featured the haunting of the *Queen Mary*. Carol Leyden was among those interviewed. She was a longtime waitress, employed since the mid-1970s aboard the ship-turned-hotel. Carol had been working there for fourteen years when something odd occurred early one winter morning.

She recalled that it was before the breakfast rush, and the restaurant was unusually quiet when she noticed a young woman seated at a table. Carol hadn't heard the lady come in, but she dutifully approached with coffee. As she served it, she couldn't help staring at her customer's lovely dress, so very pretty but out-of-fashion since the 1940s. The mysterious lady's hair was also done up in an old style, with coiled braids on the sides of her head, a popular look among young women in the 1930s.

**FRIEND SAYS MISSING GIRL HAPPY ON LINER**

Lynn Youth Tells of Chat With Jane Carey
Queen Mary Before Disappearance

JANE CAREY
Wired photo of Smith College student, and Lynn girl, whose disappearance at sea was reported when the liner Queen Mary docked at New York yesterday.

*An August 1936 newspaper article reports on the baffling disappearance of Jane Carey, a lovely young woman with everything to live for.*

The woman sat very still and did not utter a word. As Carol walked away, she stole another glance at her peculiar customer and was dumbstruck to find she had vanished. Carol had just met her first ghost.

It was Carol's encounter that inspired me to search archives for the tragic lady. Jane Carey, age twenty, was last seen on the *Queen Mary* in August of 1936, not long after the grand vessel's maiden voyage. The most widely circulated photograph of Jane clearly shows her hair in braids, coiled up on the sides of her head, just like the ethereal lady who appeared to Carol Leyden.

Jane vanished early on a Sunday morning as the *Queen Mary* glided through thick fog, three-quarters of the way through her voyage across the Atlantic Ocean. Jane's cabinmate, Mary Stewart, said they had woken at 7:30 a.m. and she last saw Jane clad in a kimono. Mary stepped out for a few minutes, and when she returned, Jane was gone. She assumed her absent roommate had gone swimming, but when an hour passed and she did not return, Mary alerted a steward. The ship was searched, but there was no sign of Jane. Nearly ninety years later, she has not been found, and her mystery remains unsolved.

It's interesting to note that Carol met the beautiful ghost early in the morning, the same time of day when Jane was last seen. Was Jane headed to the dining room when she met her fate? Could she still be waiting for breakfast, unaware of the passing years as she sits patiently at a table, wondering why no one notices her?

I had hoped to speak to Carol Leyden about her spirit encounter, so I looked her up and was sad to discover she passed away in 2010 at age seventy-two. I would have loved to share photographs of Jane with Carol to see if she saw a resemblance to the ghost she met.

Jane Carey was born on March 19, 1916, in Chicago, Illinois, to parents John William Carey and Laura La Croix Carey. John was a wealthy lumber dealer who died of pneumonia at age forty-two in 1928, leaving a large estate to his family. After his death, the family moved into the mansion of Jane's grandmother in Lynn, Massachusetts.

At the time she went missing, Jane was a Smith College honors student about to enter her senior year. She was traveling tourist-class on the *Queen Mary*, heading home to Massachusetts after a year of studying with classmates in Florence, Italy. She loved the Italian language and belonged to her school's Italian Club. Jane had two siblings, a younger sister, Dorothy, seventeen, who was attending a girl's camp in Maine when her sister vanished. Brother Pete was in medical school at Yale.

Newspaper reporters noted that Jane was the third Smith College student to vanish in the past eleven years, though her disappearance did not happen on a traditionally unlucky day. The other two victims each went missing on Friday the 13th, Alice Corbett in November 1925 and Frances Smith in January 1928. Smith's body was found in the Connecticut River fourteen months later, and officials speculated her death was an accidental drowning. Alice Corbett and Jane Carey were never seen again.

When Jane disappeared, *Queen Mary* officials were quick to conclude that she had taken her own life, and some headlines read, "Heiress Leaps to her Death from Queen Mary." But Jane had left no suicide note. Her family said that she was not depressed and that her only problem was insomnia. They did not believe she would kill herself. Jane's friend, William Prichard, had seen Jane on the ship and agreed she was not suicidal. William, a student at the Massachusetts Institute of Technology, had also been abroad for a year, studying in France, Switzerland, and England.

When a reporter reached him by phone at his home, he said, "Jane was in the best of spirits Saturday afternoon, when I met her on the promenade deck. I had talked with her at different times after we met on board the *Queen Mary*, and she seemed perfectly all right. I have known her for years, of course, since we're neighbors at home here in Lynn. I was shocked and surprised when she was reported missing Sunday. I cannot understand it, unless it was an accident." (William, too, lived with his family in a mansion, a five-minute walk to the Carey mansion.)

There had been quite a bit of confusion when it was first discovered Jane was missing because her close friends claimed her voyage was on the *Statendam* and not the *Queen Mary*. Jane had, in fact, sent her mother a cablegram, alerting her that she would travel via the *Statendam* and arrive at the Port of New York on August 14th. All but one piece of Jane's luggage was aboard the *Statendam*, left in the care of her friend and classmate, Clarissa Wells, whom she had originally planned to travel with.

Jane had switched ships at the last minute, and no one knew why—or if they *did* know, they weren't saying. William Prichard may have known more than he admitted. When reporters asked him if Jane had switched ships because of him, he denied it. He gave the impression that while he and Jane were close friends, they were not romantically involved. Reporters got the impression he had last seen Jane on Saturday afternoon, but a steward claimed he saw them dancing together on Saturday night.

I studied the passenger lists of the *Queen Mary* and the *Statendam* for August 1936 and saw that Jane and William were listed as passengers on both ships. The *Statendam* added a note at the bottom of the sheet, saying that Jane Carey and William Prichard had canceled. Jane's name was crossed off the *Queen Mary* list but was still visible. A footnote said, "Jane Carey, presumed lost at sea."

While it's possible the reporters misunderstood, news articles indicated that William said he had not seen Jane in England. Either William was not completely honest, or the reporters got it wrong because I found evidence that they *had* seen each other in England. Probably no one in America saw the story published on August 6, 1936, in Bristol, Avon, England's *Western Daily Press*:

*Two Americans who were intending to sail in the liner missed the ship, but boarded her from a tender in Southampton Water. They were Miss Jane Carey and Mr. W. Pritchard [sic], who had travelled together from London by car. Arriving as the Queen Mary was pulling away from the berth, they followed her in a tug and clambered on board soon after she left the swinging ground.*

Except for the conflicting information, there is nothing to suggest that William Prichard was anything other than an honorable young man. I have no reason to suspect he was guilty of harming Jane, but it's apparent that neither wanted to tell their parents everything. Jane could have phoned her mother from the *Queen Mary* and alerted her to the fact that the boat would reach New York four days earlier than the *Statendam*, but for whatever reason, she kept her plans a secret. On the same day Jane boarded the *Queen Mary*, she had sent the message claiming she'd be on the *Statendam*. Did Jane deliberately mislead her mother, or did she change her mind immediately after sending the cablegram?

It may be that Jane and William wanted a romantic rendezvous and a few days of freedom aboard a luxury ship without their parents knowing. If they *were* romantic, were Jane's feelings for William stronger than his for her? Could Jane have been pregnant and ashamed? Either of these scenarios would be cause for depression. Mary Stewart, Jane's cabinmate, claimed that Jane had seemed sad. But they didn't know each other well. They were rooming together by assignment because they were both tourist-class passengers.

When I speculate about what *might* have happened to Jane, I dismiss the idea that she accidentally fell off the ship. While it's possible that she took her own life, I lean toward the possibility that a stranger harmed Jane.

While researching, I found that a shocking number of women disappeared from steamers in the 1920s and 1930s. While some *were* suicides, many were cases where the victims had everything to live for and had shown no sign of depression. Surely officials must have been aware that many women were vanishing from ships. Were they so naive that they believed that *every* disappearance was the fault of the victim?

It must have crossed the minds of management that predators could have harmed their missing passengers—possibly predators employed by the ships.

Serial attackers would likely have changed jobs frequently, moving from ship to ship to avoid suspicion.

The *Queen Mary* employed approximately 1,000 crewmembers for each voyage, and it wasn't statistically possible for each one to be trustworthy. That is also true when it comes to the thousands of passengers on each voyage.

It would have been very bad for business if passengers became afraid, and I suspect that many murders on various ships were not investigated and were instead dismissed as suicides.

Whatever the reason for Jane's disappearance, it was traumatic—the kind of trauma that results in earthbound spirits. My guess is that Jane is among the *Queen Mary's* many ghosts. She may very well be the ghost once seen by Carol Leyden in the ship's restaurant. Jane may also be the dancing ghost, an apparition in a white dress, seen by many over the years. Jane vanished just hours after she was seen dancing aboard the *Queen Mary.*

After August 1936, Jane Carey's story was forgotten as the *Queen Mary* ruled the transatlantic seas, pampering the pampered, until World War II. She then became a warship, painted camouflage gray, so she blended in with the ocean. From a distance, she was almost invisible. This earned her the nickname "The Gray Ghost."

The mighty ship transported troops and was so useful to the allied forces that Adolf Hitler offered a quarter-of-a-million-dollar reward to any submarine captain who could sink her. Because of this, the ship was under strict orders to never stop for any reason.

In 1942, a much smaller ship, the HMS *Curacoa,* was assigned escort duty, and accompanied the *Queen Mary,* on the lookout for enemy submarines. The *Curacoa* traveled in a zigzag pattern, and in one horrific moment as she passed in front of the larger ship, the two collided. The *Curacoa* was ripped in two, but the *Queen Mary* could not stop to help the drowning troops. The "Grey Ghost" had no fatalities but suffered a hole in her bow. Of the 400 troops aboard the *Curacoa,* only 101 survived.

In July 1947, the *Queen Mary* finally sailed again on a postwar voyage. She spent two more decades crossing the Atlantic Ocean, finally retiring to Long Beach in 1967. Serving as a hotel, a museum, and a special events venue, the regal ship has been treasured by many, but her future is uncertain.

## More Queen Mary Ghosts

Credible witnesses have reported many paranormal experiences on the ship, including the following:

- An entire tour group witnessed the apparition of a naval officer near the swimming pool. Clad in navy whites, his figure was somewhat transparent as he strolled past the startled crowd.
- Guests spending the night in a luxury cabin awoke to see the sorrowful face of a teenage boy, staring at them with large, pleading eyes.
- Some have seen the ghost of a long-ago passenger, killed when he fractured his skull after falling down stairs. The apparition appears at the top of the stairs where his accident occurred.
- Pitiful shrieks are heard near the area that crashed into the doomed *Curacoa*. It's as if the men left to drown all those decades ago don't realize they're dead and still scream for help.

**The Queen Mary**
1126 Queens Hwy, Long Beach, California 90802
(877) 342-0738
queenmary.com

———

# Johnnie's Playground

While the ghosts of famous gunslingers and outlaws are believed to haunt a hotel in Cimarron, New Mexico, the most active spirit on the premises may be that of a naughty child. In the late 1800s, the St. James Hotel drew weary travelers for more than one reason. The rooms were comfortable and each was equipped with its own sink, a rare luxury for the era. Many customers came for the meals, prepared by owner Henri Lambert. He was a master chef and had once cooked for Abraham Lincoln.

The saloon was busy and popular with the stars of the Wild West, including Jesse James, Annie Oakley, Wyatt Earp, Kit Carson, and Buffalo Bill. The hotel, however, was not just a business. It was the Lambert family's home. Henri's wife, Mary, was the mother of five boys, and she was sometimes uncomfortable with the rowdy atmosphere. It was not uncommon for customers in the hotel's saloon to fire their guns. To this day, the saloon's ceiling is still scarred with bullet holes. The night Mary gave birth to son Fred, Buffalo Bill and Clay Allison were drinking in the bar. (Buffalo Bill eventually taught the boy to shoot and nicknamed him Cyclone Dick.)

A brothel once operated at the hotel, and business was allegedly good. Gunfights were so common that no less than twenty-six men were killed at the St. James. Those who knew the reasons for the deadly disputes are long gone. We can only guess at the reasons. Love? Lust? Money? These ingredients were available at the St. James. Add alcohol, and you've got a volatile cocktail.

One psychic who visited the hotel in the 1980s sensed that the place was haunted by a gambler who had won the hotel in a poker game. The winner, she said, was killed before he took ownership and is the entity who haunts the hotel's infamous room 18. Though often reported as fact, no documentation has been found to support this. What has been documented, however, are hundreds of reported paranormal experiences. Employees and customers tell of lights turning themselves on, objects vanishing into the floor, and sightings of a small blond figure, dubbed the Imp. No one is allowed to stay the night in the hotel's most haunted room, room 18. The present owner insists that disaster strikes immediately after anyone spends the night there.

My friend and fellow writer, Cheri Eicher, and I arrived after dark on a September evening in 1999. We stepped into the lobby and felt something watching us. Glancing up, we saw the heads of long-dead deer and moose, who stared back glassy eyed. Michele, the exhausted combination bartender and front desk clerk, greeted us and requested that we save our questions till morning. Winding down from an eighteen-hour shift, she was not up for talking about ghosts. We followed her up the staircase and down a long hall toward the Mary Lambert room. Before we reached the door, it drifted open with such a foreboding creak that I was sure it was a special effect. But no, Michele was just as surprised as we were. "This door is not supposed to be unlocked!" She sounded shaken. "And the light is not supposed to be on! She must have known you were coming."

*She?* Cheri and I glanced at each other. "She must mean Mary," whispered Cheri. Mary's room was charming but small, so we helped Michele move the bed to make room for a cot. As Michele left, she stopped short and pointed a trembling finger across the hall to the Katie Lambert room. "That door wasn't open a minute ago!" she exclaimed. "And the light wasn't on!"

We stared at the wide-open door. We all thought it had been shut a moment before. But then, we were all tired. Perhaps our minds were playing tricks on us.

As Michele made a hasty retreat down the hall, Cheri said, "The room smells good—like perfume." Though the room was named for Mary, it had actually been the prostitutes' quarters. A phantom perfume has often been reported there.

After dropping off our luggage, we visited the saloon downstairs. Michele played a video of a string of TV programs that featured the St. James's haunting. One of the shows was *Unsolved Mysteries* and featured a reenactment of a sighting by a former employee. The actor who played the ghost was a boy who looked to be about age seven.

"I wonder if a child died here," I said. When bedtime arrived, I took the cot,

*The St. James Hotel, where one little ghost never stops playing. (Leslie Rule)*

and as Cheri settled into the bed, I told her, "I want to see a ghost. If something happens tonight, wake me up." Cheri shivered and pulled the quilt up to her chin. "Okay," she promised. "But if *you* see anything, don't wake *me* up!" With the black night pressing against the window, she was losing her enthusiasm. Though two of the rooms in the hotel's newer annex next door had been booked, we were the only guests in the old building— *the haunted building*—and Cheri was afraid.

I soon fell into my usual deep sleep. Cheri slept, too, but suddenly woke up late in the night. As she lay in bed, she faced the transom window over the door. The door to the Katie Lambert room, across the hall, still stood open, and its light shone through into our room. Cheri was comforted by the light—until it suddenly went out. *Who turned it off?* She held her breath, listening for footsteps, but heard nothing. She could not get back to sleep. An hour had passed when she heard footsteps outside our door. "Leslie!" she called. "Wake up!"

"Orumfh," I replied sleepily and pulled the pillow over my head. For long minutes, Cheri listened as someone paced outside our door in the creaking hall. Then, about 3:00 a.m., I felt a soft caress on my cheek, as if a little hand had patted me. Suddenly, I was wide awake. When Cheri described the earlier events, I said, "The light probably just burned out." I crossed the hall and found the light switch in the off position. I flipped it on. How could it have turned itself off? "Maybe someone is playing a joke on us," I reasoned. "Let's see if I can walk without making noise." I stepped lightly on the sides of the hall.

No matter what I did, the old wooden floor creaked and groaned with each movement. Cheri had heard the footsteps an hour after the light went out. Had someone turned off the light and then stood there for a full hour before walking away? Unlikely. When the golden morning light sifted through our window, I said, "Let's go to the cemetery. I think we'll find answers there."

"We don't have much time," Cheri reminded me. "You have a plane to catch." The old Cimarron Cemetery was on a hill, about a mile from the hotel. I gazed over the sprawling resting place at the hundreds of stones and said, "I want to find the Lambert family plot." Cheri was skeptical. "It will take forever to find it," she said.

Remarkably, my feet took me straight to the spot, and I found myself gazing through an iron fence at the Lamberts' graves: Charles Fred Lambert, 1887–1971. Katie Hoover Lambert, 1886–1964. Catherine Hoover, 1854–1940. Baby Lambert, September 2, 1911. Johnnie Lambert, son of Henri and Mary, August 1889–February 23, 1892. "I found him!" I called out to Cheri. She rushed over, and I pointed at a broken gravestone. "Johnnie is the little boy ghost. He was two and a half when he died."

"He's too young," Cheri protested. "*Unsolved Mysteries* showed him as an older boy."

"They may have taken creative license," I argued. "I'll ask the guy who saw him."

Once back home in Seattle, I made a few phone calls and learned that Steven, the employee who had seen the ghostly boy, was so rattled by the experience that he quit. I was able to track down a number for Steven's father. While Steven had been interviewed for the *Unsolved Mysteries* episode, he was very disturbed by the encounter and wanted to forget it. Steven's father told me, "My son doesn't like to talk about it. But I can tell you exactly what he told me."

He described the early morning that Steven had been cleaning the hotel when he spotted a child sitting on the bar. The kid was spinning a bottle, and he assumed he was the naughty child of a guest. He was about to send him back to his room, but as he got closer, he realized something was not right.

The little boy wore a long, white nightgown, and his blond hair was almost to his shoulders. The boy glanced up. Half of his face was horribly disfigured, as if he had been burned. As Steven watched in shock, the kid jumped off the counter and disappeared *into* the floor.

Steven had been adamant that the child was a *boy*. If I had seen someone with long hair, dressed in a nightgown, I would have assumed I was looking at a girl. Yet, Steven had been certain that it was the ghost of a male child, and his father relayed that to me.

"How old was the boy?" I asked.

"My son said he was a *little* boy."

"A toddler?"

"Yes."

According to his tombstone, Johnnie Lambert was two and a half when he died in 1892. He was a *little* boy, the right age to be the ghost seen sitting atop the bar. The fact that the apparition had something wrong with his face was a very interesting detail, and I wondered whether it had something to do with his death. Had Johnnie died in a fire?

I contacted the New Mexico Bureau of Vital Records and was told that if I sent them a check for the fee, they would look for the death records and mail me copies. I mailed the check and waited impatiently for weeks. If I could confirm that Johnnie had an injury to his face, it would validate the ghost sighting in the bar. I was disappointed when I finally received a letter from the records department. No documents could be found for either Johnnie or Baby Lambert.

Next, I turned to psychic Nancy Myer, hoping she could provide answers. I'd worked with her before and knew she had an impressive track record. She has been featured in multiple books and television programs, including *Unsolved Mysteries* and *Psychic Detectives*. Nancy can "read" photographs, psychically picking up information. I mailed photographs of the St. James Hotel to her, but I gave her no information about the place. She'd never heard of the hotel, and I didn't reveal the location. Just as she had done with crime scene photos when she was working with police, Nancy studied the images I sent her.

*Though Johnnie Lambert is buried here, his spirit does not rest. (Leslie Rule)*

We lived on opposite coasts, so she studied the photos as we talked on the phone. She took one look and immediately said, "There have been over twenty murders here." She added that the place had once been a brothel. She was correct on both counts. I asked if she could pick up on a child who died there.

"Which one?" she asked. "There are *nine*."

"Tell me about the little boy. He was two and a half."

Nancy laughed. "That child had more energy than any one child has a right to."

"Do you have a sense of his name?" I asked.

"It's something like Joseph or Joe."

"Close," I said. "It was Johnnie. Is his face disfigured?"

"He was burned. Someone was carrying fried food in a big pot. He ran into them. They were burned, and so was he. He died from the burns, but not right away."

When I told her the little ghost was seen spinning a bottle, she laughed knowingly. It fit the description of the little bundle of energy she was connecting with. "He's still running around those halls," she told me. Johnnie was "a barrel of mischief" and was responsible for most of the paranormal activity at the hotel. His mother was also earthbound and had been trying for decades to get her son to cross over with her. "He's happy," said Nancy. "He's having a good time." She explained that his resistance to leaving his earthly playground prevented his mother from moving on.

She had just confirmed what hotel employees had long suspected—that Mary Lambert was among the ghosts residing there. She had, in fact, died in the hotel.

Nancy said that the spirits of two little girls were also there. "They died of diphtheria. It was probably in the late 1800s." The girls were sisters, ages twelve and nine, with sausage curls. One was blonde, the other brunette. She sensed their names were Andrea and Melody, with a last name of either Simple or Sample. The sisters had two brothers who also got sick but survived. One of those boys was a baby, nine months old, and though he lived, his health was weakened for the rest of his life.

Nancy added, "Their father may have been a teacher. He was very good at math." Melody and Andrea were polite girls, strictly raised, and they were now polite ghosts who were shocked by Johnnie's behavior. "The girls are aware of Johnnie, but they don't approve of him."

What about the men who died in gunfights? Nancy said that their ghosts might appear and that they are quite capable of playing jokes on the living. They stay in a cave in the hills most of the time because they felt safe there when they were alive.

## — Update —

It's been twenty-three years since Nancy read the St. James photos, and it is now easier for me to access archives to validate information. I've recently learned that Nancy was accurate when she sensed that the St. James's outlaws chose to hide in caves. While searching old newspapers, I found multiple articles that mention this. Jessie James and the others had cave hideouts in the various areas they visited.

I've often thought of Johnnie Lambert over the years. When Nancy sensed that he was running around in the kitchen at the time of his accident, I had not told her that Johnnie lived at the hotel *or* that his father was the chef there. It makes perfect sense that the Lambert kids would gravitate toward the kitchen, the place where their father spent so much time.

While I've not yet found proof that Johnnie suffered from burns, I finally found a newspaper article about his death. He had diphtheria, but the brief article didn't mention whether burns were a contributing factor in his death. The article *did* mention that there was an outbreak of diphtheria at the hotel, and that children got sick, including Johnnie's siblings. Some died, while others survived. Diphtheria, of course, was the disease Nancy had mentioned when she read the photographs. And the outbreak was in the late 1800s, just as she had said. Were the Sample sisters staying at the hotel at the time of the outbreak? I don't know. I'm still looking for confirmation of their existence.

As for Steven's description of the ghost boy in the bar, it turns out that Johnnie matched, not only in age—but in hairstyle. About fifteen years after *Coast to Coast Ghosts* was published, I found a photograph of Johnnie Lambert when his relatives posted it on an online family tree. Little Johnnie had long, blond hair, just like the apparition in the bar.

*A relative of Johnnie Lambert's posted this image of him in an online family tree, and despite the fact they are skeptical of ghost stories, they granted permission to publish the photo.*

**St. James Hotel**
617 S Collison Ave, Cimarron, New Mexico, 87714
(575) 376-2664
exstjames.com

---

# Coral Gables Most Haunted

Sumptuous. Elegant. Formidable. These three words are the first to come to mind when describing the Biltmore Hotel in Coral Gables, Florida. Six miles from Miami, the 1926 luxury hotel impresses with its massive columns, arching roofs, and grand lobby. The shimmering pool of clear turquoise water seems to stretch on forever. At 22,000 square feet, it *is* the largest pool in the continental United States.

In the 1930s, the pool was featured in events on Sunday afternoons when thousands of spectators sat in grandstands, watching alligator wrestling,

*The Biltmore was once a hospital that some patients never left. (Leslie Rule)*

synchronized swimming, and "boy wonder" Jackie Ott as he dove from an eighty-five-foot platform. Also known as "The Aqua Tot," Jackie began swimming when he was just six months old, and he was a star of the Biltmore pool performances by age four.

Rich with glamorous history, the Biltmore also saw tragedy. During World War II, the hotel was converted into the Army Forces Regional Hospital to serve the wounded. Many windows were sealed with concrete. Government-issue linoleum covered the elegant marble floors. The Biltmore remained a VA hospital until 1968 and was also home to the University of Miami's school of medicine.

When the City of Coral Gables acquired ownership of the property in 1973, the massive structure continued to sit empty for over a decade. Rumors spread that someone—*or something*—was residing in the building. Locals reported mysterious lights shining in the abandoned hotel. When daring teenagers tiptoed near in the dark of night, they ended up fleeing in fear at the sound of eerie laughter and old-time tunes.

In September of 1985, *The Palm Beach Post* reported on peculiar things experienced by the security guards watching over the Metropolitan Museum of Art, located in the old Country Club Section of the Biltmore. The area was protected by an alarm system, activated whenever someone passed through a beam of light. The alarms, however, were notorious for going off when no one was around, as if the sensors detected something that human eyes could not see.

Midnight security guard George Warden told a reporter that his team was continually baffled by an odd thing that had appeared on the video monitor on multiple occasions. When they glanced at the monitor, they clearly saw

*Do the ghosts of murdered lovers still frolic on this Biltmore balcony? (Leslie Rule)*

wheelchair marks on the carpet outside of a doorway that led to a balcony. But whenever they investigated, they found no marks. They'd return to their post, only to discover that the marks were once again visible through the monitor.

When the Biltmore reopened on New Year's Eve 1987, it was with all of the glory of its bygone days and seemed to serve as a portal to the past that allowed ghosts of yesteryear to step through. When I visited around 1999, I spoke to a dishwasher who admitted he'd seen a ghost in the Country Club Building. He'd wandered in one afternoon and was startled to see a man in a top hat playing the piano.

This did not surprise Linda Spitzer, an expert on the history and haunting of the hotel. She became the official Biltmore storyteller in 1994, with weekly sessions held in the hotel lobby. She had expected her talks to focus on history, but when employees and guests confided in her about their ghostly encounters, she realized that audiences would be fascinated by the haunting. She began to share stories of the paranormal in her talks, including a sighting she relayed to me. "A dancing couple dressed in twenties clothes has been seen in the ballroom," she said. As the spirits waltzed past the window, observers were stunned to notice they were transparent, and a moment later, the dancers vanished into thin air.

*The Biltmore reflected in a pond. (Leslie Rule)*

A guest met a mysterious lady on the thirteenth floor. It was apparent the lady was an ethereal being because she was floating several feet above the carpet. The thirteenth floor may be the most haunted area of the hotel because it's the site of one of the most dramatic events to take place at the Biltmore. Gangster Thomas "Fats" Walsh ran an illicit casino there in the 1920s. Shortly after midnight on March 7, 1929, Fats was shot and killed by a rival gangster in the middle of a gambling party.

Many believe that Fats is responsible for the mischievous pranks played on the hotel's guests. "He pesters the guests by messing with the elevator and the lights," said Linda. The elevators are regularly and *inexplicably* summoned to the thirteenth floor, though no living person is waiting for them.

In 1999, when psychic medium Nancy Myer "read" photos of the Biltmore, she sounded almost shocked as she exclaimed, "There has been a lot of raunchy activity here!" She studied my photograph of a Biltmore balcony and said, "A couple was murdered here. They were having an affair and were shot by the woman's husband." Nancy said the woman was naked—except for her jewelry.

I had spent a peaceful night sleeping in that room, and I hadn't experienced anything odd there. I was prompted to photograph the balcony when a gust of wind suddenly sucked the curtain out the open door. I shot sixteen photos of that curtain, mesmerized by how beautiful it appeared as it danced in the breeze. While I *assumed* it was the breeze, it may have been something other than the wind moving that curtain!

## — Update —

I've yet to find a case of a murder on a Biltmore balcony. If this did actually occur, it was probably during the gangster era, and the bodies could have been disposed of before hotel staff could find them and alert police.

I wish I could remember which room I stayed in. I was there over two decades ago, and I recall only that hotel management knew I was researching a book on ghosts and that they gave me an upgrade to an extra nice room to make up for the fact the pools had been drained for maintenance. Whether it was ghostly hands or just the wind that made the curtain dance on the balcony, I got a great shot that became the cover of my book *Coast to Coast Ghosts*.

While Nancy Myer shared insights about the source of some of the paranormal activity I wrote about in *Coast to Coast Ghosts*, she is best known for her work solving crimes. "About 90 percent of the time, I'm able to provide the police with new information," she said.

I met Nancy around 1991 when I was writing for *Woman's World* magazine. My editors asked me to write an article about psychics who work with police, and part of my assignment was to interview detectives who could vouch for their abilities. When I talked to Delaware State Police Colonel Irvin Smith, he said, "I've utilized Nancy's gift on many occasions. It's simply phenomenal—what she's able to recreate about a crime."

In order to best tune into a case, Nancy requests the victim's name, the date of the crime, and photographs of the crime scene. She usually "sees" the killer in her mind's eye and can sense the victim's last moments. "It's like watching a movie running in my head," she explained.

It's rare when Nancy goes to the actual site where the drama unfolded. She prefers to study *photographs* of crime scenes because her senses are overwhelmed when she visits locations where violence occurred. Once a pair of skeptical cops tricked her into going to a house where an elderly woman had been murdered. They didn't believe that Nancy had psychic ability, and they doubted she would catch on. But when she got out of the squad car, the horror overwhelmed her. Nancy screamed, "I can see her being stabbed!"

Colonel Smith was livid when he found out what the cops had done. He reprimanded them, and the sheepish rookies had nothing to say in their defense.

While many people have some psychic ability, very few have the talent that Nancy Myer has. She, and a handful of other psychic mediums, have been extremely successful in using their gifts to help victims find justice. The psychics wouldn't be nearly as successful if not for help from ghosts. Yes, the spirits of the dead can be instrumental in solving their own murders, but they can't do it alone. They need someone to hear or see or sense them. In some cases, psychics help victims, in other cases, it is investigators who come to the rescue.

In the next chapter, I'll introduce you to a man with an extraordinary ability. He solved many murders, but never called himself a psychic, and he shied away from ghost stories. Even so, he shared with me an incredible encounter he had with the spirit of a little girl. She had waited a very long time for justice, and Frank Bender was just the man to help her.

# Want to See a Ghost?
## You May Have Already Seen One!

Approximately 20 percent of Americans confide that they've seen a ghost or been in the presence of one, according to a 2009 study by the Pew Research Center. That percentage could actually be much higher because many of us have seen ghosts and not realized it.

For instance, that pale teenage girl sitting alone on the bench in the train station or the elderly woman trudging along the side of the road may not be a living being at all. Who actually stops to check each person they encounter?

Five signs it may be a ghost:
- The figure is unusually pale.
- You glance away for an instant, and when you look back, they are gone.
- The "person" ignores you when you speak to them—though sometimes ghosts do interact with people.
- The "person" is seen in an unusual place, such as on a deserted road or peering from the window of an abandoned house.
- The "person" is dressed in inappropriate or outdated clothing, such as a raincoat in the middle of summer or an outfit from another era.

# 6

## WHEN JUSTICE IS DONE

W e see countless cases of haunted sites where murders have occurred. Murder seems to be the ultimate ghost maker. Nearly as mysterious as the spirits who remain earthbound as a result of this most unjust of deaths, killers are enigmas that no one yet completely understands.

There are, of course, people who kill out of self-defense or to protect loved ones. And there are those who simply lose control—those who are truly insane because of malfunctioning brains. Then there are the killers who have no heart. They are so intent on their selfish needs or desires that they can snuff out a human life and feel no more guilt than if they swatted a fly. These are the ones who baffle the rest of us.

Murder and ghosts go hand in hand. If a killer thinks it is the end when he or she slays another person, they may be in for a rude surprise. Killers don't deserve the ink it takes to cover these pages, but they are an integral part of some of the following stories, so they must be mentioned here. And *maybe*, just *maybe*, a potential murderer may read these words and decide that taking another's life will not be worth it. Perhaps killers will understand that they don't have any power in the end—that their victims aren't really gone, and they will one day have to face them, perhaps in this lifetime.

# A Face for a Ghost

Ghost enthusiasts agree. Murder victims *want* their cases solved. And while homicide investigators and forensic experts are often hesitant to mention the paranormal events that occur when they're solving crimes, some privately admit that they may have had just a little help from the Other Side.

Little Aliyah Davis did not stand a chance. Five and a half years old and living in West Philadelphia in 1981, her fate was in the hands of her mother, Maria Davis Fox. The court had given Maria custody of her children—despite the fact that she was serving an eight-year probation for the 1974 beating death of her baby son.

Aliyah's big sister, eight-year-old Amira, was afraid of her mother and step-father, Charles Fox, who sometimes stabbed and starved the children. She wished she could protect Aliyah, her cute little sister, who wore two pigtails and smiled so sweetly. The family was watching *Dukes of Hazzard* on television

*Frank Bender with his first reconstructed face. His accuracy resulted in a killer's conviction. (Leslie Rule)*

when Aliyah had an accident in her pants. Amira and her siblings watched helplessly as Charles beat their little sister to death.

Years went by, and no one seemed to notice or care that Aliyah was not with the family while Maria and Charles continued to collect welfare checks for the murdered girl. It must have seemed to Amira that the killers would never be punished for what they had done to her sister. Then again, she had known and loved Aliyah for over five years. Perhaps she knew her sister had an invincible spirit—one that could not be stopped by death.

While world-famous forensic sculptor Frank Bender tends to be skeptical when it comes to ghost stories, he has no explanation for the unusual assistance he received in Aliya's heartbreaking case. It is as if by magic that Frank's sensitive fingers coax features from the clay that covers the unidentified skulls. The finished products are so lifelike that you can't help but jump when you first see them staring at you. Yet, it is not the fact that Frank Bender is a talented artist that is so incredible. It is his uncanny ability to give something precious back to the dead. *Their faces.*

Classically trained at the Pennsylvania Academy of Fine Arts, Frank did not set out to become a "Recomposer of the Decomposed." In the mid-1970s, while researching anatomy, he toured the Philadelphia Medical Examiner's office and viewed an unidentified woman who was killed when shot in the head. Her face had been obliterated. Moved by the victim's plight, Frank reconstructed her face, a procedure that requires sterilizing the skull and covering it with clay to sculpt a new face. Once finished, a mold is made from the original, and a copy is made.

Frank's first forensic sculpture resulted in the identification of Anna Mary Duval from Phoenix, and her killer was convicted. Frank has since created dozens of forensic sculptures with nearly as many cases solved as a result. In addition to recomposing victims, he does age projection—including one on the widely publicized fugitive John List, who hid for nearly two decades after murdering his family. When *America's Most Wanted* featured the bust of List, the likeness was so exact that the fugitive was captured eleven days later.

How does the sculptor take a skull and give it the semblance of the person it once belonged to, complete with the right hair, wrinkles, correctly colored eyes, and style of eyeglasses? *Good question.* Frank has his share of scientific answers and would rather use the word "intuition" than "psychic." Yet he can take a shattered skull with the features obliterated by a weapon and recreate the victim's exact nose, lips, and eyes.

Once a face has been recomposed, you can almost see the dignity restored in the eyes. Some of these faces are lined up on shelves in Frank's Philadelphia studio. There is a calm and challenging air about them. They seem to be daring their killers to try to get away with murder.

Each bust takes hundreds of hours to complete. It is a labor of love, and he does it for the lost ones, the victims who are so callously thrown away. When he stops to do the math, he earns pennies per hour. His satisfaction comes from knowing that many unidentified victims recover their names, and their killers are stopped from hurting others.

Frank is most disturbed by the cases of children. In 1982, Philadelphia road workers made a sad discovery beneath the Platt Memorial Bridge. "They found a steamer chest with a body in it," said Frank, explaining that the men waited to call the police. They saw the human remains wrapped in a garbage bag and sheets but pawed through the contents, hoping to find something worth money. "They completely destroyed the crime scene," he said.

She was a child of color, about five years old. But authorities had no clues to her identity. Frank went to work, his gentle fingers forming a tiny, upturned nose. He worked for hours, but the right face simply would not emerge from the clay. He was unusually stumped and frustrated. "That night I had a dream," he confided. "I was walking down a long corridor that led to a morgue." He described the scene in detail, including the shade of beige on the walls. The doors to the morgue were open, and there was nothing but darkness beyond.

A gurney sat blocking the doorway, upon it a little girl. "She sat up and smiled at me," said Frank. "Her skin was so beautiful, dark with a reddish hue, and she wore two pigtails." He studied the soft curve of her cheeks, the tilt of her nose, and her wide brown eyes. He woke up energized, the child's gaze burned into his memory, her smile urging him to get to work. "I knew it was her. I knew it was right," he said.

Though the dream had lasted only seconds, it had been so vivid that Frank remembered every detail. He completed the sculpture, duplicating the image of the dream girl, right down to the two cute pigtails that stuck out from the sides of her head. A photograph of the bust was put on flyers and distributed to police stations. It was there that some six years later a visitor happened to glimpse one of the flyers. Ronald Davis was taken aback as he recognized his daughter Aliyah, whom he had lost custody of when courts gave her to his murderous ex-wife.

*Frank Bender with the reconstruction of the face of a little girl. He helped convict her killers. (Leslie Rule)*

The proverbial wheels of justice finally began to turn. And soon Charles Fox and Maria Davis Fox were arrested. Fifteen-year-old Amira was the star witness for the State and testified against the killers. Maria was sentenced to ten to twenty years, and Charles got fifteen to forty.

Ronald, Aliyah's biological father, was overcome by the uncanny likeness Frank had created of his little girl. "He wanted to know how I knew about the pigtails, and how I got her skin shade right," said Frank. It seems he had help from a spunky little spirit.

## Dream Visits

It is a widely held theory that spirits can insert themselves into dreams. Dreamers can distinguish between dream events and actual spirit visits by the intensity and vividness of the "dreams." A spirit visit within a dream leaves a lasting impression on the dreamers who may find themselves thinking, *It was so real!*

This type of ghost encounter is especially common in cases of lost loved ones, particularly within the time frame of a recent death. Most people find these experiences reassuring.

It is thought that the dreamers are in such a relaxed and open state while asleep that they are able to make a psi connection with a disembodied soul that they may resist while awake.

Psychic people tend to have this type of spirit visit more often than others and will often connect with spirits of those they don't know. In some cases, the departed folks need to get a message across and choose a psychic as a conduit. Many of these types of spirit visits have been reported in the cases of unsolved deaths.

# The Lost Lady

*I work in the PECO Energy building in Coatesville and several times when I'm in here very early (I know this sounds strange) a ghostly lady with wet hair and a gold spot on the top of her dress comes through. She's very forlorn . . .*

So began the email I received on February 7, 2002. It came from a stranger. She was not a reader of my books or my mother's books. In fact, she had never heard of either of us. Katie Furman was so troubled by her encounters with the sad ghost that she got on her computer and went to the web for help. She conducted a search with two words, "crime" and "ghosts." Through the miracle of the internet, she landed on my mother's website, where she found my email address, and seconds later, she sent me a note, describing the pitiful spirit. She ended her email asking, *Was someone killed here?*

It's amazing that two strangers can meet at their desks, hundreds of miles apart on opposite coasts. Katie lives about eighty miles from Philadelphia, Pennsylvania, and I live near Seattle, Washington. And yet, what a *small* world. My mom went to high school in Coatesville.

Katie and I quickly formed an email friendship. She told me that she had seen the ghost three times, and each time the scenario was the same: *It is summertime, and Katie arrives before 4:00 a.m., long before dawn's cold light can creep over the building. She is always alone in her cubicle when a woman with wet hair comes down the hallway, stops in the doorway, and peers in at her.*

The first time Katie saw her, she thought that it was her fellow employee, Mary Grace, arriving at work. Concerned that something was wrong, Katie jumped up and ran after her down the hallway. "But she was gone," said Katie. "Mary Grace came in a while later."

An overwhelming aura of sadness always accompanies the encounters. "She seems forlorn, but she knows I am here," confided Katie. "I can tell. She stops in the doorway and looks at me. There is a gold patch of light on the middle of her dress over the breast. The dress seems blue-gray, as does the lady."

The spirit "moves smoothly and quietly. She goes down the aisle, and then I can't see her anymore. Now that I know she's dead, I stay in my seat and don't

*Frank Bender stands in the mouth of a tunnel at the scene where a victim was discarded in a suitcase in Pennsylvania. (Leslie Rule)*

run after her anymore." Katie, a devout Catholic, said three rosaries for the spirit, and though she did not see her again, she could not stop thinking of her.

I urged her to talk to the old-timers who worked in the building to learn if they knew of a nearby traumatic death of a young woman. I soon received a response from Katie. A coworker had told her that an unidentified body had been found a few years before, not quite two miles from the building where she had seen the ghost.

Katie looked at a police website and read the details of the Jane Doe. "I was horrified to see her legs were found very far away from her," said Katie, who explained that the ghost's legs, too, were missing. Though this is sometimes the case with apparitions, it was a chilling coincidence. In another coincidence, a friend of my mom's, forensic sculptor Frank Bender, had done a reconstruction of the victim's face. To make a long story short, I soon flew to Philadelphia to investigate.

Moved by the plight of the unidentified victim and the possible connection to the sad spirit that Katie saw, I knew this was something I had to write about. The Embreeville Police Department graciously allowed us to stop by. "They want to solve the case and need the publicity to do that," said Frank, and tactfully added, "But I don't think you should mention ghost stories."

*Forensic sculptor Frank Bender and Corporal Mark Healey with the reconstruction of a Jane Doe. Is it her ghost who is seen crying in a nearby building? (Leslie Rule)*

I understood. Not everyone believes in ghosts. And some people believe that those who *do* are unbalanced. I took Frank's advice and did not mention that the writing project I was working on involved the paranormal.

I listened as Frank and Corporal Mark Healey did most of the talking. The skull was brought out of the evidence room, and I watched Frank handle it as he recalled the sculpture he had made several years before when he had covered it with clay. He had created a mold from the original bust and made a copy before the skull was cleaned and returned to the evidence room.

Corporal Healey took us to the spot where the victim was found alongside the Brandywine Creek on Valley Creek Road. It is a lightly treed area beside a railroad trestle, a place where teenagers hang out to drink beer. Broken bottles littered the inside of the abandoned tunnel that looked out onto the site.

The woman had been found in a maroon suitcase on July 11, 1995, and had died an estimated three to seven days before. Corporal Healey showed us the puddle of water where she had been, face down, zipped inside the suitcase. Despite the horror that had been discovered there, the scene felt peaceful. A little frog bobbed to the surface of the puddle and peeked out at us, and wildflowers speckled the area. Corporal Healey pointed up the hill to the train tracks. "She might have been thrown out of the train," he told us. He had spent long hours examining every probable angle.

He'd investigated the possibility that the victim was connected to a carnival that had been in town around the time of her death. There was also a chance that she had been on her way to a nearby summer camp, perhaps seeking work as a camp counselor. Corporal Healy worked tirelessly to explore every avenue but discovered few clues.

The woman had brown eyes and brown hair, and she appeared to be between twenty-five and thirty-five. Her height was probably between 4' 11" and 5' 3", and her weight was estimated to be between 120 and 140 pounds. She had a dead tooth, pierced ears, and no scars or tattoos. She had never given birth. Her legs were found miles away in January 1996. It is our hope that a reader will recognize the victim from Frank Bender's reconstruction, and that the "Lost Lady" will find her name, so she can be put to rest. And *perhaps* a killer will be caught.

Did the spirit Katie encountered belong to the Brandywine Creek Jane Doe? Katie said the reconstruction of the victim looked similar to the ghost she saw, though the ghost appeared to have lighter hair. (But then, the whole appearance of the apparition was the color of bleached denim. Spirits often appear as white or ice blue.) Katie also pointed out that the victim was found with a denim shirt with brass buttons, and she wonders if one of those buttons was the shiny light she saw on the ghost's chest.

If indeed the ghost and the victim are one and the same, then the spirit did not have to wander far to find someone who could see her. The "Lost Lady" chose Katie, and Katie found me. As a result, the story of a woman who was thrown away is an open book for the world to read. Now it is a reader's turn to pick up the thread of this sad story and help the Lost Lady find her way home.

For more information on this unidentified woman, others like her, and missing people, visit the Doe Network at doenetwork.org.

## — Update —

Frank Bender passed away from lung cancer in July of 2011 at age seventy. I'm honored that I got to meet him and will always remember the day we spent together in our quest to learn about the Coatesville, Pennsylvania, Jane Doe. Her case remains unsolved.

# GHOSTS IN THE NEWS

## Through the Looking Glass

An American Media weekly newspaper reported that a man convicted of killing his wife in a case that shocked our nation saw her ghost just days after she vanished in December 2002. Modesto, California, fertilizer salesman Scott Peterson is serving time for the homicides of his pregnant wife, Laci, twenty-seven, and their unborn son, Connor.

The bodies of mother and baby washed ashore in Richmond, California, in the spring of 2003. The nation mourned as videos of Laci were broadcast. The vivacious brunette was always smiling, and the footage of her clowning around with her friends captured the hearts of Americans, who were outraged by the senseless murders of the mother-to-be and her infant.

The news account cited a police report that said Scott told Laci's friend, Kim McNeely, about his startling encounter with the spirit of his missing wife. Police believe Laci was murdered in their home, and Scott was sleeping there when he woke abruptly in the middle of the night. He got out of bed, and as he glanced at the mirror, he saw something shocking in the reflection. It was Laci, and she appeared to be standing behind him.

## Cold Case Horrors

The site of a horrific unsolved murder in Keddie, California, is haunted, according to witnesses quoted in a June 2001, article in the *San Francisco Gate*. Writer Kevin Fagan reported on strange activity at Keddie Resort, a once peaceful vacation destination where visitors could stay in a secluded, rustic cabin or book a room in the two-story lodge.

In its heyday, the resort in the northern Sierra Mountains was a popular place where travelers explored trails on pristine, wooded acres and dined at the acclaimed Keddie Resort Lodge Restaurant.

But the peace was shattered on April 11, 1981, when four people were brutally murdered in Cabin 28. Glenna Sue Sharp, age thirty-six, and her fifteen-year-old son, John, were killed, along with John's friend, seventeen-year-old Dana Wingate.

Sheila Sharp, age fourteen, had spent the night with a friend in a nearby cabin and came home the next morning to a horrific scene. Her mother and older brother were dead, but her two younger brothers and their friend were unharmed. The boys had apparently slept through the night, unaware of the attacks in the next room. Sheila was alarmed when she realized her twelve-year-old sister, Tina, was missing. The girl's skull was found three years later and a hundred miles away by a bottle digger.

The murders not only destroyed two families but also destroyed the Keddie Resort. With the public too frightened to visit, the resort "rotted into a refuge for squatters and hobos," Kevin Fagan wrote in his *San Francisco Gate* report.

The death house was a grim reminder, a site so filled with evil that even seasoned detectives dreaded stepping inside. Though its windows were covered with plywood and its doors nailed shut, Cabin 28 attracted homeless folks seeking shelter and curious neighborhood kids who dared each other to enter.

Many broke in, only to flee in terror. Witnesses told Fagan that they had seen eerie, floating figures, heard footsteps, doors slamming, and moans in the empty house. Some confided that they had watched objects materialize before their eyes, while others described levitating chairs.

## — *Update* —

The haunted cabin is long gone, demolished in 2004, twenty-three years after the sadistic crime. Plumas County detectives recently told ABC reporters that they were close to solving the case, but as of May 2022, no arrests have been made.

# 7

## AFRAID OF THE LIGHT

"When killers die, they never remain as ghosts." When the speaker made that bold statement, no one in the audience challenged him. I, however, wanted to leap from my chair and protest. But I had already finished giving my talk, and it was his turn to speak. We were at a paranormal conference, and I was listening to the session taught by one of my peers, a man well respected in the field. I bit my lip, wondering how he could know such a thing. He possesses no special powers. He can't know any more about the Other Side than the rest of us. He confirmed my belief that the term "ghost expert" is an oxymoron.

By their very nature, ghosts are mysterious and elusive beings. Out of reach and seldom seen, their secrets are hidden in the fleeting shadows. We can collect witness accounts, measure energy levels in haunted sites, record ethereal voices on tape, and occasionally capture images on film. When psychics scrutinize the afterlife, they sometimes provide explicit details about ghosts, but even their insights aren't certainties. We can study phenomena around hauntings but still have more questions than answers.

I suspect that the only real ghost experts are ghosts themselves. Though I held my tongue and did not contradict my fellow speaker, I and other ghost researchers have thick files on hauntings by killers. I wonder if the evil ones remain earthbound for the same reasons as the innocent. Are they confused or shocked or simply attached to this plane? Maybe murderers have an entirely different reason for staying. Maybe it is *guilt*.

If conscience does not nibble at them in life, perhaps fear does in death. Are these stuck souls afraid to meet their maker? Perhaps when they were made of flesh and bone, they dismissed the "afterlife" as a fairy tale. Smug in the belief that judgment day would never arrive, they committed their crimes, hurting others for their own gain. What happens when death curls its cold fingers around a murderer? How does a killer react to finding they have no body?

Psychics and those who have had near-death experiences tell us of a brilliant light. To go to it, they say, is to be embraced by love. Does this same light shine for evil people? Does it offer them the same love? Maybe. Maybe not. This uncertainty could prompt a killer to turn away from the light, choosing instead to cower in the darkness.

Most of us take comfort in stories of a peaceful light where our lost loved ones are waiting to greet us. But what if the dead ones waiting for you are your *victims*? Killers might not be anxious for such a reunion. When I imagine the heartless wraiths wandering the blackness of the despair they created, it's difficult to muster a drop of pity for these wretched souls who are afraid of the light.

# Lady Killer

Are killers born, or are they made? It is a huge question with no definitive answer, though experts find that a combination of the wrong genes and a traumatic childhood are usually factors when a person is without conscience. On February 29, 1956, a killer was born in Rochester, Michigan, though when nurses peered at the wrinkled newborn, they saw only a baby girl.

Aileen Carol Pittman Wuornos never knew the man who provided half her genes. Her father, child molester Leo Dale Pittman, hanged himself in prison in 1969. Aileen's troubled teenage mother abandoned her, leaving her to be raised by allegedly abusive grandparents. A bad seed planted in poisoned earth, Aileen was a thief, a prostitute, and a cold-blooded killer.

She is not the typical female killer, and this is one of the reasons people are fascinated by her story. While most female serial killers poison their victims, Aileen shot her seven male victims. She has been immortalized in books and movies. Parts of the blockbuster movie *Monster*, starring Charlize Theron as the killer, were filmed in the Last Resort Bar, where Aileen was a customer. Al Bulling, owner of the bar, portrayed himself in the movie. He thinks that she favored his pub because it's near a pawnshop where she sold the valuables that she'd stolen from her victims. Al, who has owned the biker bar south of Daytona Beach, Florida, for over four decades, confesses that he felt a little sorry for Aileen. Too often, it seemed she had no place to go when the bar closed down for the night. He frequently allowed her to sleep in the trailer behind his bar.

Much of the drama that played out in Aileen's life and death was centered around Al's tavern, including her arrest. In January 1991, undercover officers posed as bikers and lured the killer out the front door of the bar, where she was surrounded by police.

Aileen's execution on October 9, 2002, has not stopped her from visiting the Last Resort. "She's still here," Al told me, explaining that she made her presence known moments after her death, when the bar was crowded with reporters who had gathered there to watch news of the execution on TV. A tub of knives suddenly leapt off a shelf as startled witnesses gasped. "She always said that she would be back," said Al. Bartender Kelley Pleis told me that she, too, has experienced odd things at the bar, such as the quiet afternoon she was alone there. "Business had been slow, so I was reading," she said. Suddenly, the jukebox turned itself on. "It came on full blast. There was no explanation for it."

Eeriest of all are the breezeless days when the back door suddenly bursts open. As Al watches and waits, the hairs on the back of his arms stand at attention. He knows what is coming. The television suddenly switches channels, and then, in the seconds it takes for the invisible presence to walk across the room, the front door abruptly opens. It is as if Aileen Wuornos is walking the path she walked in the days she camped out back. Whenever the ghost bursts through the back door, Al tries to remain nonchalant. As unseen hands change the TV channels, Al asks, "Who pissed you off this time, Aileen?"

## — *Update* —

Employees and customers report that the ghost of the serial killer still lingers at the Last Resort. When attractive women sit at the bar, they're often startled by the sensation of someone playing with their hair. One recent event spooked a bartender who arrived to open the bar for the day. The vacuum cleaner was normally stashed in a closet, but she found it in the middle of the room with its engine roaring.

Al bulling sometimes hears the inexplicable jingle of a ringing bell but has been unable to trace the sound to its source. He proudly calls his place the "home of ice-cold beer and killer women," but even so, he sticks up for the "killer woman" who made his bar famous. Al insists that others feel as he does and that females *always* sympathize with the murderer. Quoted in the UK's *Daily Mail* in a January 2013 article, Bulling said, "I have not had one woman in here yet, I don't care if they were nine or ninety, that said she got what she deserved. Every woman felt sorry for her in one way or another."

My conversation with Al had been over the phone, and he would not have been able to make that claim if I *had* been to his bar because I do *not* feel sorry for Aileen Wuornos. It's this type of forgiving attitude that makes killer women so dangerous. We don't expect females to be evil, and even when we're told that they are, we make excuses for them. Aileen's victims probably also felt kindly toward her—*until she killed them!*

**Last Resort Bar**
5812 S Ridgewood Avenue, Port Orange, Florida 32127
(386) 761-5147

---

# "See Ya"

Warren Bridge was a man filled with hate. His life of crime began when he became a burglar at age fifteen. At age nineteen on February 10, 1980, he and his accomplice, Robert Costa, walked into a Galveston, Texas, convenience store. As they robbed the store, Warren pointed his .38 pistol at the clerk, sixty-two-year-old Walter Rose, and pulled the trigger, shooting him four times.

It was a painful battle of life and death for the victim, who died two weeks later, four days after the robbers were arrested in a drug raid on their motel room.

Prison did not end Warren's violent streak. Filled with anger, the young Caucasian racist proudly displayed a tattoo of a Confederate flag. His assaults on black prisoners landed him in more trouble. Despite the fact that Warren Bridge was sentenced to die, defense attorneys fought for his life and warded off the execution until November 23, 1994, when he was fed his last meal. He ate a double-meat cheeseburger, fish sticks, and peaches before he was killed by lethal injection.

Before he died, he nodded toward his stepfather and said, "See ya." Warren had plenty of time to contemplate his death and say goodbye to his family. He had once said, "I don't want to be hanged or ride Old Sparky. I'm not very fond of electricity. Just a plain bullet is cleaner somehow." Walter Rose was given no choice. He didn't get to pick a last meal or say long goodbyes to his family. Warren Bridge stole that from him. I admit that makes me angry. I don't want to imagine the killer, stepping into the afterlife, free to roam. But because I received a letter from a woman who knew him well, I have to entertain the idea.

Prison Guard Lorie Hopper tried not to think about the evil committed by the inmates she watched. "I treated everyone with respect," she confided. And the prisoners seemed to respect her for that. It was not her job to punish the men on death row. They were human beings who had made mistakes, and their fate was in the hands of the law. In her letter to me, Lorie wrote about her strange experience in 1994:

> *After staying home sick from work one November evening, I woke abruptly on the couch with the distinct feeling someone had just leaned over me, kissed my forehead, and whispered, "Thank you." While I did not SEE anyone, there are some things that you just KNOW, and I KNEW that someone had been there. It was not a frightening experience. Just baffling. WHO was it?*
>
> *My first thought, naturally, was that it must have been my boyfriend. Unfortunately, he was sound asleep in our bedroom. Since we had argued earlier that evening, the "thank you" made no sense. When I returned to work the next day, I learned that while I was off work, an inmate had been executed. While I had previously known that Warren Bridge's execution was scheduled, it did not cross my mind until that moment that HE might have been my mystery visitor. Several months later, I finally told my strange story to another officer, and I almost fell over when she told me she had experienced the same thing on the same night.*

If Warren Bridge visited his prison guards after his execution, it may have been just the first stop on a long road. In addition to those he had to thank, there were many waiting for his apologies.

# Locked inside the Gray

Prisons are another place where the ghosts of killers roam decades after their bones have turned to dust. Many haunted prisons no longer cage inmates because they've been turned into museums where tourists can wander freely from cell to tiny cell as they try to imagine what it was like to be locked inside the gray. The cold steel doors stand open, and the heavy keys are simply interesting relics. Yet, those who were once trapped sometimes remain. It is as if they don't see the way out. Both the guilty and the innocent linger behind the bars of the following prisons.

# Deadly Silence

When the Quakers thought up a unique way of rehabilitating inmates, they certainly did not imagine that their tactics would drive the prisoners insane. A peaceful people, they believed that their methods would send criminals along the right path. Put a man in an isolated cell, they figured, and he would have plenty of time to contemplate his wrongdoing. To accomplish complete isolation, they built the Eastern State Penitentiary in Philadelphia.

Constructed in the early nineteenth century, it had a modern feature that even the White House didn't yet enjoy—private, flushing toilets. There would be no camaraderie in a common restroom, no "Good morning" or "Please pass the toilet paper." Each cell had its own toilet, so there was no need to venture out.

Meals were delivered by unseen attendants who slid the trays beneath the cold doors with never a word spoken. The isolation was complete. A few lucky prisoners captured mice to tame for pets. Everyone else was all alone. The suffering began on October 25, 1829, when the first inmate entered the castle-like structure. In addition to the loneliness, prisoners endured cruel punishment at the direction

*Every nook and cranny of the Eastern State Penitentiary hides secrets. (Leslie Rule)*

of Warden Samuel Wood. Inmates who were caught making noise were led outside in freezing temperatures, stripped naked, and doused with ice water.

In 1833, prisoner Matthias Maccumsey was punished with the iron gag. The horrible contraption of iron and chains was inserted into his mouth and fastened so tightly that if he moved just slightly, he would suffer unbearable pain. Though the device was not designed to be fatal, it killed Matthias. Inmates, desperate to escape, dug tunnels, scaled walls, and swam through rat-infested sewers. In 1925, prisoner James Gordon escaped by hiding in a truck full of hot ashes. He was free for a year before he was apprehended in Los Angeles.

When I visited the prison-turned-museum, employees told me that they've seen shadowy figures darting in and out of the cells. The most haunted areas, they said, are the cells where the meanest criminals were housed. Sometimes witnesses hear evil cackling emanating from the dense stone walls, but they don't stick around to see who is laughing.

When infamous gangster Al Capone was jailed at Eastern, he claimed that the specter of James Clark haunted him. Shot and killed during Chicago's black St. Valentine's Day Massacre, the angry ghost apparently blamed Al, who could be heard shrieking, "Leave me alone!"

*Lonely prisoners lived long, sad lives in total isolation at Eastern State Pen. Statues of the white cats that once roamed the old prison grounds are placed throughout the popular tourist attraction. (Leslie Rule)*

When I research haunted places, Al Capone's name pops up more frequently than anyone else's. He allegedly had ties to many hotels, and I've visited several where management claims that he was treated like a royal guest and given special privileges. Apparently, the guy got around! In fact, my grandparents had an encounter with America's most famous gangster! In the following story, I'll introduce you to yet another haunted place where Al Capone spent a great deal of time, and I'll also share the story of how the Rules met the notorious character.

### Eastern State Penitentiary

2124 Fairmount Avenue, Philadelphia, Pennsylvania 19130

(215) 236-3300

easternstate.org

---

# Laugh at the Nightmare

Alcatraz Island was the site of one of America's most infamous prisons, dubbed "The Rock" because of the barren and rocky terrain. The federal penitentiary operated from 1934 to 1963, and administrators boasted that it was escape-proof because of the mile and a half of rough, cold waters that separated the island from San Francisco. A favorite unsolved mystery, however, involves prisoners who may have escaped in a makeshift boat in 1962. The drama inspired the book *Escape from Alcatraz*, later made into a film starring Clint Eastwood. Debate continues on whether the men reached freedom or drowned trying.

Today, Alcatraz is a popular tourist destination, intriguing to curiosity seekers not only because of its dark history, but because of its ghosts. Witnesses have seen shadowy figures and heard disembodied moaning, sobbing, and whispering. In the spring of 2014, San Francisco's KPIX and dozens of other news outlets around the world reported on an astonishing image captured at Alcatraz by British tourist Sheila Sillery-Walsh. She was in the visitors' block, where inmates long ago received guests, when she used her iPhone to snap a photo of an empty cell. When she looked at the picture, she was stunned to see the image of a dark-haired woman. Though slightly blurry, the photo is remarkable.

Who are the ghosts of Alcatraz? While humans have visited and lived on the island for hundreds of years, investigators suspect much of the paranormal activity stems from the violence that occurred when some of our nation's most dangerous men were locked up there. The Rock saw several deaths, including murders, during its time as a penitentiary.

In one disturbing incident in July of 1942, inmate Cecil Snow attacked Maurice Herring in the prison's basement barbershop. Both men were in their early thirties and serving time for robbery. Herring worked as a prison barber, and Snow was the bathhouse attendant. Snow slashed Herring six times with a prison-made knife. The victim bled profusely as he staggered up the stairs to a guard post and collapsed. He was treated by the prison doctor but died within an hour.

Al "Scarface" Capone was an Alcatraz resident for seven years in the 1930s. His name pops up frequently when I research the histories of haunted places, and he's been mentioned in several ghost stories I've covered. While Capone served time for tax fraud, he was never convicted of homicide—though he was allegedly responsible for numerous murders.

Al apparently had somewhat of a conscience because he did right by my grandparents. My father's parents, John and Doris Rule, were living in Chicago in the 1920s during the gangster era when Capone ruled the city's underbelly. One night, the Rules went out to dinner, and while they were in the restaurant, a gunfight broke out near their parked car. After they dined, the Rules were

*Long before "The Rock" caged America's most dangerous men, it was home to Fort Alcatraz, pictured in this antique postcard.*

shocked to find their car riddled with bullet holes. The person responsible for the damage had left a note on the car, promising to pay for repairs. It was signed by Al Capone! True to his word, Capone covered the repair costs.

Others caged at Alcatraz were also complex characters. Robert Stroud was a violent killer, yet he had a soft spot for birds. He rescued them, earning him the nickname "Birdman of Alcatraz." His research resulted in important contributions to the cure for bird diseases. Whitey Bulger is another example of an Alcatraz inmate who was both cold-hearted and kind. He was complicit in multiple murders but doted on his son, Doug. When Doug died of Reye's Syndrome at age six in 1973, it broke Whitey's heart. The complexity of these characters is fascinating. They were capable of killing and apparently felt little or no remorse over it, yet some part of each of them was honorable. These men, so filled with darkness, sometimes let in the light.

On the flip side, a man filled with light let in the darkness. He, too, lived on Alcatraz Island, but it was long before Capone and the others were locked up there. In 1890, Captain William Daniel Dietz of the Fifth Artillery was stationed at Fort Alcatraz, where he lived with his wife and son. He was a busy man that year. Not only was he the fort's assistant surgeon, but he also wrote a book, *The Soldier's First Aid Handbook*. A primary goal of that book was to teach enlisted men how to cope with medical emergencies in the absence of surgeons. (It was published in the spring of 1891, adopted by the army, and can still be purchased from online bookstores.)

The Dietz family's quarters were in a large building on the summit of the island, a concrete structure divided into apartments for army personnel. From that elevated vantage point, there was an extraordinary view of the entire island, the shimmering San Francisco Bay, and the forested land in the distance. When their many friends walked past their home, they often saw the couple sitting together on the porch, and they appeared to be content and in love. Ella Tyler Dietz was twenty-three, seven years younger than William, and she cherished her role as mother to three-year-old Wally. Reporters described Ella as a talented musician—attractive with raven locks.

While coworkers said that Doctor Dietz was normally a "jovial" fellow, they noticed he was irritable in the weeks leading up to January 27, 1891. On that day, he told a coworker he wasn't feeling well and "had a dizziness in his head." Even so, Dietz was attentive to all of his patients that night and went

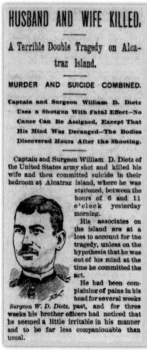

**HUSBAND AND WIFE KILLED.**

A Terrible Double Tragedy on Alcatraz Island.

**MURDER AND SUICIDE COMBINED.**

Captain and Surgeon William D. Dietz
Uses a Shotgun With Fatal Effect—No
Cause Can Be Assigned, Except That
His Mind Was Deranged—The Bodies
Discovered Hours After the Shooting.

Captain and Surgeon William D. Dietz of
the United States army shot and killed his
wife and then committed suicide in their
bedroom at Alcatraz Island, where he was
stationed, between the
hours of 6 and 11
o'clock yesterday
morning.
His associates on
the island are at a
loss to account for the
tragedy, unless on the
hypothesis that he was
out of his mind at the
time he committed the
act.
He had been com-
plaining of pains in his
head for several weeks
past, and for three
weeks his brother officers had noticed that
he seemed a little irritable in his manner
and to be far less companionable than
usual.

*A San Francisco newspaper reports on an Alcatraz tragedy that may have left restless spirits in its wake.*

on rounds several times. The last patient he saw was Frank Brandt, and he sat up with him until early morning. Brandt, suffering from blood poisoning, thought highly of him and would never get over what happened after Dietz left his bedside.

While the exact sequence of events is unknown, the lives of both William and Ella ended that morning. Ella was sound asleep and seemed to be enjoying a sweet dream because she was smiling when her husband killed her with a double-barreled shotgun. Her smile never left her lips, something that brought her friends comfort when they viewed her in her casket. Even in death, she was still smiling and looked as if she were deep in a peaceful sleep.

That was not the case with her husband. While both bodies were placed in "elegant, silver-mounted caskets," laden with floral arrangements and crosses, the lid of William's coffin was closed. He was not recognizable, and the death scene had traumatized Lieutenant Gallup, the first to arrive. It was a miracle that the gun blasts from the murder-suicide didn't wake up little Wally, asleep in the next room. The child did not witness the horror, and officers' wives cared for him while preparations were made to send him to his maternal grandparents in New York.

When investigators discovered pages of bizarre rantings by Captain Dietz, they concluded he had gone temporarily insane. They could find no evidence of conflict in the marriage, and when he had last put pen to paper, Dietz wrote fondly of his wife and child. But his thoughts were scattered, and some of his last musings could be those of a crazy man. Dietz wrote: *Is this life a dream? At the end of it, shall we awake in our little beds and laugh at the nightmare which has frightened us?* The irony of those words is that Ella died in her bed and never woke from the nightmare.

What happens to the spirit of someone killed violently while they're sleeping? Are they more confused than the average earthbound ghost if they die while dreaming? Could Ella still be wandering Alcatraz, searching for her little boy? Or did she step from her body, survey the scene, and promptly walk into the light? If so, a leading theory among paranormal researchers says that she is not an earthbound spirit, but one who can watch over her loved ones and return for them when it's their time to pass.

If Ella is free, she surely would have come for her son when his life, too, ended tragically. On December 26, 1898, nine-year-old Wally Dietz was ice skating in Sackets Harbor, New York, when the ice broke. He lived in the village with his grandparents and was skating alone that day. Nobody saw Wally fall in the water, but when the hole in the ice was found, it was clear he had drowned. His body was recovered the next day.

If Ella Dietz is earthbound, she may be the spirit caught in the Sillery-Walsh photograph. We can't be certain of the identity of the ghost in the photo, but she clearly had black hair, just as Ella did. The ghost appears to be wearing old-time clothing, but the image doesn't reveal enough to pinpoint the exact era of the fashion.

According to an 1891 news account, the Dietz apartment was in a building that sat at the highest level of the island. If that report was accurate, it means that it occupied the same space where the prison would eventually be built. I would not be surprised to learn that the Dietz deaths occurred in the same space as the visitors' block where Sillery-Walsh snapped the photo. If Ella died in the exact spot where the photo was taken, it makes it an even stronger possibility that she is the ghost in the image. The island, however, is so small at 1,075 by 850 feet, that no matter where the Dietz barracks stood, it couldn't have been far from where the prison stands today.

While I suspect Ella is the ghost in the photograph, there are other candidates. Many broken-hearted wives visited their husbands at Alcatraz. Those women didn't have to die on the island to be drawn to the place where they last saw their loves. Another dark-haired female had a fatal accident on the island. In 1970, twelve-year-old Yvonne Oakes was playing in an old

*It was a miracle that Wally Dietz didn't witness the violence that orphaned him.*

building there when she fell three stories. While Yvonne had dark hair, she did not otherwise resemble the ghost in the photo.

Another restless spirit roaming Alcatraz could be Frank Brandt, the patient with blood poisoning Dietz had been treating. A February 5, 1891, edition of the *Morning Call* reported that "when Brandt was told of the tragedy that he became so affected that he took a relapse and died." His death came four days after the murder-suicide.

My archive research revealed other traumatic Alcatraz deaths, including a July 1857 accident, reported by the *Daily Bee*. A landslide dumped several hundred tons of earth upon men at work, killing Daniel Pewter and Jacob Unger, and severely injuring a third man. A few years later, in March 1869, Andrew Roman, age thirty-six, was on guard duty when he slipped on the steps and accidentally discharged his musket. He died instantly. Enlisted man Frank Williams is yet another possible Alcatraz ghost. He was helping to load a cannon in April 1915 when it fired prematurely. He, too, was instantly killed.

With all the tragedy that has occurred on Alcatraz, it's not surprising that it is considered one of the most haunted spots in America.

**Alcatraz Island**
San Francisco, California
For tickets and ferry schedule, visit alcatrazislandtickets.com

———————

# Deadly Redemption

Recognizable to movie fans as the set for *The Shawshank Redemption* and many other films, the Ohio State Reformatory in Mansfield was filled with drama long before actors such as Tim Robbins ever set foot on the gloomy grounds. Since the Ohio prison opened in 1896, its impenetrable walls have witnessed suicides, deadly prison breaks, riots, and horrible accidents.

The real-life haunted prison is turned into a staged haunted prison during Halloween season. Actors play ghostly killers, strategically placed lights cast eerie shadows, and spooky sounds emanate from cobwebbed corners. But sometimes it is hard to tell what is pretend and what is real, for the screaming continues after the actors have gone home, the special effects are turned off, and the place is buttoned up for the night.

A scent of flowery perfume wafts from nowhere on the third floor of the administration building. Staff credit it to the gentle spirit of Helen Glattke, who once lived on the prison grounds with her husband, Chief Arthur Glattke.

Poor Helen met her fate on a quiet Sunday morning in November 1950. According to November 7 editions of Ohio newspapers, the forty-one-year-old mother of two was getting dressed when she reached up on a high shelf for her jewelry box. Her fingers curled around her husband's .32-caliber automatic pistol, a defective weapon that often jammed. This morning it was in her way, and as she tried to move it, it slipped from her grasp, discharging as it fell. A bullet pierced her left upper lung, and she later died at General Hospital.

The saddest thing of all was that she did not get to see nine-year-old Teddy and thirteen-year-old Arthur Jr. grow up. It is somehow comforting to know that her spirit is sensed in the administration building and not in the gloomy places where the evil wraiths roam. Some say they have witnessed Helen's shadowy shape and even felt her soft touch as she caressed their faces and shoulders.

### Ohio State Reformatory
100 Reformatory Road, Mansfield, Ohio 44905
(419) 522-2644
mrps.org

––––––

Not all prisons cage criminals. Sometimes the incarcerated are prisoners of war. In the following case, the great, gray fortress was a prison camp during the Civil War, and many of those trapped there have never left.

# "Longest Liver Takes All!"

Park Ranger Roby Armstrong looked up at the enormous brick fort, and her eyes were drawn to the startling image framed in one of the windows. She glanced at the two coworkers who walked beside her and asked tentatively, "Is there anyone else on the island today?"

"Nope. We're the only ones here." *Not exactly.* When Roby looked at the window again, the figure was gone. She did not tell the others what she had just seen. She kept walking, trying to convince herself that she could not have seen what she knew she had.

Fort Delaware State Park on Pea Patch Island is accessible only by boat. Smack in the middle of the Delaware River, the Union fortress was built in 1859 and caged an estimated 12,000 prisoners during the Civil War. A formidable structure with its great size and iron-barred windows, it also served to protect the ports of Wilmington and Philadelphia. Today it is Fort Delaware State Park.

Throughout the warmer months, visitors can travel to the historic site by boat from either New Jersey's Fort Mott State Park or Delaware's Delaware City. Ninety acres of Pea Patch Island serve as a bird sanctuary. It is, in fact, the biggest Atlantic Coast nesting ground north of Florida for wading birds such as herons and egrets. While the park is alive with visitors in the spring and summer, off-season it is frequented only by volunteers, park employees, and the spirits of the dead.

At one time, Roby Armstrong didn't believe that Pea Patch Island was haunted. The thirty-something park ranger has spent years in law enforcement and is an admitted skeptic when it comes to the paranormal. "I had to see it to believe it," she told me. But what she witnessed that day made no sense to her. "I saw a pirate. He was standing in the window in a beautiful green silk shirt that billowed in the wind, and he wore white silk pants."

About a year after Roby's sighting, I visited Pea Patch Island. It was in March 1999, and Roby had arranged for me to accompany her on a maintenance trip to the fort. We traveled there by boat, along with a small group of employees and volunteers. When we arrived on the island, we trudged up the long path to the fort, and as we got close, Roby nudged me. "I was right about here when I saw him," she whispered. "He was standing in that window." She pointed at one of the tall, narrow windows in the upper level of the fort. "Why would I see a *pirate*?" she asked. "I didn't even believe in ghosts, but even if I wanted to see a ghost, it sure wouldn't have been a pirate! What would pirates have to do with a Civil War fort?"

I smiled. I'd spent the day before researching at the Wilmington Library, and I told Roby what I'd learned. "This area was once swarming with pirates," I said. In fact, a June 11, 1933, Delaware newspaper article ventured that the city of Blackbird, approximately fifteen miles south of Pea Patch Island, was named for a notorious pirate. Old families, said the article, claimed Blackbird was a corruption of the name *Blackbeard.* The "swashbuckling pirate king" often anchored his ship, *Queen Anne's Revenge,* at nearby Blackbird Creek.

Blackbeard, also known as Edward Teach, went down on record as taking refuge in the area in 1717 after he and his "lily-livered rogues" panicked the "sedate Quaker city" of Philadelphia with a rowdy visit that prompted citizens to send word to the authorities for help. The "giant, bull-necked man with his barbaric beard and clanking cutlass" was a frightening sight. To perpetuate his image, he braided slow-burning wicks into his hair and lit them before a raid, so it appeared his head was on fire.

He was famous both for his hidden treasure *and* for marrying fourteen women. Once asked if his wives knew the whereabouts of his treasure, he replied, "Only the devil and me know! The longest liver takes all!" Could Roby have seen Blackbeard? Is he still roving the area, keeping an eye on his treasure? Pea Patch Island, after all, would have made a good hiding place. It was isolated, reachable only by boat, and near his favorite territory. Maybe he *is* trying to outlive the devil, so he can "take all."

Or perhaps Roby saw one of the "lily-livered rogues," searching for the treasure they suspect is buried there.

*Ranger Roby Armstrong once saw the ghost of a pirate standing in a window at Fort Delaware. (Leslie Rule)*

*Apparitions of Civil War soldiers have been seen inside Fort Delaware. (Leslie Rule)*

Mean and boisterous, the colorfully clad buccaneers frightened those who lived near the water. The plundering pirates so terrorized the shores of Delaware and New Jersey that at least one historian hints that the bad memories have been swept under the rug while "other 'nice' occurrences" are remembered and celebrated. The pirate raids are just one more chunk of history that seems to shame citizens into forgetfulness. No wonder Roby and the few Delaware historians I chatted with were not familiar with pirate raids on area shores.

Roby will never forget the hollow, scooped-out feeling that accompanied her one and only ghost sighting. Her coworker, park historian Lee Jennings, was more matter-of-fact about *his* sighting. During his sixth year working at the park, he finally spotted a ghost. "I saw a Union officer," he told me and described the early summer evening when he guided a tour of four visitors. As he led them around the outside of the fort, they were startled by the solid image of a uniformed officer. "We all saw him," Lee said, explaining that the apparition stood between the restrooms and the fort, in vivid color, his arms folded across his chest. Suddenly, he turned around and walked away before vanishing. "I think we saw Captain Ahl," said Lee. "I found an old photo of him, and it matches what we saw."

Captain George Washington Ahl was a controversial figure at Fort Delaware, with prisoners coming forward after the war to publicly share horror

*Many prisoners of war drowned when they attempted to escape Fort Delaware. (Leslie Rule)*

stories about his cruelty. Ahl's most notorious action at Fort Delaware was ordering the shooting death of a "lame" prisoner because he hobbled too slowly as he left the latrine.

Employees and visitors have also had many independent sightings of an apparition in a black cloak. The black cloak suggests that they, too, may have seen a pirate. Several other witnesses reported seeing the ghost of an African American cook in the fort's kitchen. "My wife has seen her," Lee said. "The ghost was peeking into pots."

Still others report the sound of children's laughter—when no children are present. Officers' families once lived on the island. And children *did* once run and play there as prisoners watched from the windows and longed for their own families. It is not surprising that lost souls still linger on Pea Patch Island. Pain and suffering went along with being held captive here. At least a couple of people were shot at the fort. And prisoners of war, who often arrived in sorry shape, frequently starved to death on the premises.

## — *Update* —

The Diamond State Ghost Investigators report that Fort Delaware is still paranormally active. Their documented accounts include sightings of a pacing man in the Battery Torbert area of the fort, inexplicable clouds of mist forming near the ceiling, and activity in an area staged to look like a child's room. The rocking horse in that room rocks on its own, and a depression in the little bed forms, as if a child is resting there.

Who are the ghost children of Fort Delaware? They may be the offspring of General John Newton and his wife, Anna. Several of their fourteen kids did not survive past childhood. My research revealed that the family lived on the island for years while the general oversaw the building of the fort. Two of their little ones, Anna and her baby brother Frances, were born at Fort Delaware. Anna was only three when she died of scarlet fever at Fort Delaware in April 1862. Frances died the following April.

Most of those who wander Pea Patch Island are likely the ghosts of the nearly three thousand soldiers who died there. Their lives were miserable in the crowded, unsanitary fort, yet they may be unaware that they are free to go now. The leading cause of death was starvation and disease, and some drowned when they attempted to escape by swimming across the river. When their corpses washed ashore, they were unceremoniously buried.

While the Pea Patch Island deaths are mostly Civil War related, the end of the war did not end the tragedies. In June of 1897, mechanic John Schunder, sixty-six, from Delaware City, was up on a ladder, plastering Fort Delaware's new ammunition building, when he made a grave error. It was quitting time, and in a rush to be done, he wasn't paying close attention and lost his balance. He fell backward, hit his head, and died almost immediately.

Another tragedy occurred in August of 1902 when a lovesick druggist took his own life. Robert Sloan was a member of the Hospital Corp at Fort Delaware, and he was found dead in his bed there after taking poison. The first newspaper articles about the suicide reported that his girl had fallen out of love with him and had told him so in a letter. But as it turned out, it was not a letter from his fiancée, Miss Clara Osborne, but a letter from her *father* that caused Robert distress. Clara's father had sent Robert a letter, forbidding him from seeing her.

Meanwhile, Clara was at home in Philadelphia, admiring the engagement ring Robert had given her in July and making plans for their Thanksgiving Day wedding. When Robert stopped answering her letters, she went to Fort Delaware to talk to him. She couldn't find him and asked several soldiers where he was. No one wanted to give her the news—until a drunken soldier blurted, "Druggist Sloan, do you mean, lady? Why, he was found dead in bed on Wednesday. Poisoned himself."

Clara fainted, and a nearby soldier caught her. In shock, she showed the sympathetic soldiers her ring and told them her story. Two hearts broke, and one stopped beating forever. I would not be surprised if Robert Sloan's tormented spirit is earthbound.

### Fort Delaware
45 Clinton Street, Delaware City, Delaware 19706
(302) 834-7941
destateparks.com

———————

# 8

---

# WAKING
# THE DEAD

S ome of the most haunted locations in the world are sites where tragic events took place. The most active of these seem to be the places where the basic configuration of the buildings or grounds have not been altered much. Often, when a place is drastically changed, it apparently discourages the ghosts, and they drift away—or at least go to sleep until they again find something in the environment familiar or enticing.

It's interesting to note that paranormal activity spiked in an area of Fort Delaware that was staged to look like a child's room. If little Anna Newton is the ghostly child heard giggling at the fort, then she is probably the one who curls up in the bed in the nursery. It's as if the little bed, the rocking horse, and the toys have woken her from the deep sleep of death.

Paranormal investigators in recent years have taken to bringing toys to places haunted by children. Often investigators can collect impressive EVP after they "wake" a ghostly child with a toy.

*Can we really wake the dead?*

I visited the site of one of America's most ghastly tragedies with three ghost hunters, Mark and Debby Constantino and Janice Oberding. In 1836, a group of pioneers was traveling by wagon train, headed toward California, when an early snow stopped their progress. Snowbound for months in the Sierra Nevada Mountain Range, many died of starvation while others resorted to cannibalism to survive. Today the area is the site of the Donner Memorial State Park.

The Constantinos showed me their process of recording ghostly voices. I participated, and we apparently woke the dead—unless they were talking in their sleep!

We may have been successful in capturing voices because we visited when the ground was covered with snow, just as it had been during the dark days that so many died of starvation. I'm wondering now if the ghosts would respond to food brought to the site. We didn't bring food, and it didn't occur to us to do so. This is something that future investigators might consider. If the lonely ghosts of children respond to toys, then it stands to reason that the ghosts of the starving might respond to food.

Did we record the voices of the dead? It certainly appears so, but first let me tell you about someone else who went to that location and captured something just as intriguing as ghostly voices. He visited the tragic spot a couple of years before we did, and while we trudged through snow, he walked in the sunshine.

# Little Boy Lost

It was a lovely October day in 2004 when Jason Sweeton visited Truckee, California. In the area on business, the clinical researcher for the Food and Drug Administration found himself with some spare time and decided to hike the trails at the Donner Memorial State Park. "It was the middle of the week and very quiet," he said, explaining that he passed a few folks on the path before finding himself alone in the forest. Sunshine speckled the ground, scattered like gold coins in the shadows of the pine trees. The peace was so complete that he was acutely aware of the sharp crunch of gravel beneath his every step.

Jason knew that this was the site of an appalling tragedy a century and a half before. A huge rock on the trail had been turned into a monument to those who had suffered and died here. It marked the spot where the ill-fated Donner Party had found itself snowed in and literally starving to death. In a case that horrified the world, some of the malnourished pioneers had succumbed to cannibalism to survive.

Jason had heard rumors that the place was haunted, but he did not take them seriously. "I've never been interested in ghosts," he told me. "I'm typically a skeptical individual." He simply wanted to photograph the scenery to share with his wife, Jacqueline, who was home with their baby in their Round Rock, Texas, home. He took a number of shots with his digital camera and, after a relaxing hike, headed back to his hotel, where he scrolled through the photos. Something caught his eye. "It was the undeniable face of a child," he said. The little face appeared in the bottom corner of a photo that Jason had taken of the tree-lined path.

Ever so slightly blurred, as if the child had dashed in close for a peek at him, the colors on the image are real and distinct. From the deep blue eyes to the varied tones of the flesh to the light brown hair highlighted in the sunlight, the image is as clear as any snapshot of a human being. While only the top of the head, one eye, and the rise of a tiny nose are in view, it's clear that the hair is short, like a boy's, and that his face is puffy with bags beneath his eyes. Jason picked up the phone and called his wife.

Jacqueline remembered their conversation and told me about it. "He was really freaked out," she said, recalling how he had tried to make sense of the anomaly. She told him that he would have noticed if there had been children running around. Of course, he would have! The silence had practically screamed at him. He had definitely been alone there.

*A visitor to the Donner Memorial Park was shocked by the image in the lower right-hand corner. (Jason Sweeton)*

The practical-minded Jason, who has a degree in biology, stressed, "My job mandates that I observe with a critical mind." Yet, he cannot explain how the child appeared in the picture. Since his paranormal surprise, Jason has read up on the Donner Party, but until I spoke with him, he had not heard about one particularly shocking death of a toddler.

Jeremiah George Foster was born on August 24, 1844, in St. Louis, Missouri. He was not quite two years old when he and his parents, William and Sarah, left Missouri in May 1846 with a group headed by wagon train to a new life in California. Jeremiah's maternal grandmother, Levina Murphy, thirty-six, also accompanied them. They joined a larger team and eventually camped beside the Little Sandy River in an area that is today part of Wyoming. As they sat around the campfire, the men debated about the best route to take. Some argued that a shortcut would get them to California quicker.

Instead of continuing with the large group on the known route, a new party was formed, with George Donner pronounced the leader. Jerimiah's family joined the Donner Party as they branched off from the others and continued west. No one had the slightest inkling of the suffering ahead. The new path took them over terrain so rugged that the trip took much longer than expected. By the time they rejoined the California trail, their "shortcut" had cost them three precious weeks. In the Sierra Nevada, they were blanketed by a blinding snow, which stung their faces, froze their fingers, and blocked their path. Eighty-one people found themselves trapped in the mountains.

The Donner Party split up, with one cluster camping by a lakeside and the other six miles away by Alder Creek. The oxen were killed for food, but it was not enough to ward off starvation. People began to die. Faced with either death or survival, some turned to cannibalism. While a few had forged ahead to look for help, others stayed behind. Jeremiah and his grandmother huddled in the Murphy Cabin beside the lake as they anxiously waited for Sarah and William's return.

The child's ribs were sharply outlined beneath his pale flesh, and he stared pleadingly at the adults. When Levina watched her grandson crying with hunger, it broke her heart. But there was nothing she could do to help him or the other little ones.

Among those at the Murphy Cabin was a man who has become a controversial figure. Survivors painted him as an abusive man, cruel to his wife and concerned only with himself. Some of his descendants, however, are angry with this description and insist that their ancestor has been unfairly portrayed. They reject accusations that Lewis Keseberg developed a taste for human flesh.

Yet, many believe the alleged account of little Jeremiah's last night alive in March 1847. It was another bleak evening with no hope in sight when Lewis Keseberg insisted that the toddler sleep in his bed. Levina awoke in the morning to the news that her grandson had died during the night and that his flesh would sustain the others. In shock, Levina accused Lewis of murdering the child.

Perhaps Lewis was innocent. He cannot, after all, defend himself because he is no longer here. And neither is little Jeremiah. *Or is he?* The small boy who appears in Jason Sweeton's photograph looks to be between two and four years old. Jeremiah was two and a half when he died. Other children perished, including three-year-old James Eddy, who succumbed after Jeremiah.

Jason had been walking toward the boulder that once served as a Murphy Cabin wall, when he raised his camera and caught the ethereal image. His artistic eye was framing the snaking trail, flanked by sun-dappled trees. It is a calendar-quality photograph with an unexpected bonus. Why did the little boy appear in Jason's photo? Could it be that the toddler is still waiting for his daddy and that he recognized the paternal energy in Jason?

It is sad to imagine hungry little ghosts still waiting for help. Jeremiah's devoted grandmother died weeks after he did. If he is still there, she, too, may be there, looking after him. It is a comforting thought.

# Donner Party Ghosts

Jeremiah George Foster is not the only Donner Party victim to materialize in places where the pioneers camped. Inside the Emigrant Trail Museum, artifacts from the wagon trail days are on display. A couple dressed in period clothing has been seen beside a wagon there. Visitors usually assume that they are actors, hired to add authenticity to the exhibit—until they suddenly vanish. Apparitions are also seen outside of the museum. "A ghost we believe to be Tamsin Donner has been seen by many people," said author and historian Janice Oberding, elaborating on the devoted mother's tragic ending.

Tamsin Donner was torn. While her children stayed at the Alder Creek camp, her ailing husband, sixty-two-year-old George, was six miles away at Murphy Cabin. The determined woman trudged through the snow between the two areas, desperately trying to care for both her husband and children. Tamsin, forty-five, died after George, and there was just one witness to her death. Lewis Keseberg, the questionable character who some have accused of murder, claimed that Tamsin showed up at the Murphy Cabin in an unfortunate state. She had fallen into the creek, he said. According to him, Tamsin was soaking wet and disoriented, and she babbled incoherently about how she needed to get back to her children.

When she died suddenly, Louis did not let her body go to waste. "It was the finest flesh I'd ever tasted," he allegedly commented. "Tamsin's skeleton was never found," said Janice, who suspects that she is buried beside the Donner Party memorial rock, which once served as a wall of the Murphy Cabin. If that is true, detectives could unearth the remains of Tamsin, if they were so inclined. Modern-day forensics might be able to determine the cause of death. A blow to the head or a strangling death may still be detectable.

Is Tamsin's spirit earthbound because she was murdered? Witnesses claim that her glowing figure still walks the path leading to the Murphy Cabin. When the apparition of the woman in pioneer clothing appears near the pioneer monument and floats toward the Emigrant Trail Museum, she travels the same path that Tamsin did when she was on her way to see her sick husband. Is Tamsin Donner reliving her last journey? What really happened on that trail? Did she stumble into a stream, as Lewis claimed, and suffer from fatal hypothermia? Or did she stumble upon something even more dangerous than icy cold water?

The answer is buried somewhere on the grounds of the Donner Memorial State Park. Yet another Donner Party memorial is also believed to be home to ghosts of the tragic pioneers. "Not many people know about it," said Janice Oberding, who took me to see the plaque. At the foot of Rattlesnake Mountain, the bronze plaque is situated between houses in a modern housing development in the Donner Springs neighborhood, a subdivision in Reno, Nevada.

It was here that the Donner Party camped during its last happy time. Though the members of the party were warned that the weather would soon change and that they should move quickly, they lingered. The children frolicked in the sunshine as the adults dreamed of the new life in California. "They stayed too long," said Janice.

By the time the group got moving, the mild season was running out of days. The mean winter weather crept in, its icy fists pummeling the pioneers with snow until their path was blocked. Some of the ghosts went back to the last place where life was good, theorizes Janice, who once ran a tour of haunted places in Reno.

One night, at about 10:00 p.m., she led a bus full of tourists to the old campsite on Peckham Lane. As the folks wandered around exploring, the skeptical driver stayed in the bus. He was friendly, and Janice liked him, but she couldn't help noticing how he rolled his eyes as she told ghost stories to the eager group. While Janice waited for her tourists to finish examining the place, the driver motioned to her from the doorway of the bus.

"Don't tell the others," he whispered, "but I just saw a ghost!" His hand trembling, he raised his arm and pointed to the spot where he had seen a little girl in a white nightgown materialize. She studied his face, wondering if he was teasing her, but he was genuinely shaken. "He didn't believe in ghosts before that," she said.

An enormous boulder once served as the wall of a cabin where members of the Donner Party took refuge. A memorial plaque attached to the rock honors both the victims and survivors of the Donner disaster. Some believe human remains are buried at this spot. (Leslie Rule)

The bus driver was new to the state and had no idea that it was not the first time a nightgown-clad girl had been seen in the area. A couple of years before, authorities were baffled when drivers reported seeing a child in a white nightgown near McCarran Boulevard. "It was in the dead of winter and on a cold night," Janice remembered. The story appeared in newspapers.

The girl appeared to be three or four, too young to be wandering alone on a cold, dark night. Several people reported seeing her, including a woman who said she approached the child. But the little girl ran from her, disappearing into the night. "They searched for her for days," said Janice, remembering how concerned people were.

It did not occur to the police that it could be too late to help the child. The authorities did not consider the possibility that the small girl had been dead for a century and a half.

If the evasive figure was indeed a spirit left behind by the Donner Party, it could have been Ava Keseberg, the three-year-old daughter of Lewis. The little one perished on the trail as a group of folks forged ahead. After she died, they were unable to carry her with them and buried her in the snow.

Her father was unaware of her death until he was finally able to leave the area. When he saw a piece of fabric poking from the snow, he was curious and tugged on it. The snow fell away, and he found himself staring at poor little Ava.

The ghost could have been any one of the small children who lost their lives that winter. Boys, too, wore nightgowns in that era and often had long hair.

Survivors of the Donner Party passed their stories along, each version shaded by their own perceptions. The passing years have surely distorted these accounts all the more. We can't know what was in the hearts of the desperate people who walked the frozen trails. The answers to the Donner Party mysteries are buried with the dead, their secrets unspoken on the lips of ghosts. Unless they speak up, we will never know what really transpired.

# Speaking Up

On the snowy day that I visited Donner Memorial State Park, I was accompanied by EVP specialists Debby and Mark Constantino and ghost hunter Janice Oberding. While the Constantinos ran a recorder, we took turns asking questions, addressing whatever unseen beings might be present. "Introduce yourselves first before you ask a question," Mark advised Janice and me, explaining that he and Debby always tried to be considerate of the earthbound spirits. After each question, we were to wait a full ten seconds to give the ghosts plenty of time to respond.

"The tape recorder is voice activated," said Debby. "Even though we can't hear the ghosts, we know that they are speaking when the recorder is recording." Sure enough, as we stood in the silence, we could see the indicator on the machine revealing that it was picking up some type of noise. The Constantinos phoned me several days after our trip. They were in the middle of the time-consuming task of replaying the tapes and removing background noise. "We definitely got voices," Mark said. "They are very quiet, though," added Debby. "Almost whispery."

"Did a Frank die there?" Mark asked me. "We got a voice saying, 'Frank.'"

*EVP specialists Debby and Mark Constantino prepare to record ghostly voices at the Donner Memorial State Park. The large boulder behind them once served as the wall of a makeshift cabin where doomed pioneers sheltered from the cold. (Leslie Rule)*

"Let me see," I said, as I leafed through the photographs I had taken of the site. I found an image of the memorial plaque on the giant rock. It listed both survivors and victims. Among those who had perished were Franklin Graves Sr., fifty-seven, and Franklin Graves Jr., five.

It may have been one of the Franks who spoke to us, simply giving his name. The other remarks recorded by the EVP collectors included the following: "I'm hungry," "Look for the bones," and "Please move." The recording of two simple words bothered us the most: "Help us."

While many historians suspect that Lewis Keseberg committed murder, that has never been proven. If, however, violence was a factor in any of the Donner Party deaths, it makes the possibility that the site is haunted all the more likely. Out of all the reasons for a place to be haunted, murder is at the top of the list, particularly when the murder is unsolved. We note a definite pattern of more paranormal activity in places with histories of violence. According to a leading theory, the ghosts of victims of violence often remain earthbound because they're waiting for justice.

### Donner Memorial State Park and Emigrant Trail Museum
12593 Donner Pass at Highway 80, Truckee, California 96161
(530) 582-7892

---

Two haunted sites of famously unsolved murders are now tourist attractions for ghost enthusiasts and the morbidly curious. Visitors can stay the night at both the Lizzie Borden House in Fall River, Massachusetts, and the Villisca Axe Murder House. In Villisca, Iowa, a family of six and two of their children's friends were murdered in 1912. Today, the crime scene is a popular destination for ghost hunters.

A nasty argument broke out on Facebook recently when a ghost enthusiast posted about her plans to stay at the Villisca Axe Murder House. Though the page was set up for people to chat about haunted places, a member took offense and commented that she was appalled because she was the "mother of a murdered child," and it angered her to see someone so excited about visiting a crime scene where children had died. Others immediately jumped on that mother, suggesting that this was not the page for her. I understood the viewpoint of each. Murder is not something to be *celebrated*, and it would be painful for any mother to think that the death of her child could be turned into a fun event.

Yet, the *intention* of the ghost enthusiast was not necessarily disrespectful, even if she chose the wrong words to make her announcement. What was in her heart? Did she plan to approach the house with reverence? Did she understand that even though the murder occurred over a hundred years ago that eight people lost their lives? Was she planning to pray for the poor souls who might be stuck there?

When it comes to visiting haunted sites, our intention is everything. The people who lived and died before us deserve our respect. Not a single one of us is immune to death, and though some may find that uncomfortable to contemplate, it is the reality. As disturbing as it might be to consider our own mortality, those of us who embrace the idea of ghosts know that our spirits will live on.

The young lady who was excited about staying the night in the Villisca Axe Murder House may have actually been anxious to prove to herself that ghosts exist, and, therefore, that life never really ends.

It's worth noting that both of these infamous crime scenes had periods when ghostly activity was apparently dormant. The houses were simply places for people to live, and many of those residing there never experienced anything paranormal. *The dead seemed to be sleeping.* What made them stir?

They may have been woken when new owners replicated the historical ambience of the houses. In the Lizzie Borden House, crime scene photographs were referenced so that the furniture could be placed exactly as it was on the day of the brutal attack in 1892 that ended the lives of Andrew and Abby Borden.

The owner of the Villisca House also created an environment that echoed the night of the tragedy. He went so far as to remove some of the home's modern conveniences and hang a 1912 calendar on the wall with the page flipped to June, the month of the murder.

For the unprepared, a visit from a ghost can be a disturbing experience. Yet, even those who are prepared and make a practice of contacting spirits sometimes find that the encounters are more than they can stand. The psychics in the following story will never forget the horror they felt while visiting a murder site.

# Villisca

"Slay utterly old and young, both maids, and little children . . ."
*Ezekiel 9:6 (KJV)*

Brenda Marble of Harrisonville, Missouri, cannot explain the lure of a simple Iowa farmhouse. It drew her to it, again and again. Each time she visited, she swore it would be the last. Yet, she feels there was a message that she was chosen to tell the world. The house would not let her go until she and her friends deciphered that message and passed it along.

It should have been a lovely spring day filled with the sounds of birds singing and children laughing. But June 10, 1912, in Villisca, Iowa, was the darkest day in the history of the town. The first inkling that something was wrong at the Moore house came when Mary Peckman peered down the street and noticed that her neighbors were not up and about. She grew more alarmed when she investigated and found the house tightly closed with all the shades drawn over the windows.

Worried, Mary spread the word, and before long, the brother of Joe Moore showed up and used his spare key to enter the home. He stepped into a nightmare. The usually lively home was too quiet and washed in darkness. Every window and mirror in the home was covered with blankets or clothing. As his eyes adjusted, he did not want to believe what he saw. Everyone was dead.

Someone had crept into the house and killed them with an axe. Joe, forty-three; Sarah, thirty-eight; Herman, eleven; Catherine, ten; Boyd, seven; and Paul, five, made up the entire Moore family. The children's friends, the Stillinger sisters, had spent the night. Both girls, eleven-year-old Lena and eight-year-old Ina, were dead. A crowd soon gathered outside the death house, and the curious pushed their way into the home, gawking at the mutilated bodies and trampling over evidence. The crime scene was destroyed.

Over the next years, investigators focused on three suspects. There was the Reverend Lyn George Jacklin Kelly, a minister who had been visiting the town the night of the murders. Mentally unstable, at one point he confessed to the killings and said that he was inspired by a sermon he was working on. It was taken from the book of Ezekiel in the Bible with a verse that begins, "Slay utterly old and young . . ."

As any seasoned detective knows, compulsive confessors crawl out of the woodwork to admit to crimes they did not commit. In addition, it appeared that the reverend may have been pressured to confess.

Then there was Frank Jones, a rich and powerful rival of Joe Moore's. Each owned a hardware store, and the competition had grown bitter. William Mansfield was also investigated. A suspect in the axe murder of his wife, daughter, and in-laws in Blue Island, Illinois, his modus operandi was similar to that of the Villisca killer.

The convoluted case and its investigation inspired books and documentaries. Perhaps if the case had been solved, there would not be such interest in it today. Apparently, residents of Villisca were not altogether repelled by the history of the house. When a documentary maker interviewed an elderly woman whose family had lived there after the murder, she smiled as she recalled her childhood, sleeping in the blood-splattered room.

Though no one interviewed for the documentary mentioned ethereal encounters, it may simply be that they were not sensitive enough to sense the spirits in the home. Or it could be that new owners woke the spirits from a daze. When Darwin and Martha Linn purchased the old house, they restored it to resemble the grisly day in 1912. Like a dial on a radio, the ambience was set to pick up signals from beyond. Crime buffs and ghost hunters flock there to take the tours.

When people began to notice ghostly stirrings in the house, a small but determined investigative group from Missouri got on the case. Six members of the Miller Paranormal Research team traveled to Villisca. Brenda Marble, Dee Ann Tripses, Jerry Miller, Kathy Burhart, and psychics Joyce Morgan and Misty Maeder entered the historic murder site in August 2003, equipped with their electronic detection tools and their keen sixth sense.

The stage was set to draw visitors to the past, Brenda noted, as she inhaled the heavy odor of the kerosene lamps. Those with imagination could find themselves back in the era of that brutal night. Add intuition to that, and it may be more than anyone bargained for. Joyce Morgan was so tuned into the horror that she was overcome with emotion on her first visit as disturbing images of the children invaded her senses. It was too much to deal with, and she decided to leave. But the rest of the team spent the night, one they would never forget.

It was 2:00 a.m., possibly the exact hour that the mass murder had occurred, when the spirits came alive. Investigators theorized that the killer went into action as the train roared through town, the scream of its whistle drowning out the screams of his victims. When the whistle sounded the first night that the Miller team visited, it seemed to literally wake the dead. Misty, Dee Ann, and Brenda watched in astonishment as a fog moved through the upstairs rooms of the old farmhouse. It began in the parents' room and settled in the children's room. "It was as if the whole room went out of focus," Brenda told me.

Through her third eye, psychic Misty Maeder saw a reenactment of the attacks on the children. The train passed, and the world became still. "It was so quiet," Brenda remembered. "There were no clocks ticking, and it was not raining. It was eerily silent." And then came a sound that made the hair on the backs of their necks rise. All three women heard the distinctive sound of dripping. It came from the direction of one of the girls' beds. It was the sound of blood droplets hitting the floor. "That's when it became real," confided Brenda. "With the sound of the dripping, I realized how brutal it was. It just hit me how tragic it was."

Though Brenda had planned just one visit to the murder site, she and the team found themselves heading back several more times. "The house kept drawing us back," said Brenda. "We kept thinking we were finished with the investigation, and then we would find ourselves back there again." The psychics zeroed in on two men as the culprits. One, they believe, was a hired killer, and the other was his accomplice. The accomplice was unaware that the children would become victims and has great remorse over the fact. He is, they say, so sorry that he has returned to the Villisca home.

Catherine suffered the most. "We believe that she woke up during the attack," said Brenda. The little girl, the psychics felt, hid in a closet, but the killers found her. The investigators got an audio tape recording of a young girl's voice saying, "I'm dying." It is a devastating scenario, one that seems to have no hope. Yet, amidst the cruelty and violence, a single powerful message shines through. "It is why we were there," said Brenda, who feels that the spirits of the tragedy called upon them, so they might speak on their behalf. "The Moores were a very spiritual family," Brenda explained.

Sarah, in particular, took the teachings of her church to heart. The loving mother and devout Christian carried her values with her to her death. From the

Other Side, she spoke one word so loudly and clearly that the Miller Paranormal team was able to capture it via EVP.

"Forgiveness."

*Author's note: Is the spirit of Sarah Moore really preaching the virtue of forgiveness? Has she forgiven the person or people who slaughtered her family? When it comes to forgiveness, I admit I'm on the fence. I agree that there are times it's beneficial to let go of anger and forgive those who caused us harm. But how do we forgive someone who brutally killed someone we love? I suppose some will say I'm not spiritually evolved because I don't wholeheartedly embrace the concept that everyone should be forgiven for even the most horrendous of deeds. In my opinion, before forgiveness can be considered, there must first be justice.*

### The Villisca Axe Murder House and Olson-Linn Museum
323 East Fourth Street, Villisca, Iowa 50864
(712) 621-4291
villiscaiowa.com

---

The most disturbing aspect of the Villisca case is the absolute brutality. The same can be said for the next case. When one human sets out to obliterate another, it shocks those of us with consciences. When the murder is overkill, we know it was driven by a hatred and rage that most of us can't even begin to imagine. Just as in the Villisca case, the victims in the Borden case received enough blows to kill them many times over. The sheer violence of the act might have been enough to keep the Bordens earthbound even without the décor that replicates the crime scene.

# Lizzie

*"Hi. This is Lizzie. No one can take your call now. Father's taking a nap on the sofa, and Abby is visiting a friend . . ."* The bed-and-breakfast's macabre telephone announcement makes the flesh crawl.

*"Father is taking a nap on the sofa . . ."*

It is exactly what Andrew Borden was doing when he was bludgeoned with an axe on August 4, 1892, in his home in Fall River, Massachusetts. His wife, Abby, was killed in her room upstairs. Lizzie Borden was blamed for the grisly murder of her father and stepmother. Though a jury later acquitted her, she remained guilty in the public eye, a legendary killer who inspired a rhyme that little girls sang as they played with a jump rope:

*Lizzie Borden took an axe and gave her mother forty whacks. When she saw what she had done, she gave her father forty-one.*

Today, the site of America's most infamous double homicide is the Lizzie Borden Bed & Breakfast. The house has been carefully restored to resemble the day of the murder, decorated with historical accuracy. An antique sofa was placed in the exact spot where Andrew Borden had been napping when he was attacked.

It's no wonder that the ghosts are confused! Andrew might believe it's still the morning of August 4, 1892, and that he's still napping on his sofa. An employee of the bed-and-breakfast will never forget the day she saw a fog form in the kitchen. She watched, stunned, as the wispy, white entity floated into the parlor toward the sofa. *Was it Andrew still attracted to his favorite napping spot?*

"She was a little unglued," said Lee Ann Wilber, owner of the Borden home, adding that the previous owner had seen the specter of a woman in Victorian dress in the cellar. Lee Ann has owned the place since June 2004, and though she has not yet seen a ghost, she has experienced odd things. "I was in the basement when something touched me," she confided. It was as if invisible fingers tapped her between her shoulder blades and then moved down her back.

Does Lizzie haunt her childhood home? *No!* At least that is what Lee Ann believes. "Lizzie is not here," she said adamantly. It is the murder victims who remain frozen in time in the historical home. The killing was so long ago that it's hard to wrap our minds around the fact that Andrew and Abby Borden were real people. Yet they *were.*

Andrew Borden and his first wife, Sarah Morse Borden, had three daughters: Emma, Alice, and Lizzie. Little Alice died before Lizzie was born. When Lizzie was just two years old, her mother died. Andrew later married Abby Durfee Gray. Gossips whispered that he could not possibly love the plain,

*When Lizzie Borden's father and stepmother were murdered, she was the prime suspect, but a jury failed to convict her. Some say she haunts her childhood home, a popular B&B where guests often leave spooked.*

chubby woman. Surely, he must have married her simply to get a free house-keeper and babysitter.

Lizzie and Emma never liked their stepmother. Many have said that when Andrew, a wealthy banker, put a piece of property in Abby's name, his daughters' anger toward their stepmother intensified. Andrew, they say, was so miserly that his daughters were frustrated by his refusal to supply them with the finer things, including indoor plumbing. As members of one of the prominent families in town, Lizzie and Emma longed to live up on the hill among the wealthy Fall River residents.

Was it this frustration that fueled Lizzie's habit of stealing? In addition to shoplifting in stores, she was the main suspect when valuable items, including diamonds, disappeared from her parents' room. There is no one left alive to truly understand the intricacies of the Borden family dynamics, yet many are still speculating about this and the impact that jealousy and resentment could have had on the warm summer morning that stained the calendar with a splotch of blood that a century of sunny days cannot wipe clean.

The Borden housekeeper, Bridget Sullivan, was in her attic room on the fatal morning she heard Lizzie yell, "Come downstairs! Father is dead! Somebody got in and murdered him!"

Andrew Borden was on the sofa, covered in blood. Abby, too, was soon found dead in her upstairs room, apparently cut down as she made the bed. Andrew had received ten blows, while his wife suffered nineteen. Emma Borden had an alibi. She was out of town, visiting friends.

Fingers were soon pointing at thirty-one-year-old spinster Lizzie. Her case was not helped when a pharmacist testified that she had tried to buy prussic acid, a deadly poison, one day before the killing. And she certainly looked guilty when her neighbor Alice Russell said she had seen her burning a bloodstained dress days after the homicide.

The defense claimed that the stains were not blood but paint. Emma and other witnesses took the stand to testify that the stains on the cheap dress were indeed paint, left by careless painters who had worked in their home months before the murder.

As for rumors of conflict in their family, Emma said they weren't true. Everyone was civil to each other, she insisted. She suggested that a newspaper report on a quarrel between the sisters had been planted by police. The defense attorney brought up the mysterious stranger whom witnesses had seen lurking near the Borden home around the time of the killing. Maybe *he* was the killer!

Had the brutal murder been committed by a total stranger, thirsty for blood? Had he slipped away, taking the murder weapon with him? Despite an exhaustive search, investigators could not be certain that they had found the murder weapon. A hatchet with a broken handle was discovered in the cellar, and though primitive forensics indicated a match, it was not a certainty.

Searchers took apart walls within the Borden house, but to this day, the question of the murder weapon is part of the puzzle.

During the 1893 trial, the victims' skulls were revealed. Lizzie took one look at the gruesome sight and fainted. Was she really distressed, or was it a calculated move? If it was simple theatrics, it worked. The all-male jury deliberated for sixty-eight minutes and pronounced her innocent. Somehow, they could not find the soft-spoken Sunday school teacher capable of such a grisly crime.

On June 20, 1893, Lizzie was free to go. Abby and Andrew, however, are not free. They are frozen in time, shadow people, hidden in the whispers of those who sit up all night at the B&B, debating America's most famous whodunit.

Despite warnings that it could open the door to evil, a Ouija board is available for guests who dare to contact the Other Side. Regular séances are also conducted. "We recently had a birthday party for a fourteen-year-old," Lee Ann said, explaining that they held a séance as part of the entertainment. "It was in the dining room where the temperature is always comfortable." Yet, during the séance, an inexplicable cold breeze blew from nowhere, swirling around the teens until they shivered. The entire downstairs was soon chilled.

Another recent occurrence left Lee Ann shaking her head. She was in Abby's old room, making the bed for a couple who had spent the night and were out exploring. She tidied the room and was preparing to leave when she saw a pair of diamond earrings sparkling at her feet. "They were side by side on the floor by the door, as if someone had put them there," Lee Ann told me. She wondered why she hadn't noticed them when she entered the room. She put the valuable earrings in her pocket for safekeeping. When the guests returned that evening, Lee Ann approached the wife as she relaxed in the parlor and asked, "Are you missing something?"

The woman asked, "What do you mean?" Lee Ann held out the earrings. "Her mouth popped open in surprise, and her hands went to her ears," said Lee Ann. "Her husband had given them to her years ago, and she had never taken them off." Later, the same lady was in the shower when she felt her necklace loosen and drop to her feet. She scooped it up as the suds swirled around it. It, too, had not left her neck in years. Whose ghostly hands tried to snatch the glittering jewelry?

While Lee Ann believes that the notorious Miss Borden is not one of the resident ghosts, the fact that Lizzie had a reputation for stealing diamonds makes me wonder. It's understandable that the B&B owner would shy away from the idea that Lizzie was among the ghosts.

Despite her acquittal, most people believed that she was guilty, and she was ostracized in Fall River. She purchased a big house on the hill, and though her neighbors found it pretentious, she named it Maplecroft. She further annoyed Fall River citizens when she changed her name to Lizbeth and entertained famous actors and actresses. She broke the rules of a Victorian society, but that does not make her a killer.

A nurse who cared for Lizzie years after the tragedy said that her patient had confessed the truth to her. She had had a boyfriend that Andrew did not approve of. It was he who had committed the brutal double homicide. If this is true, what happened to him? Did she continue to see him

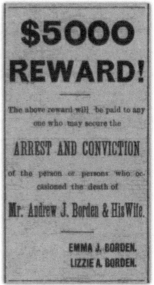

*The Borden sisters offered a $5,000 reward for the arrest and conviction of the violent killer. The reward was equivalent of over $150,000 today.*

after the trial, sneaking off to a faraway city for rendezvous? Or did she break it off, sickened by what he had done but afraid to report him for fear she would be implicated in the plot?

In America, we are "innocent till proven guilty." Yet Lizzie, never proven guilty, is rarely considered innocent. If she were innocent, would that draw her back to the scene of the crime? Is she roaming restlessly there, as visitors sit up all night debating her guilt?

Innocent or guilty, her ghost may very well be drawn to her childhood home. And she may not be alone. Could one ghost be responsible for so much paranormal activity?

Shadowy figures dart through the house, furniture moves on its own, and unseen hands tamper with the thermostat. Some have reported the sound of marbles rolling on the upper floors.

Marbles? Yes, Lizzie may have lost hers, but these marbles are believed to belong to the ghosts of two neighbor children allegedly drowned by their mother. Some say the lonely little spirits seek refuge in the Borden house. I've yet to find any documentation of the case, but Lee Ann insists there is a childish energy present in her B&B. The mischievous kids play with the thermostat, randomly turning it up or down. The children's ghosts, she said, may have moved from the house that they shared with their murderous mother and now make their home at the Bordens' old place.

## — *Update* —

In the spring of 2021, Lee Ann Wilber sold the Lizzie Borden House. Days later, she was struck by serious illness and soon died. She was only fifty, and her family and the many friends who loved her were shocked by the loss.

The house is now owned by Lance Zaal, creator of US Ghost Tours, a spooky venture operating in thirty-five states. Lizzie's old place is still open for business, and according to Zaal, it's still very haunted. In October of 2021, he told a *USA Today* reporter about an apparition seen in the Andrew and Abby Suite. Witnesses say she is clearly a woman, resembles Abby Borden, and wears a nightgown.

Visitors have also reported feeling someone tug on their ears, touch their legs, and pull the comforters off their beds at night. A group on a tour recently witnessed a chair slide across the floor on its own volition. When Zaal spent the night there, he heard murmuring voices and the distinctive sound of footsteps, though no other live humans were there at the time.

The Borden case is one of the most contemplated mysteries in America. No one knows for certain who the killer was, but in my opinion, it was Lizzie. I was more willing to consider that Lizzie could be innocent when this story appeared in my book *When the Ghost Screams* in 2007. Fifteen years later, I'm more cynical. I concluded that Lizzie was guilty after reading a credible report on a disturbing incident. She killed a family pet. I won't go into detail, but that information convinced me that she was a cold-hearted sociopath—something I

### OUR FOLKS AND OTHER FOLKS.

Miss Lizzie Borden, daughter of Mr. Andrew J. Borden, met with an accident while at work in the tea room of the Central church, Wednesday. The dumb-waiter, heavily loaded with plates, came down on both of the young lady's arms. It was feared for a few minutes that both arms were broken, but we are glad to say that Miss Borden escaped with nothing more serious than painful bruises.

*Weeks before the murder, Lizzie Borden had an accident, as reported here in this June 1862 edition of a Fall River newspaper.*

know a little about after writing a true crime book about a sadistic, murderous female with similarities to Lizzie.

As I was combing news archives for info on the Bordens, I came across something intriguing in the *Fall River Daily Evening News*. The incident *could* have changed the fate of the entire Borden family—had it played out differently. The article was published in mid-June 1892, a short time before the murder. It told of an accident that occurred when Lizzie was working in the tearoom of the Central Church:

> *The dumbwaiter, heavily loaded with plates, came down on both of the young lady's arms. It was feared for a few minutes that both her arms were broken, but we are glad to say that Miss Borden escaped with nothing more serious than painful bruises.*

It's interesting to note that the accident happened six weeks before the Bordens were killed, *and*—because broken bones can take up to twelve weeks to heal—Lizzie probably would not have been able to swing an axe by August 4 if things had turned out differently and her arms *had* been broken. If she was determined to kill, she could have done so after her arms healed, but the incident that historians have scrutinized for the last 130 years would have been dramatically changed. For example, sister Emma was conveniently out of town during the murder, but had it occurred at a later date, she could have been home and a potential witness.

When it comes to fate, we're not traveling down an unyielding path of stone. If we change our actions in the *slightest*, we can find ourselves on a different road, moving in an entirely different direction. Sometimes, events out of our control occur and change our destinies—sometimes for the better and sometimes for the worse.

If the dumbwaiter that slammed down upon Lizzie Borden's arms had been loaded with just a *few more* plates, it might have been heavy enough to fracture her arms. *It might have changed everything.*

In the next case, tragedies occurred within the walls of a famously haunted house—a house that might not have been built if a man had not stolen a boat. Would this family have suffered the same tragedies if the house on San Diego Avenue had never been built? We will never know.

**Lizze Borden Bed & Breakfast**
92 Second Street, Fall River, Massachusetts 02721
(508) 675-7333
lizzie-borden.com

---

# The Whaley Skeleton

My investigation into the Whaley House reinforced my finding that historians often mold the past to suit their needs. For some unfathomable reason, they decide that certain deaths make for "nice, clean little stories," while others are so distasteful that they must be locked away and hidden like the proverbial skeleton in the closet. With this writing, I am releasing the Whaley House skeleton. The restless spirit of the Whaley House is a disturbed woman who seeks compassion, understanding, and—*perhaps*—forgiveness. Maybe when the public learns the truth, she can finally move on.

*The Whaley House parlor, where reporters once trooped in to see poor dead Violet after her last desperate act. (Leslie Rule)*

The Whaley House Museum in San Diego's Old Town is often called "the nation's most haunted house." This reputation gained momentum in 1964 when popular TV host Regis Philbin and his crew investigated. As they sat in the dark, a female ghost floated into the parlor. Regis aimed his flashlight at her, and she vanished.

Steve Bennett, who toured the museum long ago, told me about his experience there. His visit was before the days when sheets of glass kept the public from reaching into the rooms.

As he passed the kitchen, he was startled to see the meat cleaver moving. "I reached out my hand to steady it, but it immediately started up again," he confided. This was said to happen so frequently that the curators finally put it away.

The upstairs windows flew open by themselves and set off burglar alarms so often that they had to be nailed shut. The day I visited, I was downstairs chatting with a volunteer when two men came racing down the stairs to tell us they had just heard an odd, inexplicable clicking. By the time I got upstairs, the noise had stopped. I secretly thought they were imagining things, until I read that the very sound they had described had long been a mystery there. Others say they've seen the ghost they believe to be Anna Whaley, wife of Thomas and mother of their three children. When music floats from the still piano, witnesses attribute it to Anna. One curator admitted he'd seen a lovely young woman in vintage dress. "She was unpacking a suitcase," he confided. "Only the top half of her body was visible."

I suspect the ghost he saw was the woman who copied the following Thomas Hood poem, writing it down on a sheet of paper and leaving it where everyone would see it and know exactly how she felt:

*Mad from life's history, Swift to death's mystery: Glad to be hurled, Anywhere, anywhere, Out of this world.*
— *Violet Whaley, August 1885*

Violet Eloise Whaley was a tender twenty-two years old on the sunny morning of August 19, 1885. The *San Diego Union* chronicled the horrible events.

Lillie Whaley testified as follows: I reside at Old San Diego. The person lying here is Violet E. Whaley. . . . Last saw her alive around 6 o'clock this morning. . . . Father went down to get his horse, then came up and asked where Violet was. After he went down the second time, he opened the backdoor and called to her.

Thomas Whaley called out, "Violet, do you want a peach?" His daughter was in the water closet, and she answered him with a gunshot. Lillie continued, Mama and I heard the shot. Coming downstairs I found Papa had brought her in, apparently dead. . . . My sister threatened to take her life on the 5th of July this year. Think she was tired of life. She thought no one cared for her, and her life was a burden.

Three years earlier, Violet had married a man her parents did not approve of. The newspaper described him as "a worthless fellow, with whom she lived but two weeks. . . . A divorce was procured from her faithless husband, Edson, who had several aliases, and she returned to her maiden name."

*Violet loved to play the guitar and piano and may still be making music from beyond the grave.*

We can only imagine the "I told you so's" when the union failed. In a time when divorce was a scandal, the experience must have been shattering. As the newspaper stated, "The marriage blighted her life, and its curse has built her tomb."

What a powerful moment it must have been for nineteen-year-old Violet when she unpacked her suitcase just weeks after she had filled it in anticipation of a life with her love. The moment was so painful that it imprinted upon the room, where it replayed nearly a century later when a curator peered into the bedroom and witnessed it.

The *San Diego Union* lamented the loss of lovely Violet. "Refined and intelligent, and a passionate lover of the beautiful in nature, she also worshiped the arts, and music was her passion. But the piano is now silent, and the guitar will never more wake to her touch."

The article went on to describe how reporters trooped in to see beautiful, dead Violet in repose on a "makeshift cot" in the Whaley parlor. The distraught woman had shot herself in the heart. Violet wrote in her suicide note that her life had been a lie. Now, it seems, her *death* is a lie, hushed up, all but erased from history. Oh, it is there in the library archives. But until I went digging for answers, no one talked about it. How sad for Violet. And for every other human being who is suffering from depression. Why is it okay to talk about death from cancer but not from suicide?

Violet is forgotten. Is she aware she has been obliterated from memory? Does she want her existence known? Is that why she is so active? It makes you stop and wonder about the ghostly music that has been attributed to her mother, Anna. Many have reported hearing sounds of tunes rising from instruments with no human hands in sight.

"But the piano is now silent," wrote the reporter, "and the guitar will never more wake to her touch."

Oh, really?

# Whaley Legends

The most famous story about the Whaley House concerns Thomas Whaley's first look at the site where the house sits. He and dozens of other folks witnessed the hanging of Yankee Jim, a tall, fair-haired man who had been apprehended for stealing a boat. The chagrined fellow thought that authorities were only bluffing when they placed the noose around his neck. Surely, execution was too severe a punishment. But they were dead serious. The poor man was hanged until the life seeped out of him.

Now, this part of the story has always seemed odd. It is written that as Thomas Whaley watched the loop of rope strangle the helpless man, he said to himself, "I ought to build a house here." And so, he *did!* He built a huge, two-story brick house for his family. He put the arch between the parlor and the living room in the exact spot where Yankee Jim had been executed. Mr. Whaley proudly pointed the arch out to visitors as he shared the story of the man who died there.

The brutal killing of Yankee Jim is considered one of the "nice" little stories that Whaley House historians love to tell. They suggest that the house is haunted, not just by Yankee Jim but by Thomas Whaley and his wife, Anna, who died of natural causes. Sometimes they mention Thomas Junior, the baby who died in an upstairs bedroom.

Over the years, many have claimed to smell Mr. Whaley's distinctive Havana cigars or Anna's sweet perfume. There have been sightings of the family's dog, Dolly Varden, who darts down the hall and into the dining room.

Visiting children often claim they see the ghost of Annabelle Washburn. The story goes that the girl was playing with the Whaley children and suffered a crushed windpipe when she ran into a low-hanging clothesline.

This account has not been documented. It did, in fact, come from a psychic. I and many others have sifted through the California obituaries in fruitless pursuit of proof of Annabelle's existence. I did, however, find that a builder by the name of Washburn lived in the neighborhood during the right time.

## — *Update* —

Restless spirits still pace the old floors of the Whaley House, according to visitors. Some have heard children giggling and the pitter-patter of tiny, invisible feet echoing through the house. In an April 23, 2021, article in the *San Diego Explorer*, Hedge Metreyeon wrote about a personal experience there. It happened years ago when Hedge was a kid on a class field trip and came face to face with the solid apparition of a little girl. The two stared at each other for a long moment that Hedge would never forget. The encounter happened in the dining room, an area of the home where others have reported seeing the ghost of a girl.

It's been over twenty years since I released the Whaley skeleton from the confines of her gloomy closet via my book *Coast to Coasts Ghosts*. I'd discovered Violet's suicide while going through old news articles in the reference section of the San Diego Library. In 1999, when I asked a Whaley House curator about the suicide, she told me that Whaley descendants were ashamed and that they didn't want the public to know about it. I have to admit that this made me angry. My mother's only sibling took his own life before I was born, and our family has never tried to hide that fact.

I've often wondered if Whaley relatives and the museum's curators are mad at me for telling their secret. If they are, then that is a burden I'll gladly shoulder because I think it's more important to spread the word that depression is *not* a weakness than it is to cater to misplaced pride. Many people suffer from depression, but today we have medications to balance brain chemistry that weren't available to Violet in 1885 or to my uncle, Donald Rex Stackhouse, in 1955.

For those of you in the grips of depression who happen to be reading these words, please don't give up. It can take time to find the right medicine to balance your brain chemistry, and your doctor might try a few different medications before she finds the right one for you. Prozac did *not* work for me, but I understand it helps some people.

Yes, I, too, have struggled with depression and anxiety. I eventually found the right medication and have been taking it for fifteen years. I'm not ashamed, and I hope you aren't either. If anyone tells you that you're weak because you can't "snap out of it" when you're depressed, ignore them because they have very little understanding of the workings of the brain.

I take great satisfaction in knowing that Violet Whaley's story is no longer a secret and is spoken of frequently by everyone connected to the museum. Nowadays, when visitors spy the filmy apparition of a pretty young woman, they conclude she is Violet. She is often seen on the second floor, and some say they can sense a cold loneliness there, as if she is still wrapped in her sorrow.

As for the mysterious clicking that is heard upstairs from time to time, I've thought a lot about that. It's possible that Violet practiced before she got up the nerve to put a bullet in the gun. She may have repeatedly pulled the trigger of the empty weapon. The inexplicable clicking may be the sound of Violet playing with the gun in a morose moment a century and a half ago. If you visit the Whaley House and see or hear or sense her, please greet her kindly and tell her she is free to go.

As long as she continues to be earthbound, I hope Violet channels her energy into making music, rather than playing with guns. In 1885, a reporter wrote that music was Violet's passion. Her lovely, long fingers pranced over the piano keys in life and apparently still do so in death. According to witnesses who have heard the eerie tunes, the music wafts from nowhere.

The fact that music is heard in the haunted Whaley House is not unique. Ethereal notes from unseen instruments have long been associated with paranormally active places. In some instances, the music is disembodied, while in others, the instruments in question actually exist but are manipulated by spirits. Sometimes music seems to stir those in eternal sleep. In the next chapter, we'll explore cases where melody is the catalyst for ghostly activity.

**Whaley House**
2476 San Diego Avenue, San Diego, California 92110
(619) 786-1143
whaleyhousesandiego.com

———————

## Ghostly Exposure

An astonishing infrared image, shown below, was captured by Joe Jones of Vista, California, and appeared in my book, *Ghosts Among Us*, nearly twenty years ago. (When you study this photo, ignore the *live* man, leaning into the window.) The *ethereal* being is emerging from behind a column, on the far left of the photo.

In the image beneath Joe's photo, is a comparison for clarification. Figure A shows the apparition overexposed, with her skirt shaded. Figure B illustrates what *I* see in my mind's eye—a woman in an old-time dress, partially obstructed by a column. Figure C depicts a late nineteenth century outfit, similar to the dress in Figure B.

Huge puffed sleeves were popular in the Whaleys' era, and this makes me wonder. Did Joe Jones snap a picture of Violet?

**Figure A**       **Figure B**        **Figure C**

# 9

## SONGS FOR
## THE DEAD

The armonica plays such sweet music, it was once believed to awaken the dead. Invented by Benjamin Franklin in 1761, the armonica is made up of crystal bowls that spin in unison. When sensitive fingertips touch the rims, they create a vibration that coaxes pure notes to life. In practiced hands, the armonica makes magical melodies. Famed hypnotist Dr. Franz Mesmer used one to *mesmerize* his patients. He claimed the surreal sound plunged them into deeper trances.

In the mid-1800s, superstitions ran wild. People believed the haunting music drove performers mad and evoked the spirits of the dead. In fact, the armonica was once outlawed in Germany because critics feared it was waking too many ghosts! Farfetched? *Maybe not.* Many ghost sightings seem to be surrounded by music. Sometimes the specters are making music. Sometimes they seem drawn to it, as in the following story.

# Final Curtain

It was 1921 in Memphis, Tennessee, when twelve-year-old Mary stood outside the place she loved the most, the Orpheum Theater. A pretty girl with long curls pulled back by a white bow, she wore a crisp white pinafore and matching white Mary Janes. As a horse-drawn carriage passed, disaster struck. "Mary was either kicked by a horse or hit by the carriage," explained Orpheum volunteer Barbara Jackson, whose grandparents remembered the incident and related it to her.

In shock, the child stumbled to her feet, entered the theater, and found her seat. No one knows how much of the production little Mary got to enjoy. When the curtain fell and the lights came on, she was found dead in her seat.

"The theater burned down two years later, in 1923," said Barbara. "It was rebuilt in 1928. We must have inherited Mary because she's still here." She's quick to point out that Mary has never disrupted a performance. "She's just a little girl," she emphasized. "And she *loved* the theater." But Mary does her share of mischief making. Once, when a housekeeper was scrubbing an actor's marks off the stage, her cleaning supplies vanished. After a frustrating search, the supplies were found in the commode!

Then there was the time a plumber fixing pipes in the basement spotted Mary leaping over machinery. "Hey!" he shouted at her. "You shouldn't be down here!" As he approached, he realized she was no ordinary child. Barbara, who gives October ghost tours at the Orpheum, was hoping to interview him on the details, but the frightened plumber left hurriedly "and never returned."

Though Barbara has never seen Mary's apparition, she *has* felt the puzzling cold spots in the mezzanine level of the theater that often accompany paranormal activity. "It's such an odd sensation," she confided. "It feels like hot ice."

Actually, Mary is said to share the theater with six other ghosts. But she is by far the most active. Some believe it is Mary's ghost who swings on the magnificent, twinkling chandeliers. Barbara has no logical explanation for the mysterious swaying of the fifteen-foot-tall chandeliers. "They are still raised and lowered manually," she said, explaining that because the two-thousand-pound fixtures hang over the audience, a motion detector is in place to alert the staff to any impending dangerous situation. Many times, the motion detectors have gone off, and the dazzling chandeliers are discovered swaying in the still air.

Mary's ghost may be intrigued by the chandeliers, but it is the music she likes best. Organist Vincent Astor notes that the little spirit is drawn to the tune of "Never-Never Land." "He says he can hear her tap dancing whenever he

*The original Orpheum Theater, shown here in an antique postcard, burned down in 1923. Some say that the old Orpheum's ghostly residents moved into the new building.*

plays that song," Barbara told me. Once, during practice, several women stood listening as the sweet notes of "Never-Never Land" filled the theater. Two of the women were stunned when they glanced toward the back of the theater and saw a ghostly girl in a white pinafore dancing, her curls bobbing as she kicked her little white shoes.

One of the ladies felt herself drawn to the specter and reluctantly began to move toward her. "She told me she was terrified," said Barbara. "Yet, she couldn't stop herself from walking toward Mary." Finally, she managed to get control of herself and hurried away from the eerie site.

What drew the woman toward the child's ghost? The image of the dancing spirit had an almost hypnotic effect. *Tap, tap, tap* went the little feet as the helpless woman headed toward her. It was almost as if they were moving to a cosmic beat, an unlikely duet of the living and the dead. Two worlds collided for an unreal moment as both felt the rhythm.

Could this same rhythm be what draws long-dead Mary to the stage? Is there a pattern in music that opens a portal to the Other Side? No one can say for certain, but the odd occurrences at the Orpheum certainly make me wonder.

### Orpheum Theatre
203 S Main St, Memphis, Tennessee 38103
(901) 525-3000
orpheum-memphis.com

———

Considering that music stirs passion in the spirits of the living, it shouldn't surprise us that the magic of music continues to inspire after those spirits are free of their human bodies. Cases of music and ghosts are abundant, and an especially unique case has made a Memphis, Tennessee, bar famous. The jukebox there seems to have a mind of its own, and it plays tunes that echo the moods of customers. Earnestine & Hazel's is a popular "dive bar," in a two-story brick building, erected in the late 1800s. It's across the street from Central Station, where millions of passengers have boarded and disembarked trains for over a century. The area is steeped in history.

Earnestine & Hazel's has been called "the most haunted bar in America" because of frequent paranormal activity. A disembodied voice has been heard calling out the names of employees. Piano music, footsteps, and conversation are also heard, drifting from the upstairs when no one is there. Witnesses say they've seen the ghost of a man holding a candle. He's been spotted both inside and outside of the bar.

The staff realized that the jukebox was extra special when James Brown, the "Godfather of Soul," passed away in December of 2006. Bartenders were talking about what a terrible loss his death was to the music world when the singer's voice suddenly blasted through the jukebox via his hit song, "I Got You (I Feel Good)." The machine had been sitting silent a moment before, and no one had pushed its buttons.

A newly divorced woman and her friends were marking the occasion with drinks when Tammy Wynette's voice filled the bar, singing "D.I.V.O.R.C.E." Once again, the *jukebox* chose the song, and no human hands had touched the buttons. The jukebox frequently picks tunes to match the mood, according to staff and regular customers.

**Earnestine & Hazel's**
531 S Main St, Memphis, Tennessee 38103
(901) 523-9754
earnestineandhazel.com

———

In the next story, death could not stop a man from doing what he loved the most—making music!

# Ebony and Ivory

Eileen Smith Betancourt has always loved antiques. Charmed by the beauty of old-time craftsmanship, she began her collection as a teenager. It is not just the object itself that attracts her but the *history* of a thing. When she slides the palm of her hand over the worn oak of an old dining room table, she can't help but picture the families who once ate there. And when she peers at her own reflection in an ornately framed antique mirror, she imagines the faces of those who gazed into the glass before her.

This is the way it is with antiques lovers. We like the stories that antiques tell. And many of us are aware that when we bring an aged object into our home, we also invite in its past and, sometimes, its *ghosts*.

When Eileen spotted the 1880s piano, she was not thinking about ghosts. "It was a beautiful, old upright," said the Matawan, New Jersey, artist. It was "in need of repair and very out of tune." But she sensed something special about it. Refinished, the piano glowed in cherry-wood splendor. She had the instrument repaired but ran out of funds to have it tuned. "We put it in the guest room downstairs," she confided. Within days, her friend Karen, who was staying in the room, had a complaint. "She was spooked," Eileen explained. "She heard the piano playing at night."

Shortly after, Karen awoke to see a man standing in her room. "I believed her," said Eileen. Karen was not one to make things up. A few nights later, Eileen was engrossed in a book when she heard faint out-of-key notes drifting up from downstairs. "It was Chopin," she said. "And it was being played badly out of tune!" Another friend, Lori, came to visit and slept in the bedroom just down the hall from her hostess. "In the morning, she told me she had seen a man at my bedroom door the night before," said Eileen.

Finally, Eileen herself saw the ghost. She awoke to see an elderly man peering at her. Later, she walked into the guest room and caught him sitting at the piano. "He was an elderly but sturdy-looking gentleman in a smoking jacket," she said.

Eileen, who has always had a strong sixth sense, got the impression that "he once played the piano in a men's club, where gentlemen gathered to talk, smoke cigars, drink, and enjoy male camaraderie." He was a warm, friendly spirit and welcome in her home.

But the day came when she had to move to an apartment and did not have room for the piano. "The movers were super guys," she said. "One of them fell in love with the piano." She took him aside and said, "You can have the piano, on one condition." She explained to him about the ghost. "You must promise to take good care of them," she said.

The young man broke into a wide grin and readily accepted the deal. The piano *and* the ghost went with him. "I miss that piano," Eileen said. "It had a lot of character. I hope it and its true owner are happy and well."

# 10

## POSSESSIONS POSSESSED

A musical instrument with a spirit attached is not as rare as some might think. The intense emotions of musicians are focused on their instruments as they express themselves through melody. In some cases, the instruments that play on their own are not haunted by spirits but may simply carry leftover energy. The musician may be alive and well, living in some distant place, while the guitar they left behind still reverberates with the power of the passion once directed through it.

Objects soak up energy like sponges soak up spilt milk. The more emotion that a living being focuses on an item, the more likely that object is to soak up energy. In most cases, the items demonstrating paranormal activity probably don't have actual spirits attached but are releasing stored energy. In other circumstances, investigators have concluded that the objects in question were still connected to the spirit of the deceased individuals, and witnesses have actually *seen* those ghosts. Here are some examples of inanimate objects that took on lives of their own.

# Faces in the Mirror

John Cuddeback and his son, Richard, had been in the antiques business in Canandaigua, New York, for over twenty years when they got a strange call in the summer of 2003 from a distraught woman. "Please come get my dresser," she begged. "I don't care what you pay me for it. I just want it out of here."

The old dresser was haunted. The repeated appearances of ghosts in the mirror were disturbing to her, and she was relieved when the Cuddebacks loaded it into their truck and took it away with them. According to the lady, there had been several deaths in the house, including a suicide. She felt that the faces appearing in the dresser mirror belonged to those who had died there.

The Cuddebacks put a price tag on the dresser and placed it in their shop. It was recently purchased, despite the fact that the buyer was warned about the unusual feature. (No word yet on whether the ghosts still appear in the mirror!)

When it comes to haunted objects, mirrors are among the most active. In addition to soaking up the energy of all of those who have peered into them, they may have also "recorded" the images of the people they once reflected. How many of us have glimpsed ourselves in mirrors in dramatic moments of our lives? How many of us have watched ourselves crying as we did so? I suspect *everyone* has done this at least once.

Those dramatic moments always pass, and we quickly forget as we move on to the next moment and the next emotion. Imagine if the mirror does *not* forget. Will our intense, private moment be viewed one day by an astonished witness as the mirror replays the drama it retained?

Children's toys are another example of commonly haunted items. Toys, particularly teddy bears and dolls, can have a tremendous amount of energy directed at them when children clutch them close. Sometimes, a lonely child regards a doll as their

*The faces of the dead appeared in the mirror of this dresser so often that the frightened owner got rid of it. (Leslie Rule)*

only friend. The child *believes* the doll is alive and treats them as if it were so. It's no wonder that old dolls carry so much energy, especially when they've been passed down through generations, and many children have loved them.

# Clowning Around

When Renee walked into her spare room to pick up a basket of dirty laundry, she gasped. Her clown doll was propped up in front of the basket, staring at her with his wide brown eyes. "He'd been in the corner for several months," said the Beaverton, Oregon, real estate agent. "I hadn't moved him."

She quizzed her boyfriend, Mark, and her seventeen-year-old daughter, and neither of them had moved the doll. She was a little spooked but not surprised. She had, in fact, gotten exactly what she'd shopped for—a haunted clown doll!

She had been surfing the Internet, reading ghost stories, when she entered the word "haunted" into "Search." "An eBay auction came up," said Renee. "It was about to end in four minutes." The bidding was in the hundreds for the clown doll with the big, rubber head, round nose, and straw-stuffed body. The main selling point? It was *haunted*! The doll, the seller claimed, moved on its own.

Renee, who asked that her last name be left out of this story, has always been interested in ghosts. "I grew up in Walla Walla, Washington," she said. "My friends lived in an 1800s house that was haunted, and I used to spend the night there. We would hear chains rattling and a woman screaming at night."

As she stared at the photograph of the unusual-looking doll with the mysterious habits, she made a decision. On a whim, Renee entered a bid. Moments

*Vincent Hitchcock, the haunted clown doll, poses on a dock outside of a Portland, Oregon, restaurant. The enigmatic doll sometimes moves on his own. (Leslie Rule)*

later, she received an email telling her that she had won! For about five hundred dollars, the doll was hers. Suddenly, she felt nervous. "I didn't want it to come to my house," she confided. "So I went and got a post office box and had the seller mail it to me there." Once she opened the package, the doll seemed innocent enough, so she brought him home.

He looked to be many decades old, but there were no dates or other markings on him. His clothing appeared to be from the 1960s, but Renee couldn't tell if he wore his original costume. "We named him Vincent Hitchcock," she said, explaining that he was named after two eerie cinema icons—monster-movie actor Vincent Price and suspense-film director Alfred Hitchcock.

She corresponded with the seller, who told her that he was a doll sculptor and that he, too, had purchased the clown doll on eBay. He, however, had no idea that the doll came with a ghost. He simply wanted it because it had such an interesting face. But he soon began to notice that the clown would mysteriously vanish from the places he had left him only to show up in unexpected spots.

"He contacted the previous owner," said Renee. "He asked him if there was something unusual about the doll. The guy told him, 'Yeah! He *moves!*'" That man's wife had made him put the clown in the shed. Renee, however, has a place of honor in her home for Vincent. She also has a website on ghosts with a section devoted to Vincent's activities. Since he has shared her home, he has inexplicably moved several times. Once they found him with his arm up in the air.

In an attempt to capture ghostly voices, Rene turned on a noise-activated recorder and left it beside Vincent when she turned in for the night. She did this several times, and she was rewarded with startling recordings of what sounded like a man's gravelly voice. In the clearest recording, the voice yelled, "Wake up!" When she played the EVP for her daughter, the girl was stunned because she had heard the same words during the night, spoken by the same gravelly voice. In fact, it had woken her. Vincent had been in another room, with no humans present, so there was no "logical explanation" for the recording.

Where in the world did Vincent come from? Rene speculated that the doll was homemade, with the rubber head purchased from a craft shop. Most who meet Vincent agree that there is a childlike aura about him. If a spirit *is* attached to the clown, it may be a child or someone with childlike energy. Despite Renee's research into Vincent's "life," his past is a mystery.

Children have been playing with dolls forever, and haunted dolls can be found in all cities, coast to coast, though most of these spooky creatures have yet to be discovered. After the kids have outgrown them, the dolls are stashed in attics, hidden at the bottom of overflowing toy chests, or sold at garage sales, their secrets seldom exposed.

Many a haunted doll has gone unnoticed—*until* it does something to attract attention. In busy households, no one gives it a second thought when a doll shows up in an unusual place. A child obviously moved the doll, or maybe the family dog carried it, dropping it somewhere unexpected.

If, however, the haunted doll is owned by someone in a quiet home where no children or naughty dogs live, everyone is spooked when they realize that the doll changed position or moved from room to room on its own steam.

Robert may be the most famously haunted doll in America, and he resides in one of our nation's most haunted cities. In the next chapter, I'll introduce you to the straw-stuffed fellow with some most unusual habits and the intriguing city where you can visit him. It's a beautiful place with a tumultuous history and is crawling with ghosts.

# 11

## ICE ON A BALMY BREEZE

Key West, Florida, the southernmost tip of the United States, is a festive, tropical city that borders two bodies of water. You can literally *walk* coast to coast in minutes. From the east, the Atlantic Ocean's turquoise waters nibble at the silver-sanded shores. And from the west, warm zephyrs blow off the Gulf of Mexico, ruffling the feathers of the great gray pelicans that perch upon the weathered docks. Famous for its key lime pie, snorkeling tours, and lively nightlife, Key West is perhaps *not* so famous for its ghosts. Yet they are there.

# Robert Doesn't Live Here Anymore

Artist House Bed and Breakfast is named for painter Robert Gene Otto. He was born in the 1898 Key West mansion and grew up there. There has been a lot of excitement over *another* one-time resident of the historic house. His name was also Robert, though he was an inanimate object, stuffed with straw. "Inanimate" may not be an accurate description, because the doll was actually *very* animated, and that's what made him notorious! Witnesses reported that Robert the doll moved on his own, giggled, and sometimes peered out of the windows at startled passersby.

It all began on Robert Gene Otto's fifth birthday in 1904. His favorite present was a three-foot-tall doll with button eyes that he named after himself. The human Robert blamed all his naughty deeds on the *other* Robert, his faithful doll, who willingly took the blame. The boy started going by his middle name, Gene, while the doll laid claim to his first name.

Photos of Gene as a child show him in a sailor suit matching his doll's outfit. The intense energy Gene focused on his doll was disturbing to family and friends. One story says that a playmate became so frightened of the toy that the straw-stuffed Robert was moved to the attic.

Allegedly, Robert the doll was so offended by this that he "taunted" the children who passed the house on their way to school. The kids claimed that there was something unnatural about that doll and that they were terrified to look up at the attic windows and see it moving. They were so frightened that they found a new route to school to avoid passing the house.

Many years later, when the house became an inn, Robert was a fixture there. The inn's owners had a favorite prank they played on each other. They often moved Robert from room to room, trying to trick each other into believing that the doll had moved on its own. But the joke was on them when they discovered that Robert moved without their help! Though neither one had touched the doll, he still managed to pop up unexpectedly all over the house.

Those wishing to see Robert are advised *not* to knock on the door of the Artist House as countless curious people have done. The owners are busy, and Robert doesn't live here anymore. He is now on display

*A haunted doll scared kids who saw him peering from the attic window of the Artist House. (Leslie Rule)*

at the East Martello Museum in Key West, where he is caged in a glass display case.

### Fort East Martello Museum
3501 S Roosevelt Boulevard, Key West, Florida 33040
(305) 296-3913
kwahs.org

---

## — *Update* —

Key West Ghost Tour founder Robert Sloan authored the book, *Robert the Doll*, published in 2014 by Phantom Press. Sloan's in-depth research started in 1996, and his fascinating book explores the truth and the myths behind America's most haunted doll.

*Author's note: In a strange coincidence, writer Robert Sloan happens to have the same name as a candidate for one of the ghosts at Fort Delaware, mentioned in chapter seven. As far as I know, they are not related!*

**Artist House**
(305) 296-3977
534 Eaton St, Key West, Florida 33040
artisthousekeywest.com

---

# Beautiful Birds and a Homely Doll

Audubon House may be caressed by the balmy breezes of Key West, Florida, but visitors shouldn't be surprised if they feel a chill when strolling through the lovely home where naturalist John Audubon once drew tropical birds.

The 1830 home was built for Captain John Hurling Geiger, who raised his family there. The captain's apparition has been seen in the home, but most of the paranormal activity is focused in the nursery, where disembodied voices are heard. It is there that some believe that the ghosts of Geiger children play. While some siblings died of yellow fever in that room, another son was killed when he fell from an almond tree in the yard.

*A haunted doll mysteriously vanished from Key West's Audubon House. Was she stolen, or did she escape? (Leslie Rule)*

A homely little wax doll with yellow teeth and dark circles beneath her eyes once resided in the museum's nursery. Some say that it belonged to a Geiger girl, and that when she succumbed to yellow fever, her spirit inhabited the doll. The doll has been blamed for much of the paranormal activity at Audubon House—including setting off the burglar alarms at night! The doll, however, has mysteriously disappeared. Stolen? *Or escaped?* Imagine the sickly doll, scurrying along Key West's streets in the moonlight, perhaps leaping out at you when you are least aware. Or maybe you'd rather not.

**Audubon House & Tropical Gardens**
295 Whitehead Street, Key West, Florida 33040
(877) 281-BIRD (2473)
audubonhouse.org

———————

# The Blue Lady

Captain Tony's Saloon is *the* celebrated bar of Key West. Named for former owner Tony Tarracino, the lively place hints at past wild nights with the *hundreds* of bras strung from the ceiling. Left by female customers, the brassieres are dusty testimonials that speak louder than words. As famous as the bar itself, Captain Tony was once mayor. One 1990 headline blared: "Incredible Politician Who Keeps His Promises. Key West Mayor Captain Tony Pledged to Drink, Gamble and Chase Women—*and He Does*."

Performances by talented musicians draw crowds, day and night, at Captain Tony's. "Jimmy Buffett got his start here," Tony told me. "I gave him four beers and ten dollars for his first performance. But I didn't pay much attention because I was flirting with a blonde."

While some customers are content to sip margaritas and tap their feet to the tunes, others are attracted to the poolroom, where a dead woman sleeps in the floor. Most people don't bother to walk *around* her gravestone—they walk *over* it. Embedded in the cement, the last reminder that this girl once lived reads, "Elvira Edmunds, December 21, 1822. 19 years old."

How did she get in the floor? Years ago, while building the pool room addition on the bar, Tony found the tombstone. The area was apparently once a graveyard that was buried in mud by a long-ago hurricane. When Tony discovered the stone, he simply built the floor around it. Some insist that many other bodies share the space with Elvira. One rumor says that Elvira was the lover of a married mortician and that when she became pregnant, he killed her and buried her there when the building was a morgue. But this is nearly impossible to document 179 years after the fact. Is Elvira responsible for the disembodied voices heard echoing throughout Captain Tony's? Is she the fleeting figure seen darting in the shadows? Maybe. Or perhaps another "lady" haunts Key West's most famous bar.

Captain Tony described Elvira's competition to me. He called her the Blue Lady. Despite jokes about his time in office, Tony's fans insist he was an excellent mayor who worked to preserve Key West's historical significance.

*Captain Tony outside his saloon, where he has seen the ghost of the Blue Lady. (Leslie Rule)*

His preservation efforts began in the 1960s, when he almost cut down the tree that grows in the middle of the bar. Captain Tony sat down with me in the shadow of this formidable tree. "I've never told another soul about this," he insisted.

Four decades before, he and his girlfriend, a pretty cocktail waitress, were living in an apartment above the saloon. One night after closing, they were counting the till when they glanced up to see a woman in a long blue dress in the courtyard. "That wall wasn't there back then," he explained, gesturing with his cigarette. "The bar opened into the courtyard. But the gate was locked, and there was no way for anyone to get in. "We both saw her," Tony confided. "She glided past and then vanished. We saw her several times over the following weeks." They came to think of her as the Blue Lady. "My girlfriend was terrified," he remembered. "She was so scared she moved out."

Soon after, as Tony was preparing to enclose the courtyard, he got out his chain saw and was about to cut down the tree when an old-timer stopped him. "You can't cut down that tree," cried the elderly man. "That's the old hanging tree!" A walking history lesson, the man described a macabre scenario from seventy or so years earlier. According to the man, the building that housed the saloon had once been a combination morgue and icehouse. When folks wanted ice for their lemonade, they'd chip it from the bottom of the slabs of ice where corpses lay.

"We used to come here to watch the hangings," the old-timer told Tony, and he described the day when he was a young boy and witnessed something ghastly. He and a friend had sat eating sandwiches as they watched an execution. "I'll never forget it. It took a long time for her to die." He told Tony about how the woman's face had twisted into a grotesque expression as she was slowly strangled to death.

The woman had been executed for killing her husband and children. The reason? According to town gossip, she had somewhat cryptically declared that she murdered them because she had a bad case of the "ugly-wuglies." When the old-timer mentioned that the woman had been hanged in a blue dress, Tony immediately thought of the ghost, for she, too, had worn a blue dress.

Tony agreed it would not be right to cut down the old hanging tree. Instead, he built his new roof around the old tree. Today, customers cheerfully sip cocktails at a table beneath the gnarled branches, sitting directly below the spot where a woman died in agony.

Many of the saloon's customers ask for double shots of alcohol to calm their nerves after they encounter a ghost, according to bartender Chris Smela. "When the air is still, a cold breeze sometimes comes out of nowhere and blows through the saloon," he said. He also described inexplicable banging noises and mysteriously slamming doors.

Recently, on a quiet afternoon, a honeymooner was alone in the ladies' room, sitting in the stall, when she heard a female voice advise, "Don't forget to jiggle the handle when you flush." The customer was puzzled because the door to the restroom creaked loudly whenever it was opened, but she had not heard anyone enter. She complied with the request and emerged to find she was alone. She raced out of the bathroom, her face white as snow. When she told the bartender about the mysterious voice, the regulars laughed knowingly. Many of them had either seen the Blue Lady or knew someone who had.

Is the anguished spirit stuck in those last horrible moments when she was marched up to the hanging tree? Or does she think it was all a dream—the case of the ugly-wuglies, the murder, and the death sentence? If so, maybe she is searching for her long-dead family.

Witnesses report that the apparition sometimes appears in their peripheral vision and vanishes the instant they turn their heads for a better look. Sometimes she materializes right in front of them, and sometimes they see her from across the room. Always, there is the impression of blue.

Many who see the Blue Lady may not realize they are looking at a ghost. If you visit Captain Tony's and notice a woman in a blue dress, watch her closely. She may disappear before your eyes.

I was fascinated by the account of the Blue Lady and eager to learn more. But my search for documentation was fruitless. Locals suggested that I speak with a local historian, a man I'll call Hank. "Hank knows everything!" they said. But Hank laughed when I told him the story of the hangings. "There has *never* been a hanging in Key West," he insisted.

Perhaps he would have been more convincing if he had not been wrong about the Key West lighthouse. While researching a possible haunting there, I approached Hank, who insisted that it had *never*—no buts about it—*ever* been blown down in a hurricane. Yet, *America's Lighthouses,* a meticulously researched book, noted that the Key West lighthouse was documented to do exactly what Hank said it *hadn't* in 1846. It was, according to *America's Lighthouses,* "destroyed by a hurricane that killed the keeper and his family. A sixty-foot tower immediately replaced the wrecked one."

As information repeatedly surfaces to prove historians wrong, I find myself more willing to consider word-of-mouth accounts. My gut says the old-timer who passed his tale on to Captain Tony was telling the truth. Hank the Historian probably wouldn't approve, but part of my research into haunted places involves talking to a psychic.

As mentioned in an earlier chapter, Nancy Myer is renowned for her abilities and has worked with multiple law enforcement agencies to solve crimes.

I sent her a stack of photos that included images of several locations I had photographed. I gave her no indication of the locations. She opened the envelope for the first time as we talked on the phone. When she studied an image of Captain Tony sitting beneath the old hanging tree, she had no clues, only the shades of gray on the black-and-white photograph before her. I didn't tell her that the tree was in a bar or that the location was Key West. I asked her to look at the photo with the man by the tree. "Do you sense anything from the picture?" I asked.

*Captain Tony sits beneath the old hanging tree in his Key West saloon.*

She paused and then gasped. "Leslie!" she exclaimed. "That was a *hanging* tree!" I have never gotten over the thrill I feel when Nancy is extraordinarily accurate about things that she should know nothing about. "There was a lot of Klan activity in the area," she continued.

"That's true," I confirmed. "I found an old newspaper article about it."

"Mostly black people were hanged from that tree," she added, explaining that they were innocent souls who were falsely accused of crimes. "They're still around," she said. It was a difficult reading for Nancy, who did not want to be "linked" to the horrible happenings there. "There were many evil deeds around the tree," she said. "But the tree has stayed a positive energy."

I asked her about the Blue Lady. "She had very tan skin," said Nancy. "It was one of the more recent hangings. Her name was Gertrude. She was schizophrenic."

## — *Update* —

Captain Tony passed away at age ninety-two on November 1, 2008. He is immortalized in Jimmy Buffet's "Last Mango in Paris," a song written to honor the Key West legend. I'll never forget sitting with Tony under the old hanging tree as he revealed the secret of the Blue Lady. I'm honored that he chose to give me the scoop on Key West's most chilling ghost. I'm also honored that I got to sit where Jimmy Buffet once had, listening to "the old man," and I get a little teary eyed when I listen to "Last Mango."

The historian I spoke to had scoffed at the idea of hangings in Key West, but he was wrong when he insisted that no one was lynched there. With news archives now online and searchable, I've seen the proof that history has once again proven a historian wrong. People *were* lynched in Key West, and many of them were dark skinned—probably innocent of the crimes they were accused of, just as psychic Nancy Myer had said.

While I'm still searching for validation of the Blue Lady, I've found countless cases of hangings in Key West, including the September 1897 hanging of Sylvanus Johnson, a black man accused of rape. The *Weekly Tribune* reported that as two deputy sheriffs led the condemned man to the noose, he sang, "Nearer my God, to thee."

Just as Tony had said that the Blue Lady had taken a long time to die, so had Sylvanus. For twenty minutes, he slowly strangled as spectators waited for his life to end.

### Capt. Tony's Saloon
428 Greene St, Naval Air Station Key West, Florida 33040
(305) 294-1838
capttonyssaloon.com

---

You don't have to go to Key West to visit a haunted bar. Haunted restaurants and bars can be found in nearly every city in America. In the next chapter we'll explore a few places where customers sometimes eat and run!

# 12

## EAT, DRINK, AND AND BE SCARY

# Crabby Dick's

When the employees at Crabby Dick's hear the pitter patter of little feet, they tell the kids to go to bed. It happens every so often as they're sitting in the bar after closing time, late in the night, when no one is upstairs. Suddenly, they hear the distinctive sound of a child running—the soft, rhythmic thuds echoing overhead that alert them to the fact a naughty little ghost is up past her bedtime.

Crabby Dick's, a popular seafood restaurant in the historic district of Delaware City, Delaware, specializes in dishes made from crabmeat and is known for its fun atmosphere *and* for the fact it's haunted. Ghostly encounters at the riverfront bar are not unusual, and many have seen, heard, and felt the restless spirits who cling to the landmark structure that once housed the Delaware City Hotel.

Witnesses have reported seeing the apparition of a woman who appears so solid and real that they don't realize she is a spirit until she dissolves into thin air. She appears throughout the building, most often at the top of the stairs on the second-floor landing and in an upstairs room with so many disturbances that guests refuse to sleep there.

The ghosts here hail from a time we can only imagine—an era when there were no airplanes, no televisions, and no computers. In fact, the hotel was built in 1826, before the telephone was invented, and people sometimes communicated via carrier pigeons. One wayward messenger flew into an open upstairs window on a spring day in 1892. When the hotel proprietor, Elijah Stout, found the lost bird in his bedroom, he tried to find the owner by alerting a reporter who printed a notice in the newspaper.

Despite the lack of modern amenities, the Delaware City Hotel earned a reputation as a clean and classy place soon after it opened its doors two centuries ago. Guests often came to town for fishing, crabbing, and sailing on the river and nearby canal. The hotel not only catered to out-of-towners but was also a popular place for locals who held meetings and special events there. It was once the end of the line for a trolley that connected to nearby cities, and for a period, one hotel owner granted permission for his front parlor to be used as a waiting room for passengers.

Guests arrived by trolley, by boat, and sometimes by horseback. A "first-class livery stable" was attached to the inn to accommodate the horses. The hotel was usually lively and filled with people, and things could get rowdy in the bar. In August of 1902, for instance, drunken soldiers got angry one Saturday night when the hotel bar closed down at midnight before they were done drinking. An argument between the proprietors and the soldiers ended with an exchange of gunfire. No one was hurt, but the noise woke up everyone in the neighborhood.

To the many owners who operated it over the years, the hotel was home. They lived there with their families, most taking great pride in caring for the four-story building with the stunning views of the Delaware River.

When Rebecca and Elijah Stout bought the hotel in 1886, they redecorated with fresh wallpaper and new furniture. The local paper reported that Mrs. Stout acquired "a handsome, upright piano" for the hotel parlor. It was a happy time for the family, and the three daughters were excited about their new home. At age nine, Maggie was the oldest sister. Next came Ella Belle, age seven, followed by little Ida, who turned four in March of 1887, shortly after the family moved in. Ida was an adorable child, named for her aunt, her mother's sister, Ida Hulshizer.

It could very well be little Ida who makes mischief today at Crabby Dick's. It might be the sound of her ghostly little feet, pitter-pattering in the rooms above the bar, for the child died in the hotel just eight days after her fourth birthday. On her death certificate, the doctor noted that pseudomembranous croup ended her life. While the viral respiratory ailment has effective treatments today, the medication was not available to the little girl in 1887.

It's possible that the ghosts of Ida's parents and big sister Maggie are also lurking in the shadows of the popular restaurant. Most of little Ida's family died within a decade after she did. Maggie passed away at age eighteen, in December of 1896, after a brief illness. She was visiting relatives in Philadelphia at the time of her death, but both of her parents died in the hotel. Mrs. Stout developed an illness that resulted in paralysis, and she died in February of 1896, at age fifty. Her husband succumbed to typhoid fever a year later. He was fifty-two. Only the middle sister, Ella Belle, lived a full life, celebrating ninety-seven birthdays before she took her last breath in Glenside, Pennsylvania, in July of 1977.

When it comes to the identities of the ghosts of Crabby Dick's, no one can say for certain who they are because many people have lived and died on the premises over the years. Whenever I look for the roots of a haunting, I focus on the history of sudden and violent deaths because intense paranormal activity is most often associated with murders, suicides, and accidents. I do not, however, ignore cases of death from illness, because even gentle deaths can be associated with hauntings—especially when the young die.

As I began my archive research on the history of Crabby Dick's, I was most interested in two things. First, I was looking for records of children who died on the premises, deaths that could explain why witnesses hear the distinctive sound of little feet running. I was also keenly interested in the ghost of an earthbound chambermaid that many believe haunts the place. This intrigued me because I learned that a famous psychic with an impressive record for accuracy, had tuned into the long-dead maid.

It was Nancy Myer. As my readers know by now, she's assisted me in my research of haunted places, and over the years, she's given me information that turned out to be accurate more times than I can count. It was not Nancy, however, who told me about the ghost of the chambermaid. I heard about it from John Buchheit, the bar's co-owner. When John and his business partner, Dale Slotter, purchased the building in 2006, John had an intense dream the first night he stayed there, sleeping in a room on the third floor. The dream was so vivid and felt so real that he can still recall it perfectly sixteen years later. An angry woman, dressed in chambermaid attire from the turn of the nineteenth century, appeared in his nightmare and confronted him. She ordered him to get out.

"I woke up petrified," he remembered.

He was unaware that the dream confrontation with the maid was a repeat of an argument that had actually occurred between a maid and a new owner of that very same building a century earlier. It happened in 1908. But there was one big difference. In 1908, it was not the maid who told the owner to get out. The owner told the *maid* to get out.

The century-old fight between owner and maid would have faded away with the memories of humans long dead, if not for the terrible thing that occurred afterward. This tragedy came to light through my research in old newspaper accounts, but John was completely unaware of it when he had the dream. While he tried to shrug the whole thing off as a peculiar nightmare, he couldn't quite shake it because it had seemed so *real*.

About a year after his strange dream, producers for the TV show *Psychic Detectives* asked to use the restaurant to film a reenactment with Nancy Myer for a story they were doing on a case she had solved early in her career. When John got a chance to chat with Nancy, he mentioned that the restaurant had a "myth" about the ghost of a woman who died there.

"It's not a myth," Nancy told him, and he was astonished as she proceeded to describe the chambermaid and her old-fashioned servant attire that matched the vision in his dream.

Had a maid *really* died there?

If so, I was determined to find out. The fact that Nancy had confirmed that this spirit was in the restaurant assured me that I wasn't wasting time when I spent two long and tedious days scrolling through newspaper archives, looking for evidence of the maid's existence. I normally don't get too excited when I hear that historical information about a haunted location came from a psychic because so many so-called psychics aren't as skilled as they claim. Nancy, however, has an exceptional ability, and if she said that a maid had lived and died in the building, then I was confident that I could prove her right. Near the end of the second day of combing newspaper archives, I found her.

Edna Kennedy, age thirty-three, was a chambermaid who lived in an upstairs room of the Delaware City Hotel in the early 1900s. She was a widow, struggling to make ends meet. According to the old articles, Edna had started work at the hotel in September of 1907, but in the summer of 1908, she lost her job.

Newspaper reports gave two different accounts of how that came about. In one version, the hotel had changed owners, and management let her go because of restructuring. In the other version, Edna and the proprietor, William C. Smith, had an argument. Angry words were exchanged, and he fired her.

My research confirmed that the hotel was sold in the summer of 1908. William Smith purchased it from the man Edna had been working for, John Goodwin. Most likely, William *was* making routine changes, but that wasn't the only reason Edna was fired.

## Mrs. Edna Kennedy Drank Two Kinds of Poison in Delaware City Hotel

Despondent because she was out of work and dependent on others, Mrs. Edna Kennedy, aged 35 years, formerly of this city, committed suicide last night in her room in the Delaware City Hotel, at that place. She had formerly been employed as housekeeper at the hotel, but when the hotel recently changed hands she lost the position, but was allowed to remain in the house. She had very little money and worried considerably.

*An August 1908 newspaper article reports on the shocking death of a desperate woman who ended her life when things did not go her way.*

The story about her disagreement with the new owner has a ring of truth to it. It's not uncommon for employees to bristle when management changes hands. The rules usually change, too, and workers tend to be annoyed by this. My guess is that Edna was a little too outspoken about her distaste for the new policies. She may have felt—*and rightly so*—that she knew more about the hotel because she'd been there nearly a year, while William was a newcomer. Her mistake was voicing her disapproval.

No matter how it came about, Edna was fired, and she was devastated. She lost her job and her home in one fell swoop. She was desperate to keep her job and her comfortable room in the hotel. Shortly after the blowup with her boss, on Tuesday, August 25, Edna was riding the trolley when she noticed that he, too, was a passenger. She approached and asked for another chance.

The answer was no. She could not have her job back, and he wanted her *out* of his hotel. There were few witnesses to what happened next. Edna went back to the hotel, where twelve-year-old Robert Smith, son of William, witnessed her drinking liquid from a glass at a little before 6:00 p.m. The boy later testified that Edna told him to hurry and get his father. William Smith, too, testified about the events and said that he'd heard Edna calling for help and rushed upstairs to her room. She was on her bed, writhing in pain, and admitted that she'd taken two different kinds of poison, laudanum and carbolic acid.

A doctor was summoned, but it was too late. Edna died within thirty minutes after consuming the poison. An inquest was held the next day, with both William and Robert Smith testifying. The jury determined that the poison was self-administered.

When the hotel was acquired by the new owner in 1908, it may have been the worst thing that had ever happened to Edna Kennedy. That hotel purchase started a catastrophic chain of events that resulted in her losing her job, her home, and her *life*.

Things did not have to turn out the way they did, of course. It was Edna's choice to argue with Mr. Smith and put her job in jeopardy. It was Edna's choice to drink poison. Even so, she was in an irrational state of mind and likely blamed the new owner for the tragedy she wallowed in. It was *his* fault that she had no money and no place to live. It was *his* fault that her only option was to swallow poison.

The resentment Edna felt toward the building's new owner in 1908 was so intense that it did not fade, despite the fact she was dead. It did not fade, despite the fact ninety-eight years had passed. Her resentment was so powerful that she held onto it for a century and unleashed it on another new owner in 2006 during a nightmare that was so real to John Buchheit that he woke up shaking.

Can I say for a *fact* that the ghost of Edna Kennedy carried a grudge for a century and that she was so resentful of the new owner that she stepped into his 2006 nightmare to pick a fight? No. I know nothing for certain. Whatever insight I have into the psychology of ghosts comes from patterns I've noted while researching haunted places. My perspective is not unique. It's a leading theory among paranormal experts that earthbound spirits are commonly bound to this plane by the intense emotion they felt in life and that unresolved issues can prevent souls from moving on. It is this theory, coupled with my own sixth sense, that compels me to analyze hauntings and make assumptions.

All the females in my family have a strong sixth sense, and I draw upon mine when I write. That does not mean, however, that my gift is anywhere close to that of psychic Nancy Myer. I would never say that I *am* a psychic. I'm a *little* bit psychic, just as millions of other people are. Few are born with the ability of someone like Nancy.

Even while I sing her praises, I understand that Nancy is not always correct. Nor does she claim to be. She sees, hears, and senses things and then must *interpret* what she absorbs. She freely admits that she does not always interpret correctly. When John Buchheit met Nancy in his restaurant, and she described the ghostly chambermaid, she shared an intriguing detail. Nancy told John the maid's name was Sandy.

I kept this in mind as I scoured archives for information about Edna. I learned that she was the daughter of William Curtis, a traveling salesman of farm equipment. He had divorced her mother, Loretta, when Edna was ten years old. The Curtis family had roots in Scott, Pennsylvania, and William and his siblings stayed close into adulthood.

Where did the name Sandy fit in? Why did Nancy pick up on the name, and how was it significant to Edna? I had learned the name of Edna's father via news articles about the suicide. Authorities at first believed that she had no family, and they were getting ready to have a funeral and bury her in a potter's field when they received a telegram from her father. William Curtis had heard about her death and was on his way. The poor man was overwhelmed with grief and broke down when he saw his daughter's body. Though he'd planned to bring her remains back to Wayne County, Pennsylvania, so that her final resting place would be with family, it wasn't practical. It was summertime, and too many days had passed since her death.

Edna was buried in Riverview Cemetery in Wilmington, Delaware. Her tombstone reads, *Edna F. Kennedy, daughter of Wm. O. Curtis.* It appears she was his only daughter, though he had a son with his second wife. Finding details about Edna's father and the rest of the family was a bit of a challenge because the name William Curtis is so common. I, however, had a *hint* that helped me narrow the search. *Sandy.* I kept my eyes open for that name when scrutinizing archives. As it turned out, Sandy was a *surname,* and when it popped up in an 1870 census report for one of the Curtis families I was studying, I knew I had the right family. Even so, I double-checked details to confirm that Nancy Myer's tip had steered me in the right direction.

I learned that William went by his middle name, Oscar, and that his older sister, Mary Anna Curtis, became a Sandy when she married Samuel Berry Sandy. They had two daughters who, of course, were also Sandys. Sarah Ellen Sandy, born in 1869, and Mary Emma Sandy, born in 1870. Out of all her cousins on her father's side of the family, these Sandy cousins were the girls closest in age to Edna.

Both Sarah Ellen and Mary Emma lived on Woodstock Street in Philadelphia around the time Edna worked at the Delaware City Hotel. When the cousins visited each other, they traveled by the steamboats that made regular stops at the wharfs in Philadelphia, Wilmington, and Delaware City. Travelers often took the boat from Delaware City to Wilmington and then transferred to the trolley for the rest of the thirty-mile trip to Philadelphia.

I can't help but wonder if Edna's Sandy cousins told her about the near tragedy that occurred on Woodstock Street, the very street they lived on. I learned about it while searching archives. A lovesick maid poisoned herself with laudanum, but the family she worked for discovered it in time to save her life. The newspaper reported that the girl told the doctor she'd taken the poison so that the fellow who'd rejected her would regret it for the rest of his life.

Is it possible that Edna was inspired by this other maid's actions? Did Edna take laudanum because she wanted to make William Smith regret firing her?

Did she think that she'd recover and that he would feel so bad about what he'd done that he would let her stay? She had, after all, sent Smith's son to get his father after she'd taken the poison, and she'd also called out for help. Maybe Edna believed she would recover once a doctor was summoned, just as the maid on Woodstock Street had. Or maybe Edna *had* wanted to die but changed her mind when she realized what she'd done.

Either way, Edna was in turmoil when she threw away her future. If ever there were a candidate for a ghost who refuses to move on after death, it would be the chambermaid who refused to move on in life. When Smith ordered Edna to get out, she was determined to disobey—so determined that instead of packing her bags and leaving quietly, she took a stubborn stance by swallowing poison. Maybe Edna had not really meant to die, but her wish was granted. She got to stay in the hotel.

While her flesh and bones have turned to dust, the ghost of Edna Kennedy lives on at Crabby Dick's. She made it clear to John Buchheit when she met him in his dream that she considers the place her home. She may be trying to earn her keep, if the things chef Jimmy Johnson experienced in the kitchen are any indication. More than once, "I walked into the kitchen and saw the broom and dustpan, standing up on their own, in the middle of the room," he said. Were those items *really* standing on their own, or were they held by the ghostly hands of a maid, trying to clean up?

### Crabby Dick's
30 Clinton St, Delaware City, Delaware 19706
(302) 832-5100
crabby-dicks.com

# Ghostly Exposure

"Roslyn is the most haunted place I know of," Steve Ojurovich, owner of the Pioneer Restaurant and Sody-licious Bar, said of the town he calls home. Nestled in the Cascade Mountains in central Washington, Roslyn was established by the Northern Pacific Railroad in 1886 as a coal mining town. Made famous when used as the setting for the mythical town of Cicely, Alaska, in the quirky hit television program *Northern Exposure*, which debuted in 1990, Roslyn is still recognizable to fans of the show who visit the small rustic town for the nostalgia, as well as for snowmobile and horse riding.

While known for its TV exposure, Roslyn is not yet well known for its *ghostly* exposure. Residents say the place is crawling with ghosts. In fact, Steve claims six of the town's ghosts inhabit his restaurant and bar. "I saw the first one the night I bought the place four years ago," he confided. He was in the downstairs bar area, cleaning up, when he saw a figure from the corner of his eye. "I thought it was my dad, so I called to him." When there was no reply, he went in search of him, but the place was empty, and the doors were locked.

He'd no sooner gone back to his chores when he saw him again. "He looked like a logger, with a blue plaid shirt and jeans on, and he had a beard." Since then, the bearded ghost has been seen frequently, sometimes walking in the hallway by the bathrooms and sometimes walking past the cooler. He is always accompanied by the strong scent of cigarette smoke. Who is he?

According to Steve, he just might be the fellow his grandpa once told him about—the fellow who "poked his nose where it didn't belong." Steve, a fourth-generation Roslyn resident, is a walking history book of the town's past. His great-grandfather came from Croatia to mine coal in Roslyn, and the family has been here ever since. The building that houses his restaurant and bar was once the Pioneer Grocery Store. Before that it was a Sears and Roebuck that went out of business when it couldn't compete with the other local merchants, he explained. The basement was once a Sody-licious soda bottling company where during prohibition more potent drinks were surreptitiously brewed. Secret underground tunnels hid the illegal activity, and it was there that a visiting stranger decided to snoop around. "According to my grandpa, the man was shot and killed right there," said Steve, pointing to the cooler behind the bar, where the entrance to the tunnel was long ago sealed up. "And that's where we see the ghost."

I had brought my electromagnetic field detector (EMFD) along on this trip, and I lifted the popular handheld ghost-hunting device and pointed it to where Steve gestured. It instantly measured high on the scale, indicating energy where there was no logical explanation for the source.

"And we see him over here," said Steve, pointing to the hallway that runs past the small restrooms. Once again, the EMFD registered high on the scale as I pointed it in the areas where the specter was said to walk. Upstairs in the two-story restaurant, a woman's ghost was once seen peering from the window. It was late, and Steve and the bartender had just closed up and were shooting the breeze on the sidewalk when they saw her. She stood in the restaurant window, gazing out at the street. "She wore a white blouse with puffy sleeves," said Steve. "Her hair was parted in the middle, braided, and pulled back from her face."

Steve's mother, Marianne Ojurovich, thinks she knows who the ghost is. The description matches that of the woman who owned the grocery store where Marianne's family shopped for many years. Steve was too young to have known Edna, but when he described her to his mother, she nodded her head as she remembered. Edna died decades ago of natural causes in her senior years,

*Steve Ojurovich, owner of the Pioneer Restaurant and Sody-licious Bar, often encounters ghosts there.*
*(Leslie Rule)*

but the apparition appeared as she had looked in younger days. "I can't say for certain it was Edna," said Marianne, "but I think it was her. She always wore her hair like that."

Edna's apartment had once occupied the space that serves as the Pioneer Restaurant kitchen, and Steve often senses her presence there. "She walked through me once," Steve said. "It was the most exhilarating experience I ever had." He was in the kitchen, he said, when he sensed the ghost move through him. "I felt tingling all the way to my fingertips and toes."

Steve believes that another woman's ghost shares the downstairs bar with the logger. "She doesn't know she's dead," he said, relying on his natural strong sixth sense to come to that conclusion. "The ghosts here have bothered me only once," he added, and described an incident that left him uneasy. "Against my wishes, one of my employees had used a Ouija board here. I was at the cash register when a dark shadow shot up over my head and went across the room."

Sometimes the ghosts make mischief at the Pioneer Restaurant. Marianne recalls the time that a young woman was so shocked that she never returned after a bottle of wine suddenly exited the wine rack, shot through the air, and shattered beside her. "The bottle had not been opened," Marianne said. "I could see it was unopened because I picked up the broken glass myself. There was no way that gasses could have been built up to cause the bottle to explode."

Another time, Marianne's husband, Joe, was sitting quietly in the same area when a bottle of gin lifted up off the bar and dropped at his feet. "He doesn't believe in ghosts," said Marianne, who smiled when she remembered how unsettled he was by the unexplained occurrence. "He doesn't like to talk about it."

## — *Update* —

Pioneer Restaurant and Sody-licious Bar has closed down. Residents of Roslyn are waiting for another business to occupy the space. Whether or not the newcomers will welcome the ghosts remains to be seen!

# Hide-and-Seek

Next door to the Pioneer Restaurant is the Brick Saloon, where many *Northern Exposure* scenes were filmed. Fans might gaze around the familiar rustic watering hole and expect to see the characters Holling and Shelly serving beer behind the bar. While the actors have moved on, *others* have left something behind. Quite possibly, their souls.

Bartender Jeremy Kaynor still seemed shaken as he set down a tray and told me about the encounter he had when he began working at the Brick in the summer of 2003. He and a roommate shared an upstairs apartment, and one night, shortly after moving in, they glanced at the security monitor, which kept them tuned in to the scene at the bar.

The bar was closed and buttoned up tight for the night, but movement on the monitor caught their attention. "There was a little girl staring at us!" said Jeremy. He pointed out the tiny white camera in the corner of the ceiling. "See that camera?" he asked me. After scrutinizing the ceiling for a moment, I noticed it and nodded. "She was just standing there, staring up at the camera," said Jeremy. She was little—about as tall as the pool tables. Her blouse was white with puffy sleeves."

When his roommate got up and started running to go check out the scene, Jeremy watched the monitor and saw the little girl run at the same time, as if *she* could see them through the camera too. "She ran behind the pool tables," said Jeremy. The guys searched, but there was no sign of anyone there.

When a coworker later learned that Jeremy had seen a ghost, she casually asked him, "Oh, did you see the man or the little girl?" That was it for Jeremy. He gave notice to move out of his apartment. "I'll work here, but I'm not going to live here," he said, and related another incident when owner, Wanda Najar, heard the sound of someone chopping wood in the bar in the middle of the night. Again, the bar was closed, and the doors were barred from the inside. "Jeremy, are you making that noise?" Wanda called to him. "Are you chopping wood?"

He answered in the negative, and together they went downstairs and found that a chair in the bar had been chopped into pieces. This brings to mind the logger's ghost, who has been seen frequently next door at Steve's Sody-licious Bar. A logger, of course, would be adept with an axe. Does the bearded specter wander between the two places? Or perhaps it was the ghost of one of the miners who once populated the town. They, too, used axes in their work.

While Roslyn's bars don't allow *minors*, they couldn't stop *miners* from frequenting their establishments even if they wanted to, for the ghosts of these dead men are persistent. Steve mentioned a house in town where his friends looked into a hole beneath it and saw something unexpected. "They saw the faces of the miners," he told me.

Today Roslyn's population is about one thousand, far less than at its peak in 1910, when four thousand folks lived there. Over twenty different ethnic groups lived together as the men in the families worked the coal mines. In its heyday, nearly two million tons of coal a year were produced. It was an honest living, but it was hard, dirty, and sometimes dangerous work. Accidents happened, and miners were sometimes killed. According to Marianne Ojurovich, the carbide lights on the miners' hats produced acetylene gas, which at times built up and created deadly explosions.

When the steam locomotives were replaced with trains powered by diesel engines in the 1920s, coal was no longer in high demand, and the mines gradually began to shut down. Logging became the major occupation there for a while. Loggers, miners, or merchants, they've all bellied up to the bar at the Brick, the oldest licensed bar in the state of Washington. It opened its doors in 1889 and has seen some rowdy characters come and go.

Worn wooden floors, high brick walls, and a spittoon that runs like a little river beside the bar all add to the rustic ambience. In addition to the apparitions seen there, witnesses have also heard phantom piano music. Staff have left shots of whiskey out on the bar at night, hoping to appease the rambunctious spirits. The glasses are often empty by morning.

Downstairs, the remnants of an old jail cell recall a time when lawbreakers were locked up there. Curiously, a tombstone for a man named William Thomas sits in one of the old cells. Is he buried there? If so, is his ghost one of the restless ones who roam Roslyn? Many of the mysteries of the historic town are buried and may remain that way forever.

*When you drink at the Brick in Roslyn, Washington, the ghosts of miners might join you. (Leslie Rule)*

## — *Update* —

Word on the street is that when the Brick changed hands a few years back, the new owners weren't as enthused about the ghosts as the previous management was when I researched this story twenty years ago for my book *Ghosts Among Us*. Insiders say that despite how the saloon's new owners feel about them, the ghosts are still there!

**The Brick Saloon**
100 W Pennsylvania Avenue, Roslyn, Washington 98941
(509) 649-2643

# Trapped in Tacoma

Theresa Ricon took a break during a quiet time at Alfred's Café in Tacoma, Washington. As she sat down to enjoy a few moments of rest between customers, she glanced at the mirror and noticed someone at one of her tables. "When I got up to wait on them, I realized that no one was there," said the part-time waitress and mother of two young children. She shivered a little as she told me the story. "It scares me," she admitted, as she glanced around at the mirrors in the historic building.

Every inch of the walls of the popular restaurant and the adjoining diner is covered with mirrors. They reflect back upon each other endlessly in a dramatic effect that enlarges the space and, perhaps, creates a passage for ghosts.

Housed in a one-time hotel on Puyallup Avenue, a few blocks from the icy waters of Puget Sound, Alfred's Café serves up classic American food on the ground floor while the two upper floors are used for storage. Opened in 1888 as the Hotel Brunswick, the three-story building originally sat a couple of blocks up the hill, beside the train station. The building was moved in 1907.

While it is easy to find old postcards of other historic hotels in town, apparently none were printed of the Brunswick. It seems that customers were not eager to write home and brag about their stay there. Perhaps they did not want their friends and relatives to know that they were visiting a *brothel*.

The hotel, tucked discreetly next to the railroad tracks, was not the most reputable place in town. During an era when proper ladies' skirts swished about their ankles and divorce was a scandal, the secrets within the walls of the Hotel Brunswick would have shocked the respectable citizens of Tacoma.

The hotel's second and third floors were chopped into small rooms, none much larger than a horse's stable. There, the liquor flowed freely, and the women were not shy. Over a century later, the rooms are still intact, complete with their original doors and transom windows. Worn linoleum and aged wallpaper, installed sometime around the 1930s, remain in place. Old wiring and new fire codes prevent the owners from opening the space to the public.

Today, the upper floors are a dusty place. Some of the tiny rooms are empty, while others are filled with tangled heaps of chairs and various dining artifacts. The storage room is clean and tidy, stacked with huge cans of the standard restaurant staples. "I don't like to go upstairs," Theresa told me. And she is not alone in her apprehension. Some other employees have also refused to venture upstairs alone.

It is usually the dishwashers' job to fetch supplies. They must adhere to the task at hand and try not to think about the mysterious noises that emanate from above. For sometimes, the staff is startled by the sudden, loud clomping of footsteps and the thud of objects falling to the floor. "We'll look around and see that all of the dishwashers are accounted for," said Theresa. "We realize that no one is upstairs."

Employees shudder and shoot each other knowing glances as they try to concentrate on taking orders or mixing drinks. Braver employees have searched for the source of the noise and are baffled to find nothing out of place.

Who are the ghosts of the old Brunswick Hotel? Some may be from the days of the brothel, while others may have visited or worked in the building during another era. For many years, a popular tavern occupied the ground floor. A bartender who died decades ago has materialized in the restaurant. A waitress reported that she arrived in the morning to see the fellow standing behind the bar.

An Alfred's bartender told me that things inexplicably disappear from the place. "Right now, we're missing the chore book," he said. "It lists side work, and the waitresses check off the jobs they complete each day. It's been missing for a few days." He also admitted that he has closed the place up at night and turned off all the lights, only to return in the morning to find the lights blazing.

Whoever haunts the place likes to tease the waitresses. Rebecca Sheiman was behind the bar after closing one night when she felt a sharp tug on her hair. "I turned around and there was no one there," she said.

Theresa Ricon was in the same area when she felt someone pull on her apron strings. While a number of spirits may linger in the historic structure for a variety of reasons, at least one may be grounded in sorrow. A former cook saw her and told Theresa about it. "The cook left the month I started here," she said, as she recalled the frightened awe in his voice as he confided in her.

*Employees have seen apparitions in the mirrors of this Tacoma, Washington, restaurant. (Leslie Rule)*

He had gone upstairs for supplies. When he passed the foot of the open antique staircase on the second floor, he glanced up to see a woman in a long skirt, standing on the third-floor landing. He glimpsed her for only a moment, but a few details registered. Not only was her outfit from the early part of the twentieth century, but the area around her was also from a bygone era.

"He saw pictures on the walls," Theresa said. The cook was stunned by the image from long ago. His eyes were drawn to the woman's slender white arms that were covered in bruises. The scenario vanished before he had time to question it. His shocking encounter gives us a poignant clue to the identity of one of the building's ghosts. The woman had been abused and most likely worked in the brothel. She was probably at the mercy of the strangers who visited her in her confined room. She may have been killed by one of the patrons, her body tossed in Puget Sound and lost forever in the vast, salty depths. *If* anyone had cared enough to report her missing, she would not have been a high priority on the detectives' agenda.

## Alfred's Cafe
402 Puyallup Avenue, Tacoma, Washington 98421
(253) 627-5491

# 13

## GHOSTS ON THE ROAD

When my book *Coast to Coast Ghosts* was published on September 11, 2001, my publishers, Andrews McMeel Publishing, had no idea that that day would be one of the most tragic in American history. My publicist had scheduled my first ghost interview for that afternoon, and I had train reservations to travel from Tacoma, Washington, to Portland, Oregon, where I would meet with Diana Page Jordan, host of the radio show *Between the Lines*.

As it turned out, that interview had to be rescheduled because our country was under attack by terrorists. National security suspended all train and plane travel until further notice. The tragedy also changed the publicist's approach to promoting my book. She was quite clever and had ordered coffin shaped boxes for *Coast to Coast Ghosts*. The coffin boxes were almost the exact size of the book, with just enough room for her to sprinkle in little plastic spiders. She planned to send the spooky packages to radio hosts, inspiring them to schedule me for their Halloween shows.

With the sudden death of thousands of Americans, however, coffin boxes no longer seemed like such a cute idea. A relative of the publicist worked at a place targeted by the terrorists that day, and while he escaped unharmed, she had suffered hours of worry before she learned he had survived. She scrapped the coffin boxes and mailed the books in plain envelopes.

Andrews McMeel is a Kansas City, Missouri, publisher and syndicator, celebrated for supporting their creators. They bow to the creative preferences of their writers and artists and invest energy in promoting them. They discovered Garry Trudeau when he was cartooning for a college newspaper in 1968, recognized his talent, and—despite naysayers—they launched and syndicated *Doonesbury*. The comic strip won a Pulitzer Prize and became one of the most popular in the world. Their other successes include *Calvin and Hobbes* by Bill Watterson, *The Far Side* by Gary Larson, and *Garfield* by Jim Davis.

My agent, Sheree Bykofsky, advised me in 1999 that I'd be in very good hands with Andrews McMeel, and she was right. While many publishers are tightwads when it comes to promoting their authors, Andrews McMeel Publishing assigned a publicist to work with me full-time in October 2001 to promote *Coast to Coast Ghosts*, and (with my permission) she scheduled me for seventy radio interviews in the two weeks leading up to Halloween. The interviews were "phoners," so I could do them from home. Most days, my last interview ended at midnight, and the next one started at 4:00 a.m. I didn't sleep much, and I told the same ghost stories over and over again, so often that I got sick of my own voice.

That autumn of 2001, I learned that the world was not as safe as I believed it was, and I learned that I could wear pajamas while I spoke to thousands of people and that no one would mind. They didn't mind because they didn't know. They couldn't see me, of course, because it was radio. This was before podcasts and apps such as Skype and Zoom had been invented. My voice was all that mattered, so I sometimes didn't bother to brush my hair and instead focused on enunciating as I tried to sound interesting. More times than I can count, I said, "You may have seen a ghost but didn't realize it."

The radio host would then ask me to explain, and I would say, "Some ghosts appear so solid and real that we can't tell they're ghosts unless they disappear before our eyes." Then I would ask the host, "Do you check everyone you pass on the street to see if they're alive?"

This, of course, would give witty hosts a chance to make all kinds of jokes, something I knew they relished. Part of my job was to make the hosts look good, so I'd laugh at whatever quips they came up with before I'd suggest ways to tell if a person on the street was a live human being or ghost.

I would explain that if the person is wearing out of style clothing, it could be an indicator they're a ghost. At this point, the host usually made another joke, sometimes about their own outdated clothing and sometimes about the outfits of their cohosts.

After we had a good laugh, I'd adapt a more serious serious tone and elaborate on other ways to spot a ghost on the street. Was the "person" there one more moment and gone the next? Did you turn away for a second and then look back to see that the "person" had gone—leaving much too quickly than humanly possible?

Were you the only one who saw that "person," even though you were not alone and those with you should also have seen them? (Often, with ghost sightings, not everyone in a group of people will see apparitions. Children, animals, and those with a keener sixth sense are more likely to see ghosts when others don't.)

Despite the fact I repeatedly explained ways to identify a ghost on the street, I had failed to recognize the most intense spirit encounter of my life. I saw a ghost on the road in 1987, over a decade before I went on the radio and gave advice on how to spot ghosts. But I didn't realize that the man I saw was a disembodied spirit until a decade *after* those radio interviews. In fact, it was only six months ago when I finally and absolutely confirmed that I had seen a ghost on a rainy night in Oregon three decades earlier.

I knew him before he was a ghost when we worked together at the Walrus and the Carpenter Restaurant in Lake Grove, Oregon. In my twenties in the 1980s, I waitressed for seven years, with four years at the Walrus, my last restaurant job. It was a slightly upscale place featuring seafood dishes. The fast pace and sometimes belligerent customers made it a stressful job, but I was fond of most of the people I worked with.

One of the chefs, Scott Maixner, was a kindhearted, husky young man, and he took great pride in the meals he created. His teenage brother, Dustin, worked as the Walrus dishwasher for a few months. I remember the night their father and stepmother came in for dinner, and Scott was so excited about it. Ray and Barbara Maixner were seated in a booth in my section, and Ray told me, "We want Scott to personally make our dinners."

Scott proudly prepared their meals, and after they were done eating, Ray handed me their plates and said, "We want Dustin to personally wash these dishes." I thought it was funny, but when I relayed the message to sixteen-year-old Dustin and handed him the dirty plates, he was not amused.

In October 1985 on a drizzly Sunday night, Scott and his friend went out drinking. Both were twenty-one, and they liked to party. Scott was a passenger, and his inebriated friend was behind the wheel. Alcohol and the rain-slicked road were factors in the head-on collision that killed them and sent the four people in the other car to the hospital with life-threatening injuries.

Everyone at the Walrus was devastated, and it was a very dark time. Within days after the accident, I was in the side station, dishing up salads to serve to my customers, when I noticed a very unusual slice of purple cabbage. The kitchen staff had prepared the salad, slicing lettuce and cabbage before delivering the concoction to the waitress station. A piece of sliced cabbage had perfectly formed Scott's initials in a cursive writing shape. S.M. It was probably not a paranormal incident but a fluke. Even so, it was so odd that I showed it to the other waitresses.

One waitress, who I'll call Carla, got very frightened. She turned pale, as her eyes got big and she began to tremble. If the initials in the cabbage were

Scott's way of saying hello, I would not find it frightening, but reassuring. Carla, however, was spooked. I didn't realize just how scared she was until the next night when she confided in me. She said she feared that Scott's ghost was under her bed at night and that he was going to reach out and grab her.

"Oh!" I cried. "Scott would never do that! He wouldn't want to scare you. He was a nice person."

This was years before I wrote books about ghosts, but I knew even back then that kindhearted people don't turn into cruel monsters when they die. This is something I learned growing up in a house that my parents insisted was haunted by the benign spirit of my great-grandfather, Reverend Rule. As a child, I felt he was somewhat like a guardian angel and watched over our family.

I knew Scott was gentle. A few months earlier at an employee picnic, a group of us was playing volleyball when someone accidentally ran into me. They hit me so hard that it knocked me to the ground. I was not hurt, but so stunned that I didn't get up. The first one by my side was Scott. I'll never forget how he knelt beside me and spoke in a soft, soothing tone. In that moment, I recognized a kindhearted soul.

Carla seemed somewhat reassured as I explained to her that it was not in Scott's nature to want to scare her. I don't know whether she continued to be afraid because we never discussed it again. A couple of years later, I was no longer waitressing but working in a weight loss clinic in Beaverton, Oregon. It was a rainy, autumn night, and my husband, Dave, had picked me up from work at about 9:00 p.m., and we were nearly home when I saw Scott.

We were on Firwood Road, a very long, pothole-infested road. It was necessary to travel very slowly because of those potholes. As we approached a streetlight, I saw Scott. He was wearing his favorite coat, a long, beige-colored trench coat that fell to his ankles. His face was tilted toward the light, and he was crying.

Shocked, I cried, "It's Scott's ghost!" I raised my arm and pointed. In the next instant, we had driven by him, and I immediately started laughing at myself. "*Oh!*" I said. "It was *Dustin!*" My brain had almost instantly found a logical explanation, and I embraced it. I figured that Dustin had grown up to look just like his brother. He was grieving because this was the time of year Scott had died, so he had put on Scott's coat, and was walking around in the rain crying.

Dave said, "What are you talking about? I didn't see anyone." He sounded annoyed, and I, too, was annoyed because there was no way he could *not* have seen him. The person we had just driven by had been on the driver's side of the road, and our car had passed within five feet of him as we moved at a snail's pace. The crying man was right beneath the streetlight, and anyone with eyes couldn't have missed him. I figured that my husband needed to get his eyes checked, but I didn't have time to worry about that because I was already focused on a plan to help Dustin. We turned the corner then and pulled into our driveway on Bonaire Avenue. I leapt out of the car and raced back toward Firwood, arriving within less than a minute.

I looked down the long, shadowy road. The streetlights brightened it enough that I expected to see Dustin, but there was no sign of him. "Dustin!" I called. I'll never forget running down Firwood on that rainy fall night, calling Dustin's name. I was determined to bring him back to my house, give him tea, and help him through his grief. It bothered me that the kid looked so miserable. I had seen him very clearly beneath the streetlight, and his face was etched with pain.

Our neighborhood was a quiet one, and at nearly 10:00 p.m., the houses along Firwood were dark and buttoned up for the night. I wondered where Dustin could have gone. I ran about a quarter of a mile looking for him, stopping every so often to call his name.

I finally gave up and went home. I had had a few paranormal experiences by that point in my life, but I didn't realize that ghosts could appear solid and look exactly like live human beings. That's probably why I had immediately dismissed my initial reaction. While I believed that spirits existed, I doubted that a deceased person—a person I had known—would suddenly appear on the street where I could see the tears on their face, note their lumbering gait, and even recognize their coat.

Scott had lived with his family on Inverurie Road, the street behind my home on Bonaire Avenue. In fact, if there had not been houses built on the lots where Bonaire and Firwood intersected, then Firwood would lead directly to Inverurie, close to the Maixner home. The spot where I saw Scott couldn't have been more than 600 feet from his house, but that shortcut was accessible only to ghosts who could walk through walls. Had Scott walked from his home to Firwood when he was living, it would have taken fifteen minutes because the connecting road was a quarter of a mile away.

While I'm analyzing the experience now, I gave it very little thought until three decades had passed. It was a morning in 2012, and I had just woken and was still in bed, cuddling with my cats as my thoughts drifted aimlessly. I don't know what triggered the memory, but I found myself thinking of Dustin crying in the rain. For the first time, I realized that the scenario had two key elements of a ghost sighting.

My former husband, Dave, had not been able to see what I so clearly could. And though I had returned to the street less than a minute after we'd passed the crying man, he had disappeared completely. In my need for a "logical" explanation, I had concluded that Dustin had grown up to look exactly like Scott. While they had a brotherly resemblance when I worked with them, they were in no way identical.

I knew Scott's face very well because we had worked together five nights a week for over a year, and dozens of times each shift, I peered at him through the window to the kitchen as I handed in my orders, and he placed plates of food on the ledge and called, "Order up!"

If it was Scott's ghost on the road that night, it was the most intense spirit encounter of my life. I wanted to get to the bottom of the mystery, so at the risk of looking like a nut, I found Dustin on Facebook and sent him a private message. He did not respond.

About another decade went by, and in February of 2021, I found myself again thinking of that rainy night on Firwood Road. I found a phone number for Dustin, called it, and he answered on the second ring. He told me he had abandoned his Facebook page shortly after setting it up and had not seen my message. He did not remember me from the restaurant, but he was happy I called. I shared my good memories of Scott with him. Dustin was open to the idea of ghosts, and he didn't dismiss me as a nut. He confided that he thought about Scott every moment of every day and missed him tremendously.

Dustin assured me that it was absolutely not him wearing his brother's coat and crying in the rain that night. He has some of Scott's clothes, but he waited many years before he wore them. Dustin didn't remember the coat. It had kind of a rock-star quality to it, and I had often seen Scott wearing it in the restaurant after work. I remember when he got it, and I had complimented him on it. It was apparent he was proud of it. I suspect he was wearing it when he died.

Why did Scott appear to me, and why was he crying? My feeling is that Scott is not earthbound but is full of regret about decisions made the night his life ended. Many people were hurt, both physically and emotionally, and that's why Scott showed me his sorrow. If those on the Other Side have the ability to see the future as a leading theory suggests, then Scott knew that I was destined to write books about ghosts. He may have wanted his story told and for me to remind people to stop their friends from driving drunk. I also feel he wanted me to reach out to Dustin. I feel privileged that Scott chose me to see him.

While the experience was unusual for me, it is not unusual for ghosts to appear on roads. In fact, roads are near the top of the list of places where ghosts are most commonly seen. On some streets, spirit sightings may be a one-time occurrence. Other streets, however, are haunted by frequent incidents. In the next story, we'll explore a haunting at what may be the most famous intersection in America.

# Hate on Haight

Haight-Ashbury. Two ordinary green street signs mark the California corner that was the heart of the hippie haven in the 1960s. Janis Joplin, Jefferson Airplane, and the Grateful Dead were among the famous rockers who lived and frolicked in the San Francisco district that is synonymous with the Summer of Love. The 1967 movement beat with the pulse of young people throughout America. Free spirits roamed "the Haight," an approximate six-square-block area bordered by Golden Gate Park. They attended free concerts on Hippie Hill in the park. They let their hair grow, danced barefoot, and wore peace sign pendants. They dropped LSD, questioned authority, and preached love.

After four decades, some have passed on. Others are senior citizens, and most long ago turned their ideals in for nine-to-five jobs. And some are ghosts, stuck in a groove like repeating drumbeats on a warped record album. The district now caters to tourists who wander through the hip coffee shops and rows of stores that sell tie-dyed T-shirts, strawberry incense, and black-light posters.

Though the Summer of Love has faded like a pair of bleached blue jeans, throngs visit the Haight to remember and honor the era. And some visit to hear about, and perhaps glimpse, the earthbound spirits who remain. "The area is totally haunted," Tommy Netzband told me. He is the creator and guide of the Haunted Haight Walking Tour and is well aware of the fact that love was not the only emotion promoted there. Hate, too, played a part, and all of the bumper stickers in the world could not obliterate it. Charles Manson, the crazed cult leader who persuaded his followers to commit mass murder, spent time in the Haight, with some accounts alleging that he lived on Page Street.

Over the years, many in the neighborhood were victims of crime. Sadly, an innocent teenager was caught in the crosshairs of hate at the intersection of Haight and Ashbury. "People still hear him running," said Tommy, who took me to the fatal corner one chilly fall night. He showed me the spot where the victim's blood had stained the sidewalk decades ago. "I deliberately don't tell people what happened here," he said, explaining that he waits to see if anyone will sense the energy before he shares the tragic story.

"I've had a number of people tell me that they hear the sound of running footsteps just as we are walking down the hill," he said. The phantom footfalls trace the same path the teenager took as he ran for his life. "Some people have trouble breathing here," he added, explaining that sensitive folks on his tour may empathize with the victim so much that they experience the anxiety of his last moments. He pointed to a house across the street. "A candlemaker lived there. When he saw the kid running by, he shot him from the doorway."

Tommy, a longtime resident of the Haight, is also the founder of the San Francisco Ghost Society and is well versed in theories pertaining to the paranormal. He raises the possibility that the spirit of the youth has moved on and that the activity is the result of a "residual haunting." In other words, the boy's soul is free, but his energy left an imprint on the intersection. In addition to collecting ghost stories, Tommy also delves into the history of the Haight to authenticate the cases. My own research confirmed Tommy's information. A February 1969 edition of the *San Francisco Chronicle* reported that police had arrested two candlemakers suspected of shooting a teenager on February 26. The men had lived in the house that Tommy pointed out to me.

Robert J. Robinson, twenty-four, and Loren Morell, twenty-three, were questioned in the death of seventeen-year-old Larry Watts. The suspects were white, and the teenager was black. As Larry ran down the street with two friends at about 5:15 p.m., witnesses heard a man shout, "Hey, you! Stop!"

Bullets from a 30-30 rifle struck Larry, and he died instantly. In my quest to verify the horror on Haight and Ashbury, I unearthed another account of a death at the very intersection. The fatalities occurred thirty-five years apart *to the day*. On February 26, 1934, Mary E. Van Detton, a seventy-five-year-old retired postal worker, crashed into the side of a railway car on Haight and Ashbury. She was rushed to the hospital but died before she could be treated.

Yet *another* article surfaced about a man with a similar name who crashed his car on the next block up, on the intersection of Page and Ashbury. On August 28, 1910, Thomas *Morrow's* automobile collided with a trolley, and the impact scattered the car's passengers over the street. Sixteen-year-old Emily Scott was seriously injured. A bystander carried her to a hospital a block away where she regained consciousness several hours later. In the telling of

*Shirts silhouetted in a store window resemble headless apparitions as they stare out onto the tragic corner of Haight and Ashbury. (Leslie Rule)*

the Morrow account, the *Chronicle* noted that the location had been dubbed "Death Hill," because of all the accidents there. As of this writing, however, my searches have failed to turn up more details about violence or accidents between Page and Haight on Ashbury, and I do not know if Emily Scott survived the car wreck. Let's hope that she lived a long and happy life. The district has plenty of ghosts without her.

For a corner associated with peace and love, Haight-Ashbury has a horrifying history. It is no wonder it is haunted.

hauntedhaight.com

---

## — *Update* —

When the story about Haight-Ashbury appeared in my book *Ghost in the Mirror* in 2010, I didn't share the paranormal experience I had there. It was not a ghost story, but an experience that reflects the strength of the sixth sense of my mother, the late true crime author, Ann Rule.

As I was photographing the Haight-Ashbury Street corner, a tabby cat strolled by, and I was immediately alarmed. It was a very busy street, and I feared the kitty would come to harm. My friend April was with me, and we examined the cat's collar, relieved to find an address and phone number on the tag. We were on foot, and the cat's home was half a mile up the hill, but I scooped him up into my arms, and we headed toward his address. It was a rather difficult journey, however, because every few steps, the cat jumped from my arms. I kept scooping him up as we forged ahead.

Finally, we reached the cat's apartment building, and I called the number on the tag. A woman answered, and I told her "I'm outside with your cat. I found him wandering around by the corner of Haight-Ashbury!"

"He does that all the time," she replied. Not the least bit concerned about her cat, she was irritated that I'd bothered her. She refused to come outside and get him.

I was shocked because my cats aren't allowed to wander. I learned many years ago that cats live much longer when they're protected from the dangers in the world.

The next day when I talked on the phone with my mom, she said, "I had the strangest dream last night. I dreamed I was in a strange city, and I found a cat. I was carrying him in a box, but he kept jumping out of it." Her dream was very close to my experience. I was far from home, in an unfamiliar city, and I had found a cat that kept jumping from my arms. The only difference between her dream and my reality was the box. I had no box, so I carried the cat in my arms.

My mom and I were very psychically connected, and we sometimes had the same dreams on the same nights. Her sixth sense was strong, and she occasionally saw ghosts. As she wrote in the foreword of my book *When the Ghost Screams*, she sensed that the victims she wrote about in her true crime books were often with her as she worked, though she never saw them.

# Sunday Drive

Sometimes it is the smallest action that determines our fate. It can be something as simple as lingering over a second cup of coffee, forgetting to return a phone call, or passing another car on the road. Normally not life-or-death decisions, we usually don't give these small acts a second thought. But when such a little thing prolongs our lives or brings swift death, we never forget it. It was Sunday, February 24, 1946, when Elmer Lawson of Charleston, South Carolina, made an unforgettable choice that irrevocably altered the lives of eight people and left a macabre apparition behind.

The drama played out on the Cooper River Bridge, also known as the John P. Grace Memorial Bridge. When it was built in 1929, it became the fifth-longest bridge in the world at 2.71 miles long. The superstructure spanned two wide waterways, Cooper River and Town Creek. Suspended 150 feet above the water, it cut a beautifully intricate silhouette in the moonlight. The bridge was a great convenience for area residents and a cherished landmark.

Thousands of cars had passed safely over the bridge that Sunday, just as they had done every other day. Bill Clapper had no way of knowing that he was on a fatal path when he steered his family's green Chevrolet onto the bridge. He and his wife, Dorothy, had had a pleasant day at the beach on the Isle of the Palms and enjoyed watching their son, one-year-old Billy, play in the sand. As they started their journey across the bridge, they glanced at the river below but didn't notice the freighter plowing toward them.

The *Nicaragua Victory* was a hulking ten-thousand-ton ship and not easy to maneuver. Moments before, it had been anchored in nearby Charles Harbor. But a terrible mistake had been made by the ship's crew. They'd misunderstood their captain's orders to remove the slack from the anchors, and instead, they pulled the anchors up. The monstrous freighter was now adrift and heading straight for the bridge.

The Lawson family was in a car lagging behind the Clapper's Chevy. Elmer Lawson was at the wheel of his green Oldsmobile with his wife, Evelyn, beside him. His mother, Rose, sat in the back seat with the children. Robert was seven and little Diana, only three.

As their car reached the arch of the bridge, Elmer sped up and passed the Clappers' Chevy. Dorothy Clapper noticed the Lawson youngsters waving as they passed. Why was Elmer in such a hurry?

We will never know. His sudden decision to pass the Clapper car sent him and his family to a watery grave. The timing was deadly. An instant after Elmer's car overtook the Clapper car, the runaway ship slammed into the bridge.

A 240-foot section of the bridge collapsed on impact, and the Lawson car shot off the road and plummeted to the river below. The Clappers braked in the nick of time. In a 2005 interview with Tony Bartlelme of Charleston's *Post and Courier*, Dorothy Clapper recalled the pivotal moment when the Lawsons passed them. "I told Bill that if that car hadn't passed us, we could have been the ones that drove off the bridge. . . ."

The newspaper also quoted Jesse Morillo, who was on board the ship. "I couldn't believe my eyes," he said. "When we hit the first section, it collapsed like a child's Erector Set. And we didn't slow down." As the car fell, he was horrified at the sight of two small children, their hands pressed against the windows. The Lawson family was entombed in their car for days before their bodies were recovered.

*A creepy apparition sometimes appears on the Cooper River Bridge, a grim reminder of a tragic Sunday.*

Six months later, the bridge was repaired, and drivers tried to put the tragedy out of their minds as they traveled over it. A few people, however, could not forget, because as they passed over the Cooper River Bridge, they found themselves side by side with a ghost car with passengers of the dead.

According to the guides of the Haunted Charleston Walking Tour, there have been multiple sightings of the ghastly apparition. One family of witnesses was headed home from an outing on a February day when they drove onto the bridge.

They noticed an odd, out-of-date, green Oldsmobile ahead of them. The car kept starting and stopping, so the driver decided to pass the strange car. As they began to pass, they were startled by a shocking image. Inside the vehicle was a lifeless family, dressed in 1940s fashion. A man and woman, with glazed and sunken eyes, sat in the front seat. A grandmother and two pale, limp children occupied the back seat. The terrified driver slammed on his brakes and allowed the ghostly car to pass him. It drove ahead and disappeared.

Was the Lawson family still trying to make it over the bridge? Why did the car hesitate, stopping and starting so erratically? Was poor Elmer trying to relive the crucial moment that sent his family plummeting to their deaths? If so, he once again made the wrong decision.

After nearly eight decades of service, the old bridge was dismantled, replaced by an adjacent structure, the eight-lane Arthur Ravenel Jr. Bridge. Some ghost enthusiasts have speculated that this will not stop the death car from appearing. They theorize that there will soon be sightings of the Lawson family traveling through the air in the space the old bridge once occupied. If you are easily frightened and you plan to drive over the Ravenel Bridge, maybe it is best to keep your eyes on the road.

# Roadside Attraction

Phillip Rouss can't help but smile when he remembers how much fun his parents had taking car trips together. "Dad was the regional manager of the United Shoe Machine Company," he said, describing how the senior Phillip's route covered a 400-mile radius near Memphis in the 1960s.

Sadie and Phillip Rouss, Sr. sang along with their Guy Lombardo eight-track tapes and sometimes wrote their own songs to sing in the car as the miles flew by. They were happy times for Sadie, who, at ninety-two, has spent over a dozen years without her husband. "Dad passed away in 1991," said Phil, Jr., who is privy to an unusual memory his parents shared. "Dad talked about it till the day he died."

Sadie, too, will never forget the odd encounter on a lovely spring afternoon. She and her husband were driving home from an Atlanta trip and were on Highway 78 about halfway between Holly Springs, Mississippi, and Memphis, Tennessee, when they saw some other travelers who seemed out of place and out of time on the side of the two-lane highway. "They saw a wagon train," said Phil. They stared at the sight that seemed right out of an old western. An elderly couple sat in the front of the horse-drawn wagon train. The man held the reins, a pipe clenched in his teeth.

"The woman wore a white bonnet," Sadie remembered. The Rousses were so stunned they traveled two blocks before Phillip senior said, "We have to meet those people!" Figuring that the unusual travelers must be involved in making a movie, they headed back to the spot where they'd seen them less than two minutes before.

"They were gone," said Sadie, who still shakes her head in awe. How could the wagon train have vanished so quickly? The couple got out of their car, puzzled. They examined the wet ground, scrutinizing it for the track marks that should surely have been left there but found none. The Rousses drove around the area, searching for the elusive travelers. They were nowhere to be seen, and there were no nearby roads they could have ducked onto.

"Mom and Dad couldn't wait to get home and tell my sister and me," said Phil. But when the parents excitedly shared their experience, Phil and his sister mocked them. "Yeah, yeah, yeah," they teased the elder Rousses. "They got mad at us," Phil said, laughing a little at the memory. Phil senior and Sadie were shaken by the episode. "I could see the fear in Dad's face," said Phil. They didn't know what to make of the odd event.

The apparition had been so vivid that they could describe the curl of smoke rising from the old pioneer's pipe, the big black hat on his head, and the rope and the water keg that hung from the side of the wagon.

When they saw their grown kids' reaction to their experience, they extracted a promise from them. "They insisted we never tell anyone about it," said Phil. "They were afraid people would think they were nuts." Until now, they shared this incredible episode with family only. Sadie is still baffled by the mystery.

Did they see the ghosts of pioneers? Perhaps. Or the apparition may have been a place memory, a phenomenon where a dramatic event is inexplicably impressed upon the environment. If it *was* a ghost encounter, the figures seen could have interacted with witnesses. And if indeed the old pioneers *were* ghosts, they would have been mighty confused by the sight of motor cars whizzing by along with such new-fangled gadgets as eight-track tapes. Time marches on.

When we're on the road, we see thousands of cars and don't give most of them a second thought. Chances are some of the vehicles whizzing by are *ghost* cars, but unless they vanish before our eyes or do something else of an unusual nature, we will never know it.

Sadie and Phillip noticed the wagon train because it was out of place and out of time. If they had not gone back to meet the wagon train people, they would never have realized they were not of this world.

The next story is another case of a vehicle, out of time and out of place, and while it didn't explicably vanish, it did something equally strange.

# Dead Man's Detour

It was a hot summer afternoon in 1995 as twenty-one-year-old Angela Boley headed toward a three o'clock class at the Art Academy of Cincinnati in Ohio. As she drove along Wooster Pike, she noticed something odd. The normally busy road was quiet. In fact, she saw only one other car. "It was an ugly tan car from the 1970s," she said. "It looked like a Buick, and it was really loud, like it had a hole in its exhaust. It was covered with big bumper stickers that said things like 'Free Ireland.'"

Angela pressed her foot to the gas pedal, moved to the other lane, and left the Buick behind. But when she reached the stoplight, she was startled to see the same car—*in front of her!* "I knew no one had passed me, and I had left that car in the dust."

But it appeared to be the *exact* car she'd passed. "All the bumper stickers were the same, it made the same sound, and it had rust in all the same places," she said. She was baffled. She'd passed no exits, so there was no way he could have found a shortcut to get ahead of her, but somehow, he *had*.

As she pulled up beside him, she glanced through her open window at the teenage driver, a pale, skinny boy with short black hair. He wore dark clothes that seemed too heavy for such a warm day. He stared straight ahead, apparently unaware she was watching him. He appeared to be a cautious driver with his hands placed precisely at "eleven o'clock and two o'clock on the steering wheel." He never moved. "He didn't even blink," she remembered.

An overwhelming sense of dread washed over her, and she had the distinct impression that she was seeing something not of this world—something that she should *not* be seeing. Even so, she wasn't frightened.

She and the other driver passed through the town of Mariemont, headed toward Columbia Parkway—a stretch of highway notorious for fatal accidents. "I slowed down as we went through the dangerous 'dead man's curve' on the highway, a near perfect U-shaped bend marked with yellow flashing lights," Angela explained.

She watched the other driver and noted, "He didn't even turn the wheel at all as he went through the bend. He was completely immobile! It was like the driver was frozen in time, like a 3-D photograph." Determined not to lose sight of him, she watched her rearview mirror, but soon he was left behind and she was alone on the road again. "I thought the car got off at the Red Bank exit, but when I stopped at another stoplight, there was that very same car waiting for me."

She suddenly thought of a 1976 hit song by Kiss. "It's called 'Detroit Rock City,' and it's about a kid killed in a car accident on the way to a concert," she said. Along with the tune, a thought popped into her head. "He's dead. He was killed on this stretch of highway and wants attention. He wants me to follow him." Prior to this revelation, the word "ghost" had not entered her mind. "I had to turn off to go to Eden Park Drive, but the car continued on Columbia Parkway, and it looked like it was headed straight for downtown Cincinnati. I wanted to follow it to satisfy my curiosity, but I had class."

Nine years after Angela shared the road with the mysterious boy, she is an artist with a fine arts degree and still lives in Ohio. When she remembers the inexplicable experience, the thing that stands out the most is the *stillness*. "He was like a statue," she said, recalling the unblinking apparition with his hands placed so precisely on the steering wheel. She told me she wished she'd followed the freakish car to the end of the journey, but I'm glad she didn't.

I don't think the boy was visiting *our* world. I think Angela was visiting *his*. Surely, there were other cars on the road at that time, yet Angela didn't see them. I suspect that's because she was somewhere *else*. I certainly can't explain what occurred, but it's not the first time I've heard of someone moving temporarily into another realm.

I've spoken with hundreds of people who have seen ghosts, and most of the time they had at least one foot planted firmly on this plane while they witnessed something paranormal. In some cases, however, they seemed to leave our world and move into a surreal place for a detached moment or two. I don't know what to make of Angela's peculiar encounter with the creepy car, but she has a theory. She suspects that the boy in the car was the ghost of a teen, killed on his way to a concert in the 1970s. She wonders if the boy was trying to demonstrate that he was a careful driver—that the accident was *not* his fault as his parents believed.

She explained to me that the boy was traveling on a road that once had a curve so dangerous that it was known as "dead man's curve," but it's now been altered to make the road safer. Whenever I think of Angela's inexplicable journey, I get chills. And I wonder if anyone else has taken Columbia Parkway's "dead man's detour."

Sometimes, as we travel down the road, we catch a glimpse of a moment long gone. Perhaps we see a snippet of the past so ordinary that we don't stop to question it. For instance, who would give much thought to a group of pedestrians waiting at the crosswalk for the light to change? Though the people may be long dead, we'd never think that they were anything but flesh and blood, breathing beings, unless they vanished before our eyes—*or* if they beat us to the next block despite the fact that they were on foot and we were in fast-moving traffic.

Sometimes this happens with roadside ghosts. I once corresponded with a woman who had this type of recurring roadside encounter. One night, she and her husband were driving along a quiet stretch of highway. They passed an older man in a beige overcoat who stood on the side of the road beside an automobile with its hood up. They continued by and did not think much of the scene until they'd traveled perhaps another eighth of a mile and saw him *again*. The same man stood on the roadside, in the same beige overcoat, beside a car that was identical to the first, also with its hood up.

After the woman and her husband witnessed the anomaly, they grilled each other for details just to be certain that they had seen the same thing. How could the man and his immobilized vehicle appear in both spots just seconds apart? There is no answer that fits within the guidelines of conservative rules of time and space. The couple concluded they had seen a ghost.

If they had not seen the fellow twice, it would never have occurred to them that he was anything other than an ordinary man with car trouble. When the scene takes on a morbid twist, however, witnesses are more likely to have questions, especially when the "people" seen are dressed in dated clothing.

Anita Scheftner had such an encounter, and it was so startling that it stays with her as clearly as if it were yesterday, despite the fact that nearly three decades have passed. It was April 1979 when Anita and her husband were living in Waterville, Maine, and had just become new parents. They often took Sunday drives with their infant daughter, Wendy, and marveled at the beauty of the New England scenery.

As the young family traveled along a country road, enjoying the spring day, Anita noticed something odd by the side of the road. A small cluster of people in colonial dress were engaged in a cruel task. The men were piling rocks upon a person who lay beneath a sheet of wood. "I thought that they were acting out for a colonial days festival," she said. "As gruesome as that sounds, it was the only thing that made sense." As they drove past the peculiar scene, Anita cried, "Did you see that?"

"See what?" asked her husband.

"Those people were putting rocks on someone!" she said. Though her husband was focused on driving, Anita thought that he should have noticed the activity. The people, after all, *were* on his side of the car. But he hadn't seen anything other than grass and trees. Anita insisted that he turn the car around and go back. Though only a moment had passed, there was no trace of the scene Anita had just witnessed. She knew that centuries earlier people in the area were sometimes crushed to death as punishment. She had read about Giles Corey, the elderly seventeenth-century man accused of witchcraft, who had been executed in that manner in Massachusetts.

Had such a horror once taken place beside the quiet country road in Maine? Had Anita been treated to a macabre peek into the past? Though she doesn't have the answers, she will always remember the strange scene she glimpsed from a car window.

Maine, a little over two hundred miles north of the infamous Salem, Massachusetts, was not immune to the horrendous mass hysteria that plagued New England around the turn of the eighteenth century when neighbor reported neighbor for drummed up charges of witchcraft. The false accusations of witchcraft spread to Wells, Maine, where former Massachusetts resident, the Reverend George Burroughs, was arrested on May 4, 1692. He was brought back to Salem Village, put on trial, and then executed there, a little over three months after his arrest.

Many of the horrors experienced during that era are lost to history. It's possible that Anita *did* witness a scene from the past, related to the witch trials.

I have a special interest in the atrocities that occurred in the New England witch scandal because I'm connected to one of the accused. We share DNA. In the next chapter, I will introduce you to Margaret Rule and the haunted grounds where she once strolled.

# 14

## WITCH HUNT

*I do testify that I have seen Margaret Rule in her afflictions from the invisible world, lifted up from her bed, wholly by an invisible force, a great way towards the top of the room where she lay; in her being so lifted, she had no assistance from any use of her own arms or hands, or any other part of her body, not so much as her heels touching her bed, or resting on any support whatsoever . . .*

—*Witness my hand, Samuel Aves*

Samuel Aves was one of several men who signed sworn testimonies stating that they had witnessed Margaret Rule levitate. The accusation came in the wake of the 1692 Salem witch trials. Though few people think of Boston, Massachusetts, when it comes to the infamous witch episode, it, too, suffered from the irrational worries that the Puritans forced upon Salem.

Margaret Rule was seventeen in 1693 when she was accused of being a witch in Boston. I have a special interest in her dramatic saga because a drop of her blood runs through my veins. We are family. Born nearly three centuries apart, we, of course, have never met. Yet we are bonded by a thin thread of genetics that spans time.

*The Boston Common may be the most haunted site in town.*
*(Leslie Rule)*

I learned about Margaret Rule when I was a child. My father told me about her and the fact she had sprung from a branch of our family tree. He showed me a book that mentioned Margaret and her connection to the New England tragedy. I was fascinated, but many years would pass before I could research her in depth.

In 2006, I flew from coast to coast—from Seattle to Boston—to see what I could learn. I spent a day at the Boston Public Library, researching in the Archives and Special Collections Room. Precious papers, dating back to long-ago centuries, are kept there and can be examined only on the premises as librarians keep watch. I read the testimonies of Margaret's accusers on fragile, yellowing paper and realized that I was probably the only Rule relative to lay eyes on them.

*As night creeps close, the trees cast long shadows upon the Common. (Leslie Rule)*

My first view of Boston was from a 747, my forehead pressed against the cool glass of the window, an airsickness bag clutched in my hand. A plane full of people had just heard me being sick, but I didn't care. With a horrible headache and a stomach that threatened to rebel again, I felt too ill to care what anyone thought.

Was it a bad sandwich from the Sea-Tac Airport, or was this an emotional response to the horrors that the city below had once inflicted upon so many people? I had wanted to visit Boston all my life, but now the view from the sky made my head hurt more. The city looked brown and barren. I could not stop thinking of how frightening it must have been to be marched to the gallows. Were the accused witches sick to their stomachs, as I was now?

By the next day, my stomach had settled, and I began to appreciate the historic views that Boston offered. I had chosen a hotel one block from the Boston Common, the haunted park where accused witches were hanged and where ghosts are seen by visitors. Since 1634, the people of Boston have claimed the Common as their own. The once scrubby land of rolling hills served as a place for citizens to graze their cattle. Families were limited to one cow or four sheep apiece.

The site, however, was not merely a peaceful, pastoral scene. It was a place of dark deeds—deeds sanctioned by law but so horrible that the victims still cry for justice.

*When caretakers lock the gate of the Common's Central Burial Ground, they keep the living out but cannot keep the dead in. Centuries of weather have washed away the names of those buried here. (Leslie Rule)*

Though the Boston Common retains the basic configuration of its early days, Puritans would probably not recognize it. A spider web of paved paths cuts through the forty-plus acres. Features include a bandstand, a baseball field, and the Frog Pond, a small lake that sparkles in the sunshine. Countless couples fall in love on the Common, babies giggle with delight as they toss nuts to the squirrels, and families picnic here. Despite the happy times, tragedy still marks the environment.

Before my Margaret, there was Margaret Jones. A midwife from nearby Charlestown, she was convicted of casting a spell to kill her neighbor's cow. On June 5, 1648, Margaret Jones was hanged on the Boston Common. A magnificent elm tree was used for the many hangings of those of whom the Puritans did not approve. They also hung pirates and Quakers from the old tree.

On October 27, 1659, authorities hanged Quakers Marmaduke Stevenson and William Robinson on the Common. Quaker Mary Dyer was next in line. As she stood with a noose around her neck and the bodies of the others dangling before her, her son convinced the men to release her. They escorted her from the city and told her to stay away.

Less than a year later, Mary returned. She was hanged on the Common on June 1, 1660.

Margaret Rule's troubles began about three years later, on September 10, 1663. She and her parents, from Cornwall, England, had come by ship to the new land and lived in north Boston. Her parents had a reputation as "sober and honest." But Margaret was judged by her own actions when she "fell into odd fits" in public. Her friends carried her home, and nosy neighbors came by to peer at her. Some suspected that Margaret's affliction was caused by a "miserable woman" who was once jailed for witchcraft. That woman claimed that she could cure people by chanting over them. The night before Margaret's mysterious ailment, the self-proclaimed healer had threatened her. Investigators believed that my relative was being "assaulted by eight cruel specters."

The "cursed specters" allegedly demanded that she put her hand on a thick red book and vow to become a servant of the devil. How in the world did anyone come to that conclusion? Did Margaret *say* she saw eight specters?

What was wrong with the teenager? Perhaps she had epilepsy. Perhaps she had an overactive imagination. Whatever the reason, Margaret was in serious trouble. As I wandered through the Common, I wondered if she had also walked the grounds. What did she think when she saw the enormous elm with its thick, reaching branches? Had she been present for any of the executions? Did she have any idea that she could soon be swinging from the death tree, a rope around her frail white neck?

I was about Margaret's age when I found myself in a similar predicament. Though there was never any danger of hanging or incarceration, I, too, became known as a witch. I was attending Mount Rainier High School in Des Moines, Washington, when I made a silly, flip comment about my nail polish. Another girl had

*A plaque marks the ground where Boston's hanging tree grew until 1876. (Leslie Rule)*

commented on the glitter-embedded polish, and I jokingly said, "Oh, I'm a witch. They turn this way every year around Halloween."

*A ghostly woman has been spotted on the Boston Common. (Leslie Rule)*

Within two weeks, I could not walk down the hallway at school without someone putting a mock spell on me or shouting, "Witch!" To this day, there are people in my hometown who still believe the rumors that exploded from the stupid joke I made about my nails. The experience gave me just a little taste of how fast a rumor can grow. Is that what happened to Margaret Rule?

According to archives, Margaret fasted for nine days. Yet, witnesses claimed that she remained "fresh" and "lively" and "hearty." When food was forced upon her, she gritted her teeth. In addition to swearing that they had seen Margaret levitate, people said they had witnessed unseen hands force her mouth open and pour "something invisible" down her throat. Some alleged that they saw the substance spill on her neck. Margaret screamed as if "scalding brimstone" had been poured on her. It was also said that Margaret looked sad when she claimed that ghosts threatened to drown a young man in the neighborhood. It was later determined that at the exact time she made the prediction, a man had nearly drowned.

Cotton Mather, one of those who examined Margaret, noted that the specters surrounding her were identical to those seen surrounding the accused witches in Salem, months before. It has been written that if it had been up to Cotton Mather, Margaret and others would have been executed. But Robert Calef, a prominent Boston merchant, also studied the girl. He stated that she was either faking or under a delusion. After a few trying weeks, she began to feel normal again. Margaret and her parents returned to Cornwall, where my great-grandfather was born a few generations later.

If Robert Calef had not made his levelheaded assessment, Margaret Rule could have been one of the ghosts who wander the Boston Common. The ethereal image of a woman has been seen in the old graveyard there. The cemetery is on the edge of the Common, bordering Boylston Street. Many of the stones here are so old that the lettering has worn away.

Holly Mascott Nadler, author of *Ghosts of Boston Town: Three Centuries of True Hauntings*, reported a ghost sighting in the Common cemetery. On a drizzly afternoon in the 1970s, a dentist named Dr. Matt Rutger decided to wander in the tranquil beauty of the ancient graveyard and encountered "a total deviation from reality as most of us know it," she wrote. As the dentist attempted to read the worn lettering on the weather-washed gravestones, he was startled by a tap on his shoulder. When he swung around to see who had touched him, no one was there.

According to Holly, the incident repeated itself until it escalated to a violent tug on the back of his coat collar that nearly knocked him down. The frightened dentist had turned to leave when, he said, "I saw a young girl standing motionless in the rear of the cemetery, staring at me intently."

The girl in the white dress was eerily still. When the dentist turned to the opposite direction, the ghost "relocated." Holly wrote that the apparition continued to appear each time the dentist changed his path. When he reached the sidewalk, he felt a hand slip into his pocket and watched, stunned, as his keys levitated and then dropped to the ground. I was fascinated by Holly's account and wondered if the ghost belonged to one of those buried in the old cemetery on the Common.

Or was she the unhappy spirit of someone long-ago lynched? While the formal graveyard is neatly lined by a tall metal fence, it is not the only place where bodies are buried in the Boston Common. In the old days, authorities liked to make an example of the executed

*Do the ghosts of executed Quakers, pirates, and accused witches wander the Common? (Leslie Rule)*

*Buildings along Boylston Street rest on top of the old graveyard. The tenants of the desecrated graves may be responsible for the odd noises that emanate from the basement of the cigar shop. (Leslie Rule)*

and would often leave them in public view, long after death. The insult was unbearable for the relatives of the dead, and some tiptoed into the Common in the midst of night to hastily bury their loved ones in unmarked graves.

I explored the Common in the light of day, stopping passersby to ask if they had ever seen ghosts there. I admittedly got my share of odd looks. Every other person had a phone pressed to an ear. I shouldn't have been surprised that they hadn't noticed the dead when they barely noticed the living!

I ventured into the shops on the streets that lined the Common to continue my inquiries. In an art store on Tremont Street, I learned that an employee had seen a shadowy figure darting through the basement. Bouncers at a nightclub on the same street are spooked by the shenanigans of an unseen presence. Sometimes, after the club has closed and the doors are locked, the sound system will come back on, the volume turned to full blast.

Boylston Street, too, has paranormal activity. The old cemetery once extended to the space that the street now occupies. A huge section of the graveyard was lopped off to make room for the street. As shovels churned up the earth, the skeletons that surfaced were plucked out and buried in a common grave. The rest of the dead reside below Boylston Street and its buildings, sleeping restlessly in their desecrated graves.

Stephen Smith, of L. J. Peretti Co. Tobacconists, has heard the inexplicable rattle of chains in the early morning hours when he is alone in the building. The metallic clanks emanate from the empty basement, where there is no reasonable explanation for the sound. Though he can't say for certain that the noise is of a paranormal nature, he admitted the incidents are chilling. *Chains?* Some quick research revealed that accused witches and other prisoners in seventeenth-century New England were often bound with chains.

## — *Update* —

History buffs have recently begun debating whether Quaker Mary Dyer was actually hanged on the Boston Common. The naysayers insist that their research proves that hangings did not occur on the grounds during Mary's era, but I've yet to see the documentation that they're referring to.

I'm now living in Arizona, too far away to visit the Boston Public Library's Research and Special Collections Room to search for confirmation, but I *can* comb through Boston newspaper archives that reach back hundreds of years. The articles contain many references to Mary Dyer's 1660 execution on the Boston Common, so until I see evidence to the contrary, I'm confident that the *Boston Globe* reporters got their facts right in the 1800s.

As I was searching, I stumbled upon an article about another unjust punishment. A reporter for the *Boston Evening Transcript* wrote in the February 28, 1896, edition about a shocking incident over a stolen hat. Referring to a "carefully preserved document" from "the State House," the reporter told the story of Rachel Wall. On the night of March 18, 1789, Rachel was walking down the street when she saw Margaret Bender.

Whether or not the two ladies knew each other, the reporter did not say, but Rachel apparently admired Margaret's bonnet. She ripped it right off her head and took off with it. At a cost of seven shillings, the bonnet was considered valuable. Margaret screamed for help, and Good Samaritans apprehended the thief. About seven months later, on October 8, Governor John Hancock (*the* John Hancock!) signed the order for Sheriff Joseph Henderson to hang Rachel. She was executed on the Boston Common, near Mason Street, about two weeks later on October 20.

This occurred within days of President George Washington's visit to Boston on his New England tour. Was George aware of the hanging? Did he agree that Rachel deserved to die? Did he believe that stealing a hat was worse than chopping down a cherry tree? As every school child learns in the month of February, the man whose face graces the dollar bill famously told the story of chopping down his father's cherry tree, only to refuse to lie about it when confronted.

I don't condone stealing, but I think it's far worse to chop down a cherry tree than it is to steal a bonnet. If I were Rachel, I'd be angry, and if her restless spirit is roaming the Boston Common in protest of her murder, I don't blame her one bit.

# Ghosts of Salem

When most folks think of Salem, Massachusetts, they conjure images of witches in tall, crooked hats, riding brooms against a full moon. It is an image that the city has done little to discourage. It was 1692 when teenage girls began acting silly and sparked a hysteria that burned through Salem Village. The little town (now known as Danvers) was near today's city of Salem.

The teenagers' odd behavior was blamed on the devil, and soon neighbor was accusing neighbor of witchcraft. Many residents were jailed as accused witches, including a four-year-old girl. In the horrific end, nineteen people were hanged and one was crushed to death. The murder of twenty innocent people may very well account for the paranormal activity that swirls around the area today, including some of the following places.

# First to Die

According to the managers of the Lyceum Restaurant, the classy eatery was built atop Bridget Bishop's old apple orchard. The very first villager hanged for witchcraft, Bridget was a colorful character who managed to annoy her neighbors with her flamboyant dress and her tendency to speak her mind. It is Bridget's spirit who is responsible for the odd noises heard at the Lyceum, say employees.

In addition to its connection to Salem's infamous witch scandal, the brick building that houses the restaurant has other historic significance. The hall was once used as a gathering place for meetings, for auctions, and for demonstrations—most notably by the inventor of the telephone. A plaque attached to the front of the building states: *In this building on February 12, 1877, Alexander*

*Graham Bell presented the first public demonstration of long-distance telephone conversations.*

When my friends Anne and Hilary Ferraro and I visited the restaurant, the manager invited us to explore the unoccupied upper floors. We were tired after walking around town all day, so after we had ventured up to the

*Some employees refuse to venture upstairs in the Lyceum Bar and Grill. This view is from the loft, where strange noises often emanate. (Leslie Rule)*

second floor, Anne turned to her daughter, twenty-one-year-old Hilary, and said, "Go up to the loft and tell us if there is anything worth seeing." Hilary obediently started up the stairs. She was three-quarters of the way up when an ominous creak sounded from above, and suddenly Hilary was flying back down the stairs.

We all headed up to investigate. What could have caused the creak? It was so loud that we had all heard it. It had sounded like the creaking door in a scary movie. I tried all the loft doors but could not duplicate the sound.

According to the manager, a film crew had visited recently to document the haunting and was baffled when the batteries were inexplicably drained on every piece of their recording equipment, a common occurrence in haunted locations.

## — *Update* —

The restaurant has changed hands since my visit in 2006. It was purchased nearly a decade ago by the Turner family, well known in Boston for their six decades in the seafood business. The Turners opened the new restaurant in 2013, renamed Turner's Seafood at Lyceum Hall.

While management does not advertise their ghosts, they do acknowledge the reports of paranormal activity in the building—including sightings of the apparition of a woman. The mysterious figure appears on the staircase and also manifests in the restaurant's mirrors. Some say it is Bridget, still lingering at her favorite haunt. Bridget also gets the credit for the overwhelming scent of apples, occasionally wafting from nowhere. It's apparently her way of reminding customers of her long-gone apple orchard.

### Turner's Seafood
43 Church Street, Salem, Massachusetts 01970
(978) 745-7665
turners-seafood.com

-------

# Joshua Ward House

A formidable brick house, erected in 1784, may be home to the ghost of Sheriff George Corwin. The Joshua Ward House, which today houses offices, was built on the foundation of the home of one of Salem's most detested people. George Corwin was a cruel man who orchestrated the arrest of villagers accused of witchcraft. Many hated him after he tortured the accused in his home. He also stole the victims' belongings after they were executed on Gallows Hill.

When George Corwin died, he was buried in his own basement to prevent his enemies from desecrating his grave. He was later exhumed and buried elsewhere, but many believe the despicable man's spirit remains.

It is a woman's ghost, however, that has been spotted in the house. One witness saw the pale woman sitting in a chair in the home, while others have spied her peeking from the windows or floating down the stairs. Many believe she is one of the accused witches who died as a result of Sheriff Corwin's actions.

### Joshua Ward House
148 Washington Street, Salem, Massachusetts 01970
(The Joshua Ward House is not open to the public.)

-------

# Evil Avoided

While hunting for ghosts, I not only found my roots but discovered an enemy. If Cotton Mather had had his way, I would not be here today. Not only did the self-righteous Puritan oppose Margaret Rule, from my father's side of the family, he proposed selling my ancestors on my *mother's* side into slavery.

My great-great-great-great-great-great-grandfather, Thomas Stackhouse, traveled here via ship with William Penn in 1682. When Cotton Mather heard that twenty-three ships carrying Quakers were on their way from England, he proposed kidnapping the passengers and selling them into slavery. His bright idea came a decade before he stirred up the Massachusetts witch controversy.

But destiny had its own plan. Both the Stackhouse and the Rule lines survived, and here I am, seven generations later, researching the ghosts of those who died at the hands of Cotton Mather. "I wonder how many people he killed?" said my mother, Ann Stackhouse Rule, as she pondered the evil deeds of the Boston minister.

I have walked the paths that Mr. Mather walked, and I've spoken to those who have encountered the ghosts of his victims. I've stood on the dock in Old New Castle, Delaware, where William Penn and my ancestor arrived on October 27, 1682. It is here, on the Delaware River, where headless apparitions have been witnessed. I did not see the ghosts, believed to be Dutch soldiers, but could almost hear the sound of their whispering beneath the rush of the waves.

History's harsh lessons and the ghosts they have wrought make me acutely aware of the fragility of life. From the murder of accused witch Bridget Bishop

*Who peers from the windows of the Joshua Ward House? (Leslie Rule)*

in Salem to Quaker Mary Dyer hanged on the Boston Common, the deaths were cruel and ugly. While the unjust killings silenced the heartbeat, they did not stop the spirit. Survivors carry family names. Ghosts still wander their old homesteads. And, despite Cotton Mather's objections, William Penn founded Pennsylvania.

Cotton Mather is buried in Boston's Copps Hill Burying Ground. I won't be putting flowers on his grave.

*William Penn first landed in Old New Castle, Delaware, near this site. When I stood on this dock, I had a profound sense of connection with the area but did not yet know that my great-great-great-great-great-great-grandfather Thomas Stackhouse had been here with William Penn. Not only did Cotton Mather want to execute my relative, Margaret Rule, but he also wished to sell William Penn and my ancestor into slavery. (Leslie Rule)*

# 15

## SCHOOL SPIRITS

S chool is out, and the students have left, but the empty hallways echo with the distinctive thump of footsteps. Somewhere, a locker slams shut. A chair scrapes across the floor. Eerie, childlike laughter floats from an empty classroom, and the custodian is a little nervous as he rushes to finish his mopping. This is a familiar scenario on hundreds of campuses across the country. Janitors, students, secretaries, and teachers are among the many witnesses of ghostly activity at schools.

Most schools have seen many generations of pupils move through their halls. Wherever there are people, there is death, sometimes sudden death. And wherever there is death, there may be ghosts not ready to move on.

# Helen

An odd thing happened at Coe College while preparations were being made to renovate historic Voorhees Hall. The story was covered by the *Gazette*, the local paper of Cedar Rapid, Iowa. A September 2000 edition reported that an architect went to the hall to photograph the building, inside and out. He needed images that showed the structure, *not the students*, so he made sure nobody was near as he took each shot.

Afterward, when he studied his photographs, he was puzzled—so puzzled that he brought the images to school officials and pointed out the one that bothered him. There was someone on the staircase, though he was certain no one had been there when he framed the shot. The figure was lit from the back by an explicable light.

The photographer assumed it was a student, but he had no idea how or when she had stepped into his shot. He was stumped, but others weren't. They knew *exactly* who she was. *It was Helen!* The former student and Voorhees Hall's resident ghost, Helen Esther Roberts, has been haunting the building since she died there at age nineteen in 1918.

The *Gazette* reported that the stairs where the apparition appeared were outside the infirmary where Helen lost her life to the Spanish influenza, a deadly flu that killed fifty million people, worldwide. Helen was a freshman from Strawberry Point, and she was just two weeks into the school year when she fell ill. As the pandemic swept the campus, Voorhees Hall was turned into a makeshift infirmary where students with fluid-filled lungs struggled to breathe. Helen did not survive.

A year after her death, she began to appear in Voorhees Hall, and over the past century, she has startled many students. She wears a white dress or nightgown and is usually seen very late at night in a hallway. People catch fleeting glimpses of her before she vanishes. Is Helen aware she's been dead for a century? Probably not, and she may be confused by the changes in the building. When it was renovated and turned into housing, the stately exterior was preserved, but the inside was altered dramatically, sliced up into rooms of varying sizes for the nearly two hundred female students living there.

Some of those students report peculiar things they blame on Helen. They've answered the phone to hear the weak voice of a young female. She never identifies herself, and the connection is lost before questions can be answered. Perhaps it's just a wrong number, but some believe it's Helen, calling from beyond.

Residents have also confided that someone yanks the blankets off their beds as they sleep, turns electrical appliances on and off, locks them out of their rooms, and knocks pictures from the wall. The ghost has been heard slamming doors, stomping up the stairs, and playing the piano. Sometimes Helen makes her presence known with a sudden, chilling breeze that wafts from nowhere.

While school officials acknowledge their ghost, they are quick to reassure students and their families that she is harmless. She may be mischievous but never malicious.

Shortly after she died, Helen's parents donated a grandfather clock to the school in her memory. Legend has it that she can be seen emerging from that clock on October 19, the anniversary of her death. In the year 2000, a webcam was set up by staff of the Cedar Rapids *Gazette*, its lens trained on the clock so that witnesses around the globe could tune in to watch the ghostly figure exit the clock. Helen, however, was a no-show.

# Poasttown Elementary

Scott Wise, founder of Ghostly Gateway Paranormal Investigations, was with his team for an all-night investigation at a famously haunted school in Middletown, Ohio, in October of 2021, when he decided to spend time alone in "the Bad Teacher's Room," a nickname given to the third-floor room because so many odd things have occurred there. It was after 2:00 a.m. and eerily silent when a door suddenly slammed. Scott felt the hairs on the back of his neck rise. It wasn't like his team to make noise, and he suspected they were not responsible for the banging door.

He was right. A moment later, team member Teresa Kraft walked into the room. Teresa, Scott's cohost of the podcast *Paranormal Gateway Paratalk*, didn't know *who* had slammed the door, and in fact, she had not even heard it. But she did hear something else—the sound of murmuring voices, engaged in conversation. She heard the voices as she approached the room. She was sure that Scott must have been talking to someone, but he was alone in the room and had *not* been talking to himself.

Scott Wise is one of hundreds of paranormal researchers who have investigated Poasttown Elementary School since Darrell and Brenda Whisman made it their home. Both had been students there decades before and have good memories of the place. The school was built in 1937 in the typical design of its day. It's a large brick building with three stories, counting the basement, and a grand, pillared entryway. After the school closed its doors in 1999, it sat abandoned for five years before the Whismans purchased it in 2004.

*Though they were the only ones in the old school, investigator Scott Wise and his team heard the voices of unseen people, mischievous giggling, and the unmistakable sound of a slamming door. (Sharon Wise)*

Darrell wasn't sure if he believed in ghosts and hadn't considered the possibility that the building could be haunted, so at first, he dismissed the odd noises echoing in the empty hallways. It was just the sound of an old building settling, he told himself. But there were things he could not explain. One day, Brenda was painting a stairwell and felt her husband's hot breath on her neck. Annoyed, she cried, "Quit it!" When he refused to stop, she figured he was teasing her, so she whirled around to dab paint on him. She was smiling, but her smile froze when she realized he was not there. She was alone in the stairwell.

Something similar happened to a repairman working on the top floor. The guy was bent over with his back to the doorway when he heard footsteps approaching. He assumed it was Darrell, but when Darrell began to breathe down his neck, it was too close for comfort. He turned around, but there was no one there!

Many have glimpsed shadowy figures darting about the old school. The Whismans' grandchildren have seen the full-figured apparition of a boy on more than one occasion. The first time Darrell became aware that the children could clearly see the ghosts, he and his grandson, age five, were sitting at a picnic table outside. The kid pointed at the school and commented about the boy gazing out the window. Darrell turned to look but saw only empty windows. He felt a chill move through him as the child asked, "Why do you always scare the boy away, Grandpa?"

At least three of the Whisman grandchildren have seen the boy's ghost in the gymnasium, their favorite play area, but Darrell has not grilled them for details. He doesn't want to frighten them by making a big deal out of it.

Darrell is not afraid, and he maintains a matter-of-fact attitude as an example to the youngsters so that they, too, will take the haunting in stride. While Brenda and Darrell have not *seen* the ghosts, they've heard them. The disembodied voices of both adults and children frequently drift from nowhere. "The children always sound happy," said Darrell.

Who are the ghosts? One legend says that a girl student was killed after she fell or was pushed in the stairwell, but no documentation has been found. One of Darrell's teachers died when he was in the fourth grade. "It was the first funeral I ever went to," he confided, but he has no idea if she is one of the lingering spirits.

Some paranormal investigators suspect that thirty-six fatalities from a July 4, 1910, train wreck resulted in earthbound spirits. According to historians, there were no nearby hospitals, so triage was done on the site where the Poasttown School would one day be built. Those who survived were whisked away to the closest hospitals, while those who died may have become attached to the land.

While combing archives, I came across an account of an untimely death of a student, though he didn't die on the premises. It happened *after* school in May

**BIKE JUST FIXED**

# Young Cyclist Rides to Death

Special to The Daily News

MIDDLETOWN, May 26—A 13-year-old boy was killed here yesterday when he apparently lost control of his bicycle on a steep hill near State Route 4, struck a tree and catapulted into a creek bed.

RICHARD'S FATHER said the boy had repaired the bicycle only Thursday so he could ride it this summer.

An honor student at Poasttown elementary school, the eighth-grader would have graduated next week.

*A 1962 article reports the tragic death of Richard, a Poasttown Elementary School honor student. Could he be among the mischievous spirits who haunt the school?*

of 1962. Richard was an honors student at Poasttown Elementary, and he was looking forward to graduating from the eighth grade. School was about to end for the summer, and his father had fixed his bicycle so that Richard could enjoy it in the sunny days ahead.

Only a day or two after the bike was repaired, the thirteen-year-old went out for an evening ride. When he had not returned by dusk, his parents started to worry. They searched, but there was no sign of their son on the dark roads. They were frantic by the time they called police, and an all-night search began. The missing boy's family joined searchers as they scoured the area.

At about seven o'clock the following morning, Richard's parents and brother spotted his bicycle at the edge of a steep hill, near Brown's Run Creek. His body was in the creek. At first, it appeared he had drowned, but it was later determined that he died of a head injury. He had been riding at the top of the hill when he lost control, hit a tree, and was thrown from the bike. It was a shock to all who knew him.

While the A-student didn't die at the school, it was a huge part of his life, and he had unfinished business there with graduation coming up. Could he have returned to the place where he'd spent so much of his time? Is he the boy that the Whisman grandchildren see peering from windows and in the gymnasium? He is not the only Middletown youngster who did not survive childhood. Some drowned in the Miami River, a stone's throw from the school.

It's possible that the ghosts originated from *other* schools and that they came in with desks and blackboards and various paraphernalia, recycled from those schools. In 1936, not only did the Madison Township Rural Board of Education post announcements about plans for the building of the Poasttown Elementary School, but it also announced a June auction to sell Madison Township's old East Mansfield School building to the highest bidder. In 1942, about five years after Poasttown opened, the school board *again* auctioned off a school building. This time it was Bridgeport School on South Main Street

Road in Washington Township. The school board surely stripped the old school buildings of useful material and furniture before auctioning them off, some of which could have ended up at Poasttown. An old desk, moved from an old school, could have come in with the ghost of a child attached to it.

Darrell Whisman believes his building is filled with the spirits of past students who had fond memories of the place. He figures they grew old and died elsewhere, only to return to a place where they played during an innocent time.

Paranormal investigators continue to search for answers. It's not necessary to be an investigator to visit the building. Anyone interested in spending time with ghosts can book an overnight stay at the Poasttown Elementary School. If you're a skeptic, that's fine with the Whismans, though they expect you'll change your mind after a night in their building. Their motto is "When you leave, you believe."

### Poasttown Elementary
6600 Trenton Franklin Road, Middletown, Ohio 45042
(513) 464-1330
poasttownschool.com

---

# Mother Kidder

Beloved librarian Ida Kidder may be a benign presence in Oregon State University's Waldo Hall, but students are nonetheless spooked when her misty figure materializes in the second-floor hallway. Nicknamed "Mother Kidder" soon after she went to work at OSU in 1908, she loved books, and she loved the students. A nurturer, her good deeds included visiting a hospital to read to sick kids.

Ida fell ill with heart problems at Christmastime in 1919 and was confined to her room in Waldo Hall. She never recovered, and she died there in February 1920 at age sixty-five. When she was laid out in the library so that mourners could pay their last respects, the floral arrangements were so plentiful that they overwhelmed the area. It was clear that both faculty and students were as attached to Mother Kidder as she was to them. And that could be the reason that her spirit still lingers.

*Though dead for over a century, a beloved librarian still roams the halls of Oregon State University's Waldo Hall, pictured here in this antique postcard.*

# Never Nineteen

While Mother Kidder might have chosen to stay at the school she loved, a ghost in Fayette, Missouri, may be earthbound because she doesn't realize she is dead. Virginia Emde died in a freak accident, and many students say they've seen her spirit on the campus of Central Methodist University. It was a stormy Tuesday afternoon in the spring of 1937 when the freshman was tragically killed outside of her dorm. As the wind blew furiously, Virginia and several other girls scrambled to get inside their dorm in the Howard Payne Building.

Virginia had just raced up the steps and was on the porch when a branch flew off a tree, hit the building, and dislodged a brick. The eighteen-year-old was struck on the head by the falling brick and knocked unconscious. Soon after, she seemed to recover. Her parents were notified of the accident but told it was not necessary for them to come because their daughter was doing fine. She took a turn for the worse, however, and was taken to Lee Hospital, where she died shortly after midnight.

A month shy of her nineteenth birthday, Virginia was a vivacious girl, excited about life. She competed in tennis tournaments, performed in school plays, and sang in mixed choruses. She should have lived a long life—if cruel fate had not placed her on that porch in the wrong spot at the wrong moment. If Virginia had been just a *little* faster or a *little* slower as she ran for her dorm, the brick would have missed her.

The shock of her sudden death may be what's keeping Virginia earthbound, say students who have seen the apparition of the long-dead girl. The glowing figure materializes outside of the Howard Payne Building on stormy nights and gives the impression she's still trying to find her way back to her dorm. The ghost girl most often appears inside the building on the fifth floor—possibly the location of Virginia's room. Residents report that an invisible presence knocks on their doors, runs tap water, and turns on electrical appliances.

# A Dark Premonition

The students in the Technological Institute huddled over their books, trying to ignore the odd noises emanating from the walls. There was no time to entertain the idea of ghosts or to discuss silly legends. They were, after all, serious pupils of one of the most selective colleges in the country, Northwestern University in Evanston, Illinois.

Sarah Bailey, however, managed to pry a student or two away from their books long enough to get the scoop for the school newspaper, the *Daily Northwestern*, in October 2004. Late-night studiers, she wrote, sometimes heard the sound of flasks and glasses clinking against each other. The noise was followed by a rattle and then an indefinable whisper.

More than one student reporter has speculated about the identities of the ghosts of the old college near the shore of Lake Michigan. Various legends are entertained, including the often-told story of the ghost in the Tech Building. A 1950s chemistry student allegedly drank a tube of cyanide after his doctoral dissertation was rejected. Others believe that two female students committed suicide in the late 1800s after their fiancés deserted them. Witnesses swear that they've heard the spirits weeping and commiserating with each other. Another spirit is said to be that of a heartbroken student who hanged himself in the

University Hall's bell tower. The Annie May Swift Hall is believed to be haunted by the girl it's named for. Annie was a student at the school and died in April 1889, after being sick for months with typhoid fever.

I have unearthed another possibility for the source of the paranormal activity. I dove into the newspaper archives and discovered a story buried so deeply that few on campus are aware of it. I found it by accident. I was researching another haunted location when a shocking news story surfaced. It chronicled the sort of death that often results in earthbound spirits. My investigation into the ghosts of Northwestern University was backward. Normally, I first learn about paranormal activity, and then I research the history of a place for answers about why it's haunted. But in this case, *first* I found the death, and *then* I looked for ghosts where the tragedy had occurred.

My sixth sense told me that while many spirits roam the campus, a 1921 student was probably among them. Those familiar with my books know that my intuition often guides me as I track ghosts. I had a very strong feeling about this case—almost as strong as the victim himself felt when he made a gloomy prediction. Freshman Leighton Mount had a special affection for an older woman, twenty-four-year-old student Doris Fuchs, who did not return his feelings. "You made me love you," he wrote in a last note to her in September 1921. When asked by a reporter about her relationship with Leighton, Doris insisted that there was nothing romantic between them. "We were what you might call pals," she said.

Was Leighton sincere, or was he just trying to get Doris's attention when he talked to her about the various ways that he could end his life? He dismissed the idea of drowning, because his body would resurface, she remembered. She was so used to his ramblings that she didn't take him seriously when he said he would "disappear

*The Annie May Swift Hall at Northwestern University, depicted in this antique image, is home to the ghost of young Annie who succumbed to illness while attending college here.*

during rush." Doris heard the statement as a half-hearted suicide threat. Was it a threat? Or a *premonition*?

Leighton was nervous as hazing week approached. When he told his mother he had reservations, she advised him that he had better participate or he would "look like a sissy." The barbaric "fight week" pitted freshmen and sophomore males against each other in tortuous "pranks." Did Leighton and his roommate, Roscoe Fitch, really have a choice? The rowdy, testosterone-driven event rushed over the campus like a tidal wave, picking up everything in its path and leaving the hapless wounded in its wake. Some of the students were terrorized in the lake. Student Arthur Persinger, for instance, "was tied to a plank which was placed parallel with the water, and so low over it that the waves would splash over his face," according to one witness.

Young men kidnapped and tied each other up, sometimes abandoning angry and embarrassed students naked and far from campus. Almost everyone seemed to get through the September 1921 rush intact—everyone *except* for Leighton Mount. Just as he had told Doris he would, Leighton disappeared. At first, none of the students would admit to knowing what had happened to him. But then Northwestern's star student athlete, Charles Palmer, let something slip. He worked at a bakery, and he told a girl he worked with that he knew where Leighton was. When she pressed Palmer for details, he clammed up.

Leighton's parents were worried sick and hired a private investigator. Meanwhile, rumors circulated on campus. At least one student told university authorities that they had heard that Leighton had been kidnapped by a newspaper reporter. The reporter was hiding him but planned to release him and get a great scoop for his paper. And then, at Christmastime, his parents received a telegram, signed "Leighton." Was he alive? Or was someone trying to throw them off the trail?

In April 1923 another fight week turned tragic when freshman Louis Aubere was killed in a car wreck. The cars were loaded with students, and witnesses said that the crash was deliberate. As Aubere's friends grieved, a grisly discovery was made by the Lake Street Pier, south of the campus. A twelve-year-old boy was playing on the shore there and discovered some odd bones. Puzzled, the kid took them home to show his mom. She called the police.

Leighton Mount had been found. The bone found by the boy turned out to be one of the missing student's shin bones. Leighton's mother identified bits of clothing and a belt buckle, stamped with the initials L.M. His dentist made a positive identification.

While many said the death was suicide, there was no dismissing the rotted bits of rope found with the skeleton. It was the same type of rope that the boys had used when they bound each other during rush. Prosecutor Robert Crowe argued that Leighton had been kidnapped at midnight on Wednesday, September 21, 1921. The hazers had tied him beneath the pier and, when they returned the next day, found him dead. They then made a pact to keep the death a secret.

Twenty months later, dozens of people were subpoenaed as authorities demanded the truth. The truth, however, was difficult to pinpoint. Some of the students changed their stories, including Leighton's roommate, Roscoe Fitch. Newspapers reported that after four trying hours and eight versions of his story, Roscoe burst into tears and cried, "I'll lose my credits! I'll be kicked out of school if I tell! I dare not talk, for I have been warned by men at the top to keep quiet, and I must do so!"

The school president, Walter Dill Scott, had his character questioned when he was accused of knowing more about Leighton's disappearance than he'd admitted. His detractors questioned why fifteen students had been mysteriously expelled immediately after the young man vanished. Evidence surfaced suggesting that police had altered their reports to favor one of those accused in the hazing. In the end, a grand jury concluded that Leighton's death was not a suicide and that guilty parties were involved.

News of a promising lead appeared in the July 17, 1923, issue of the *Indianapolis Daily Star* when a witness claimed that he had watched a group of men lower Leighton beneath the pier. The paper announced that the case could soon reopen. A few months later, the witness admitted he had lied.

In May 1933, Walter Dill Scott offered $10,000 to "anyone who could solve the disappearance and death." A woman came forward to say that she'd been sitting near the lakeshore on the night Leighton was killed and that she'd heard the men who "felled" him discuss taking him away in an automobile. The witness acknowledged that she'd come forward after hearing about the reward.

Apparently, nothing came of her testimony because an archive search produced no more articles. Leighton Mount's name dropped from the news. The ivy on the old buildings grew thicker, the trees towered higher, alumni lived out their lives, the guilty walked free, and Leighton Mount was forgotten.

Some of the guilty must have felt remorse as they lived out their lives, the secret a prickly bur in their sides as they tried to forget. If still alive, the culprits would be near one hundred years old. Perhaps someone with guilty knowledge told someone. And maybe that someone was a son or daughter who will now come forward with the information, especially when they learn that Leighton may still be in pain.

HAZED STUDENT WHOSE BODY WAS FOUND IN THE LAKE AND HIS MOTHER. Leighton Mount. Northwestern university student who disappeared after class fight in September, 1921, and his mother, Mrs. J. L. Mount, whose search for his body was finally rewarded yesterday.

*A drawing of Leighton and his mother, shown here in a May 1, 1923, edition of the Chicago Tribune, was published shortly after bones were discovered on the beach.*

Most of those who loved Leighton are dead. Does he know that? Or is he stuck in the nightmare of a September morning in 1921? Is he still trying to escape his terrifying, watery grave where he was so callously abandoned until his last breath was replaced by cold lake water, and the skin floated from his bones? Imagine the terrorized spirit trying to make his way back to campus. Imagine it and you will very likely come up with an image that is much like the apparition seen near campus. They call him "Seaweed Charlie."

Chicago ghost researcher Richard Crowe is well aware of the specter seen near the Evanston campus. Despite his grasp of Chicago history and the fact that he is related to the prosecutor who handled the fatal hazing case, the murder of Leighton Mount was buried so deeply that even Crowe hadn't heard of it. Yet, he had known about "Seaweed Charlie" for years.

The tortured spirit is seen both crawling and walking from the water by Sheridan Road, near the Lake Street Pier where Leighton met his fate. Witnessed by many over the decades, the description does not vary, said Richard Crowe. One encounter occurred on a summer night in 1993, he told me. "Two girls, Lisa Becker and Jenny Trisko, were driving south along Sheridan Road around midnight," he said. "Suddenly, they noticed the car in front of them swerving, as if to avoid something in the road."

There in the middle of the street was a man wearing a heavy trench coat. He had come from the direction of the lake. "It was too nice [outside] to be wearing a coat," Lisa told Richard. Jenny said that the man was tall and thin and glowing. The ethereal being emanated an eerie light as he lumbered across the road. The girls had never heard of the Sheridan Road ghost, and when they excitedly described their encounter to friends, they learned that the mother of Jenny's boyfriend had seen the specter at the same spot ten years earlier.

*Star athlete Chuck Palmer bragged to a coworker about his shocking secret. (1922 yearbook)*

When Richard Crowe speculated on the identity of the ghost, he had several ideas, including the theory that the ghost belonged to an instructor from the Glenview Naval Air Station who crashed his plane in the lake in May 1951. My research confirmed the plane crash, along with details about two rescuers who drowned while trying to retrieve the pilot's body. They were on the lake just off campus when their boat capsized. According to Richard, some who have seen the Sheridan Road ghost say that he is dripping with seaweed. Are any of these men "Seaweed Charlie"?

Maybe. But what about the fact that the ghost is encountered around midnight, the same time that Leighton suffered his fate? Weigh the terror that was surely suffered by each lake victim, and Leighton wins the dismal contest. Bound for hours beneath the pier in icy darkness, he was alone with his own tormented thoughts.

What did he think of in his last moments? Did he think of Doris and how he would never again see her lovely smile? Did he imagine the grief his parents would feel if he let the lake take him? Discovered dead and blue, he was further insulted by the cover-up. If there was ever a candidate for a spirit to remain earthbound, Leighton is it.

If you should travel along Sheridan Road, say a prayer for Leighton Mount as you pass the Lake Street Pier. If you see the wet and glowing ghost, do not be afraid. It is probably just Leighton, a naive young man in love with a girl named Doris.

## More Haunted Campuses

### 1. University of Washington, Seattle

The campus hangout, the College Inn Pub, is haunted by the ghost of a man who was murdered while visiting the campus decades ago. A frightened waitress once heard his gravelly voice call out, "Ten feet beyond the wall! Ten feet beyond the wall!"

### 2. University of Minnesota, Minneapolis

Students and security guards have witnessed odd things on the Minneapolis campus. Mysterious howling has been heard in the Walter Library, and a guard claims an unseen presence threw a phonebook at him in Nicholson Hall. According to lore, Pioneer Hall is haunted by a dorm official who was murdered by a religious cult.

### 3. Yale University, New Haven, Connecticut

Phantom music has been heard by half a dozen witnesses as they stood beside the old organ in Woolsey Hall. In addition to the ghostly organist, Professor Harry Jepson is believed to haunt the hall that he had refused to set foot in while he was alive.

*Yale students heard an unseen presence playing an eerie tune on an old organ in Woolsey Hall.*

### 4. Vassar College, Poughkeepsie, New York

The house advisor's apartment in the east wing of Jewett House is reported to have a closet that is home to a gentleman ghost who wears a Panama suit. Children shouting and laughing are often heard in another room of the same apartment. A resident there claimed he was alone in the shower when he felt something brush his leg. Occupants believe the place is haunted by an advisor. The campuses and main building and library are also thought to be haunted— the last by a deceased librarian who is seen on the stairs.

### 5.   South Eugene High School, Eugene, Oregon

The auditorium of this school is haunted by a boy who died there in 1957. He was crossing a catwalk when he stumbled to his fate onto the seats below. An eerie, cold sensation washes over those who sit where the boy died. Inexplicable sounds emanate from the area, and some report seeing a ghostly blue light. A brick once dropped from overhead, narrowly missing a student beside the haunted seat.

### 6.   University of Nebraska, Lincoln

Two ghosts are believed to haunt the Lincoln campus. Lucy was a free-spirited hippie whose short life came to a sad end when she jumped from the fifth floor of her dorm. Her waiflike specter has been seen in nearby Pound Hall where books inexplicably pop from shelves. The other ghost is a student who was studying acting in the 1940s, spending his days rehearsing for a part in *Macbeth,* when he climbed the overhead rigging, slipped, and crashed to the stage. Witnesses report spying his ghost near the stage whenever *Macbeth* is performed.

### 7.   University of Missouri, Kansas City

The Epperson House, a Tudor-Gothic Mansion on campus, is notorious for paranormal activity. Witnesses have frequently heard inexplicable footsteps and organ music here, and apparitions have also been seen. In an October 2013 issue, the *Kansas City Star* reported on a peculiar incident. Startled observers saw "a blue-suited arm that appeared out of nowhere, clawed at a light switch, and disappeared into the darkness when the light went out."

*UMKC's Epperson House is believed to be one of the most haunted houses in America. (Leslie Rule)*

# 16
---
# PARANORMAL
# PETS

It might surprise some people to learn that spirit encounters with pets are very common, but it never surprised me. I've always known that animals are spiritual beings. I have an extra special connection with furry creatures, and I've been a vegetarian since 1975 because of that. I've rescued many animals over the years, and at the peak of my efforts, I lived on an acre with a permanent shelter that I had had built for my strays. The population was seventeen cats and two dogs. I saw each one through to the end of their lives, and most lived well beyond the normal life expectancy.

One by one, the pets grew old and died, but because I believe with all my heart that animals' spirits live on, just as humans do, it's easier to accept their deaths. In my book *Where Angels Tread*, I shared an experience that my mother and I had when we said goodbye to a very old, very sick cat. We knew Siren was over sixteen because she had been with our family for that length of time and was already full grown when my brother found her. She was a gentle calico cat, and when she got sick, I wanted to give her every chance to recover. But the veterinarian told me it was no use. She was very sick and in great discomfort. It was time to let go.

*At the end of Siren's long and happy life, her yellow eyes focused on something—or someone—only she could see. (Leslie Rule)*

The vet told us to take some time to say goodbye, and I held Siren as my mom placed the oxygen cup over the kitty's mouth and nose, as the vet had instructed. Siren's breathing was labored, and she was very still in my arms. It was clear that she was near the end. About two minutes before the vet returned, Siren suddenly became alert. She lifted her head to gaze intently at something that only she could see. And then she turned and looked over my shoulder, her yellow eyes wide, as if she saw someone behind me.

"What is she looking at?" I asked my mother. "She sees someone!" While Siren had lived with various family members over the years, we didn't know her full history. She was a grown stray when my brother found her many years earlier. For all we knew, her original person had passed away and was now here to take her home. Or maybe it was the spirit of Siren's *feline* mother, there for her.

My mother agreed with me that Siren saw someone, and that either an angel or a spirit was there, waiting to take her home. Neither of us have ever doubted that this happens when we're near death. I was about seven years old when my mother told me about a scenario that played out when an elderly relative was on her deathbed.

The lady had never been very tactful, and she had a bad habit of blurting out thoughtless comments. As is often the case when people are dying, the elderly aunt could see the spirits of dead relatives from the Other Side, and she began to talk about the people in the room that only she could see. She pointed and exclaimed, "Why, there's Tom! And I see Sarah! Who is the fat one in the corner?"

When I first heard this story as a child, I felt sorry for "the fat one in the corner," because I was certain that her feelings must have been hurt by the

insult. Now, I realize it was unlikely that "the fat one" was bothered by the comment. The spirits were there for the dying woman, and they appeared in earthly form for her sake.

When my mother died, spirits were there for her too. I wasn't sure if I should share this because deathbed stories are personal, but I thought about it and decided that my mom would want me to. She cared about people, and if her story could bring comfort to a reader, she would like that.

In the summer of 2015 at age eighty-three, my mom got very sick. The doctors told us that she would die soon, and they moved

*Ann Rule and her dog Willow in 2012. Ann believed that we will have joyful reunions with our lost loved ones—including our pets—on the Other Side. (Leslie Rule)*

her to hospice. Before they did so, they removed all of the wires and tubes. The tube in her throat had been so uncomfortable that she was unable to speak after it was taken out. But she could hear, understand, nod her head, and mouth words.

She communicated to a relative that she had seen her mother. This made my mom very happy, and her face filled with joy. I felt reassured knowing that my grandma would be there for her when she crossed over.

My mom was a big animal lover, too, and I know she had the spirits of many pets there to greet her as she moved into the light.

A doctor friend of mine once worked as an oncologist and spent time with hospice patients. I learned from her that it is very common for our pets to greet us when we leave our bodies. She had witnessed many patients take their last breaths. She explained to me that terminal patients frequently wait until their relatives leave the room before they pass. It was often up to her to tell those relatives about the last words spoken by their loved ones.

The dying people commonly called out names in their last moment, as if they were greeting someone on the Other Side. Many times, when my friend told the families about the names spoken by their loved ones, they would tell her that the names belonged to deceased pets—often pets who had passed away decades earlier.

Our pets don't always wait until the end of our lives to make appearances. My friend Wendy Yadock was devastated when her cat, Goofer, passed away. He was a once in a lifetime cat who was always there to comfort her when she felt sad. When her heart was breaking over losing him, Goofer did not let her down. Wendy was struggling with the loss and confided, "I tried to work through my grief in the next few weeks and thought of him often. One day, I was on my couch when I saw him. He was walking through the room, holding his tail up high."

She stared in amazement at the slightly transparent cat before he vanished. Since then, Wendy has seen him three times, and her son has spotted him once. "I miss my cat," she said. "But I feel comforted in knowing that we are really still together." While Wendy's story is heartwarming, it is not unique.

Usually, people are comforted by spirit visits from their pets, but Nevada writer Louisa Swann admitted she was shocked. She was ten years old when she attended her first and last séance. It was a sunny afternoon when she and several younger neighborhood kids were playing in their backyard playhouse. "Our dog Blackie had just died," said Louisa. The regal border collie mix had been a faithful member of her family for sixteen years.

The kids decided to try to contact Blackie's spirit. They lit candles in the dark playhouse and joined hands as they imitated a seance they had seen on TV. Speaking in a hushed voice, Louisa asked, "Blackie, are you here?"

There was no reply. Louisa waited patiently, and the others giggled. After a long moment, she tried again. "Blackie, if you are here, speak to us now."

Nobody laughed *this* time, for she was answered by a loud "Woof!" It was beloved Blackie's distinctive deep bark. "We all took off running," Louisa admitted.

Just as Blackie appeared on command, the ghostly pet in the next story also seemed to respond to someone's wish to see him.

# Cranbury Cat

When the waitress saw the elderly lady seated at a table at the Cranbury Inn, she approached her with a smile. But the waitress's smile vanished when the woman did—right before her eyes. The small, white-haired lady has appeared several times over the years, always at the same table. She always disappears the instant anyone walks toward her.

The Cranbury Inn in Cranbury, New Jersey, is a special place. It was created from historic buildings, including two eighteenth-century stagecoach stop structures that started the inn's tradition of warm welcomes nearly 300 years ago. Today, it is stunningly beautiful with an open interior that makes it a choice spot for weddings. It's also known for its fine cuisine and for the fact it's *haunted*.

It's a peaceful kind of haunting, with benign spirits attached to the place that held significance for them when they were living beings, though the histories of the people they once were is not always clear. Owners Tom and Gay Ingegneri suspect the dining room ghost is Mrs. Mac, a lady who once lived in a room on the upper floor and passed away in 1972. If Mrs. Mac had pets, that might explain why the apparitions of animals are also seen at the Cranbury Inn.

"We have five people ghosts and a ghost cat and a ghost dog," Gay told me. "The cat has been seen by a bartender and many of my customers." She often feels the kitty brush past her ankles and has caught glimpses of it from the corner of her eye.

Many people have described the ghostly cat and dog to her, but Gay is tightlipped when it comes to describing the pets' colors and markings. When someone describes the ethereal pets in the exact way that others have, Gay can be certain the sighting is legitimate.

I spoke with customer Sharon Hecker about the night that she and two friends, Joanne and Roseanne, enjoyed Christmas dinner at the inn. While they dined, the topic of the haunting came up. They had heard about the inn's ghostly pets and were intrigued. When the trio went to the ladies-room after dinner, Roseanne said, "I've never seen a ghost! I would love to see one!" She ducked into a stall, and Joanne and Sharon were chatting by the sink when they witnessed a surprising sight. "It was the back end of a cat," Joanne told me.

"We saw its back legs and tail," Sharon added. "And then it disappeared." Roseanne exited the stall too late to see the ghostly cat. "I *always* miss the good stuff!" she cried. As they left the restroom, "All three of us heard a resounding *meow*!" said Sharon. "To say we were startled is an understatement."

### The Cranbury Inn
21 S Main St, Cranbury, New Jersey 08512
(609) 655-5595
thecranburyinn.com

---

# Little Joe

Wally. Uncle Wally. Beasty. Booty Girl. Turtle. Piggy Piggy. Sister Smudge. Amber. Snickers. Little Joe. Before they found refuge in Anita Morris's Portland, Oregon, backyard sanctuary, these ten beautiful felines lived the hard life of America's millions of feral cats.

Feral cats are simply cats born without homes and not tamed by humans. They seek shelter in places like abandoned buildings and overgrown blackberry bushes. They live on rodents and garbage pail scraps. Unprotected, their lives are often short, but the population continues to grow as they breed. And breed. And breed.

Anita first became aware of the feral cat dilemma when an elderly wheelchair-bound neighbor began feeding a couple of stray cats. Not spayed or neutered, the cats bred and before too long, over one hundred cats were swarming the neighborhood. It tugged at Anita's heartstrings to see the scrawny, homeless creatures. "I got involved with the Feral Cat Coalition of Oregon," explained Anita, a grandmother of five. She began trapping the strays in the humane Have a Heart Traps and got them spayed and neutered. Nineteen years later, she is still doing her part to help the hapless kitties. In fact, she and her husband, Joe, have turned their backyard into an oasis for feral cats, complete with cozy little houses.

While most feral cats are wary of humans and won't let them close, one special cat won Anita's heart, and she won his. Little Joe was a big white and gray boy with a little dot beneath his nose. He loved to play with the humans. "He liked to fetch acorns," she remembered fondly.

They nicknamed him "the Mayor" because he always welcomed new cats. Whenever a strange cat wandered into the yard, Little Joe would eagerly greet him and then show him to the food dish. "It was like he was saying, 'This is a great place! Look, they have food and toys!'" Anita smiled at the memory but her eyes saddened as she told me of Little Joe's tragic end. He was hit by a car

*The spirit of little Joe, the third cat from the left, stands up behind the dish. Note that he is white and grey and slightly transparent. (Anita Morris)*

and she and her husband were devastated as they prepared to bury him. "I wish we had gotten a picture of him," she said sadly. As they looked around at the surviving cats, they realized they had no photos of any of them. "We rushed out and got some film."

Anita got out her Olympus camera and took a roll of pictures of her backyard kitties. When she and Joe went to pick up the photos, they sat in their car and looked over the snapshots. Suddenly, Anita gasped. And then they both started crying. For there, smack in the middle of a photo, was the undeniable image of Little Joe. He sat behind the food trough, between Amber and Booty Girl.

Little Joe is slightly transparent, allowing the lines of the shed behind him to show through his body. But other than that, he appears just as he did in life. I learned of the extraordinary photo (taken with ordinary film) through a friend of Anita's, and it took some coaxing for her to allow me to include her story in this book. "I don't want Little Joe to be exploited," Anita insisted.

"Little Joe's story will help a lot of people feel better," I told her. "It will comfort them to see his picture and to know that their pets' spirits live on."

She finally agreed to allow me to use the amazing image of the cat's ghost. "I'd like the best possible print," I told her. "It would be better if you could have one made from the original negative, rather than a copy."

Anita misunderstood my request, so when she couldn't find the negative, she sent the photo to Kodak to have a new negative made. She soon received a phone call from a puzzled Kodak employee. "There's a problem with the photo," said the woman.

"Oh?" Anita replied.

"The cat is transparent," said the woman.

"Yes," said Anita.

"He looks like a ghost!" said the woman.

A picture tells a thousand stories!

For information on how to help feral cats, please visit feralcats.com.

---

# The White Dog

When Kathleen Lee is asked about the scariest incident of her life, she casts her memory back to the 1960s when she was a cute twelve-year-old girl with fire-red hair that fell to her waist. The Ontario mother of six remembers how her own mother struggled to raise five kids alone. The year she started junior high school, Kathleen, her sister, and her three brothers moved with their mother to a drafty farmhouse in the middle of six acres of land in Whonnock, British Columbia. "It was a rental house," said Kathleen. "It once belonged to a Japanese family, and they lost it when they were sent to an internment camp during the war."

The kids found old, faded Japanese newspapers in the attic. Kathleen felt sad for the family she knew had once loved the home. The long driveway that led to the secluded two-story house was lined with Japanese cherry and plum trees, and the overgrown land still harbored beautiful oriental shrubbery, long ago planted by loving hands.

Sometimes Kathleen and her siblings were a little spooked on the isolated property, especially when the kids at school talked about the nearby institute for the criminally insane. "It scared us," she admitted. "We worried someone would escape."

One dreary February afternoon, the family was surprised to find a visitor at their door. "It was a beautiful white dog," said Kathleen. "He was *so* beautiful that even my mother was impressed, and she is not a dog person." The husky-like dog had a thick, fluffy coat. Her fur was pure white. Oddly so. Most white dogs, Kathleen pointed out, have a little yellow or beige tones mixed into their fur. But the Carnegies' visitor had startling snow-white fur.

The dog watched the children with inquisitive, friendly eyes. "My brother tried to touch her, but she backed away," she remembered. The curious canine seemed to want to join the family, yet she shied away when anyone came near.

The Carnegie kids put food and water out for the dog, hoping their mother would let them keep her. She had a collar with a tag hanging from it, but they could never get close enough to her to read it.

Meanwhile, their dog, Scampy, a medium-sized mixed breed, stayed in the backyard. This was a little peculiar, as Scampy normally raced around the house, his tail wagging, eager to greet visitors, dogs and people alike.

That night Kathleen watched television until she fell asleep on the living room sofa. It was 2:00 a.m. when she woke with a start to an odd mixture of noises. The static of the TV was drowned out by the keening howl of Scampy. Kathleen sat up quickly. "I thought something was wrong with Scampy," she said. Then she realized that the white dog, still on the front porch, was also making noise, a low, throaty growl.

Puzzled, Kathleen got up. The moon was full and filled the room with a cold white light. Kathleen glanced at the front door and froze. There, silhouetted against the door's window, was a tall figure. The bright moonlight behind him blotted out his features. For a second, she wondered if she were looking at her own shadow. "I moved my head, but he didn't move."

Cold terror filled her belly, and her feet seemed stuck to the floor. "I could see the outline of his shoulders, neck, and jaw, but he was so big that he was taller than the door. I could not see the top of his head. I knew he could see me. I was so frightened it seemed like my heart stopped. I could not even scream. I just couldn't believe that this was happening to me. We were locked there, with him watching me. He was menacing. I knew whatever was on his mind couldn't be good."

Suddenly, the white dog's growl turned into a ferocious roar. Kathleen could not see the dog, yet she knew the animal had lunged at the intruder. "I saw the man's head move from the window." Kathleen ran to her mother's room and watched from the window as the white dog chased the stranger up the long driveway. "It was too dark to see the man." Only the dog was visible, glowing white in the moonlight as she raced away.

"I went looking for the dog the next morning," said Kathleen. But the animal had vanished as quickly as it had appeared. She stood on the porch, wondering what had become of the mysterious creature.

Then her eyes fell on the dishes they had set out for the dog. "They were still filled to the brim," she said. "The food and water had not been touched. I showed my mother," Kathleen remembered. "When she saw the food hadn't been touched, she said, 'That dog was sent by God to protect us.'" The dog, they decided, had to be either an angel or a ghost.

They checked with all the neighbors, and no one else had seen or heard of the pure white dog. "Scampy refused to come around to the front of the house for several days," said Kathleen. "My brother Gary tried to drag him, but he wouldn't budge."

Was the white dog an ethereal being? The fact that she had not touched food or water for the twelve hours she had sat on the porch was strange. And why did no one in the community know anything about such an unusual-looking dog? Wouldn't someone else have noticed the animal?

Scampy's behavior, too, suggested that the white dog may have been from another world. Why wouldn't the friendly Scampy interact with the dog? The menacing intruder was another puzzling element. Was it possible that he, too, was a ghost? Or was he a patient, escaped or discharged from the nearby criminally insane institution?

If his presence was ghostly, could it have anything to do with the Japanese family who was removed from their home? Was the white dog a ghost of a pet of the Japanese family who suffered the injustice of internment? Perhaps she had come back to make sure another family would not lose anything precious.

Helpful entities may be angels or simply the spirits of those who have passed. While a dog appeared to save Kathleen, the rescuers in the next chapter are believed to be the ghosts of human beings.

# 17

## A HELPING HAND

Many people become frightened when they witness paranormal activity because they assume something wants to harm them. Where does this fear come from? Most likely, preconceived notions about spirits and their intentions dictate our reactions. If we're raised by parents who are terrified at the thought of ghosts, then we, too, learn to be afraid.

I've found many more cases of haunted places where the ghostly presences are *helpful* rather than frightening. My book *Coast to Coast Ghosts* includes the case of Brian Sykes, a young bachelor who lived alone in a haunted apartment in Burien, Washington. He often left a sink full of dirty dishes when he went to bed at night. He would wake in the morning to find the dishes washed, dried, and put away. "When I moved out, I actually invited the ghost to come with me," he confided. (Apparently, the ghost did not move with him, because he got no more help with the dishes.)

While Brian's friendly ghost helped with chores, other spirits have assisted in extraordinary ways. In the following story, a young woman had an amazing connection with a man who died before she was born. Even so, he loved her, and he proved it in a very big way.

# Love from Beyond

It was a hot summer afternoon in Houston, Texas, and five-year-old Dawn sat on her bed, quietly playing with her Barbie dolls. Movement caught her eye, and she looked up. There, standing in the hallway, was a man she had never seen before.

"We looked each other up and down," Dawn told me, recalling the distinctive image of the dark-haired man. "He was wearing an undershirt with black pants and shiny black shoes." She assumed he was simply a visitor but was puzzled when he walked into the bathroom and did not shut the door. "We were taught to *always* shut the door after going into the bathroom," Dawn said.

When the man did not emerge from the bathroom, she grew curious. She investigated, but the bathroom was empty! When she reported the visitor to her mother and grandmother, they looked at each other, their eyes wide with amazement. *It couldn't be!*

Dawn had described the grandfather she had never met. "He died before I was born," she explained. *Had she seen his ghost?* When Dawn suggested this, her grandmother did not want to hear it and said firmly, "I don't believe in ghosts."

"But, Googie!" Dawn protested, using her pet name for her grandma. "I *saw* him!"

Today, Dawn Edwards, manager of a video store and mother of an eight-year-old boy, speaks of her grandfather with awe. "He is my guardian angel."

Hubert Clark Scott was a handsome six-foot-tall salesman with a kind heart and a winning sense of humor. After a long battle with cancer, he succumbed months before Dawn was born. Incoherent on his deathbed, he rambled senselessly when Dawn's mother and grandmother visited in the hospital.

"My mother was pregnant with me," said Dawn. "Everyone was sure I would be a boy because of the way she carried me. They even had a boy's name picked out."

But as Dawn's mother stood by her father's bed, he suddenly spoke in a startling moment of lucidity. He reached out his hand and curled it around her belly. "Take care of my granddaughter," he said. In the next instant he was again confused. Dawn believes that in that moment, she and her grandfather formed a bond that could not be broken. She has sensed him throughout her life. "He was in World War II," she said. "I wear his dog tags. Whenever I am at a parade, I feel my arm go up to salute the men and women in the service as they walk by. I was never taught to salute. I feel a tingling in my arm as this happens."

It is just one of the dozens of ways that Dawn senses her grandfather beside her. Skeptics might explain away these things as products of an overactive imagination. But who can explain what happened to her as she waited in her car at a red light?

"My son and I were both in the car," said Dawn. Suddenly, she had the unmistakable sensation of a hand on her chin. "It guided me to look in the rearview mirror." At the same time, a man's voice shouted, "Look up, damn it!" Though startled by the disembodied voice, Dawn obeyed and saw a huge dump truck speeding toward them. She quickly moved the car to the side of the road, and an instant later the truck whizzed by. "It would have rear-ended us. At the speed it was going, it could have turned my car into a heap of metal and killed both me and my son."

Dawn says that her experiences with her grandfather's spirit prove to her that there are ghosts among us. "I believe they are good and bad," she said.

"I am blessed to have such a loving one. For without him, I would not be here to raise my son, and my son might not have lived through the speeding dump truck ordeal."

While many report getting assistance from their friends and relatives on the Other Side, the ghosts of strangers, too, can step in to help. In the next story, no one knew the identity of their unusual visitor, but they are very glad she stopped by.

# Mama's Little Helper

Rhonda Lillie stirred in her sleep. As she awoke, the dark filled her eyes. It was 3:00 a.m. and she'd been snoozing soundly in the Oxnard, California, rental home where she lived with her husband and two daughters. A noise had woken her. *What is that?* she wondered as she sat up and tried to make sense of an odd tinkling sound. "Wake up!" She nudged her husband. "I hear something." He pulled the pillow over his head and ignored her.

*(Left to right) Amanda, Angel, Rhonda, and Ashley all get goose bumps when they talk about the sad little ghost who once played at the Lillie home. (Leslie Rule)*

Rhonda got out of bed and headed down the hallway, past her daughters' rooms. The noise was louder now, and she moved toward it. The dust of her dreams had cleared. Alert now, she could identify the sound. It was her kids' electronic toy, a ball that sings whenever it's played with. "I knew my kids were asleep," said Rhonda. "The ball makes noise only when it is touched."

Yet, she wasn't frightened. She opened the door to the playroom, flicked on the light, and saw the ball wiggling and "singing" in the middle of the room. A shrill siren sounded near her ear, and she turned to see a toy police car on the dresser. The little blue light atop its roof blinked as the car moved forward on the dresser. But before it reached the edge, it backed up and then moved forward again. It repeated the action, each time stopping before it reached the edge of the dresser. It was as if an invisible hand guided it, stopping it just before it crashed to the floor.

"You don't have to do this," Rhonda spoke calmly to the empty room. "I know you are here." She turned off the toys and went back to bed. She doesn't believe the toys themselves were haunted. They were simply playthings for an ethereal little girl who shared their old white stucco house.

While some people might have been disturbed by the 3:00 a.m. wake-up call, Rhonda took it in stride. In fact, she would not have had it any other way. "I'll always be grateful to her," she confided.

She first became aware her family was not alone one summer afternoon when she was in the bathroom. "The door was open, and I glanced up just as a ball flew past. A second later a little girl rushed by, chasing after it."

Rhonda figured it was her daughter, four-year-old Angel, so she shouted, "Hey, don't throw the ball in the house." But when Rhonda came out of the bathroom, the house was quiet. Angel didn't answer her when she called, so she went outside, where she found her, happily splashing in the plastic wading pool. She started to scold her for throwing the ball, but Angel protested. "I wasn't in the house!"

One day, soon after, she was doing housework when she heard Angel chattering away in her bedroom as if involved in an animated conversation. She asked Angel later who she'd been talking to, and the child replied, "I was playing with the girl." Rhonda assumed her daughter had an imaginary friend, but Angel insisted her playmate was real. According to Angel, her friend was definitely *not* imaginary. Today, at thirteen, she vividly recalls playing with the unusual little girl. "I looked into my room and saw her playing with my things," she confided. "At first I was mad, and then I decided she'd be fun to play with."

She stared for a moment at the strange figure. "She was glowing and blue," said Angel. "She was a Hispanic girl about six, with long hair that fell to her waist." The little girl was clutching Angel's teddy bear as Angel sat down beside her. "She kept staring at me. She looked kind of strange. She had squinty eyes, as if she was crying. Her hair looked damp. Every once in a while, she'd laugh. But she would not say a word."

Though a bit apprehensive about her odd playmate, Angel was glad to have someone to play with. There were no other children in the neighborhood, and she was lonely. "I knew she wasn't like normal people," she remembered. When Angel tried to take back her teddy bear, the glowing girl clutched it tightly, refusing to give it up. The visit ended when the strange child tossed the teddy bear across the room. "I went to get it, and when I looked back, she was gone."

She saw the girl again a few days later when she awoke shivering from a sound sleep. "I was so cold it woke me up. I looked up, and there was the little girl staring down at me. It frightened me. She looked so sad."

A year passed, and it was summertime once again when the girl made another appearance. "Angel was playing in the wading pool, and I stood at the kitchen sink, watching her as I did the dishes," remembered Rhonda. "My one-year-old, Amanda, was just out of sight of the window when I heard a voice in my head."

It was more than a thought. It was as if someone were speaking to her, yet the voice did not ring in her ears. The warning was louder than any spoken word. *The baby is choking.* In that instant, Rhonda saw the little ghost at the edge of her vision. "She was about six with long brown hair, and she was wearing a white dress."

Rhonda whirled around, and the girl vanished. She rushed outside to find Amanda sitting on the ground, her face red and her mouth filled with dirt. She reached into the choking baby's mouth and pulled out a huge dirt clod. "She was okay," said the grateful mother. "But if a few more seconds had passed, she might not have been!"

Years later, as Rhonda and Angel recalled the unusual little girl, they wondered if she could be the spirit of a child who died on or near the property. Angel had noticed that the girl's hair appeared to be damp. Could she have been the ghost of a drowned child? And what about the fact that the encounters occurred in the summertime? Could that also be a clue? Was there a drowning death in the neighborhood, one that occurred in the summer?

A pattern is sometimes noted in ghost sightings, with correlations between time of year or time of day. In some cases, a ghost in a haunted place might appear only during one season of the year. Sometimes they are seen more often at a particular time of day. This could be because they stir when the conditions remind them of intense moments of their lives, such as their *last* moments.

# GHOSTS IN THE NEWS

On February 18, 1999, the *Orlando Sentinel* reported that a ghost saved the life of forty-year-old Maria Tejada in Kissimmee, Florida. She was watching television when she heard her deceased father's voice. Tejada was quoted as saying, "He told me to get up off the couch. I didn't listen the first two times he said it, but the third time I got up and went over to the loveseat."

It was at that instant that a 1982 Chevy crashed through her front door. The automobile knocked over the couch and demolished an interior wall. The seventeen-year-old driver and his passenger were on their way to school when they took their disastrous detour. The kid claimed his brakes failed, but officials found nothing wrong with them. The teen was presented with a ticket for careless driving. Interestingly, the house had a reputation for being haunted. Neighbors had long gossiped about the slamming doors, strange noises emanating from the attic, and phantom footsteps associated with the home.

Though Tejada insisted it was her father's voice who warned her, she said he was not responsible for the other paranormal activity there. It was, she said, the ghost of a man who had hanged himself in a big oak tree beside the house twenty years before. She and a neighbor had once heard his ghost walking on her roof.

# A FINAL WORD

When a fellow ghost author was featured on a documentary-style show about hauntings, he was interviewed in a haunted hotel and it quickly became apparent that the producers wanted him to act as if he were frightened. He refused to pretend to be afraid of ghosts, but that didn't stop them from getting the footage they wanted!

When the episode aired, my friend was startled to see himself running from the building as if he were fleeing in terror. The scary music left no question in viewers' minds that he was frightened. After he got past his surprise over the scene, he laughed out loud.

He had not really fled in terror, but he knew exactly how the producers were able to make it appear as if he had. During a break in taping, he'd rushed out of the hotel to retrieve something from his car, and he had no idea the cameras were still rolling. The camera had captured him running out the door on his hurried errand, and with a little crafty editing, the producers achieved their goal of creating a terrifying show.

Why has Hollywood created so many scary ghost stories? I suspect that many of those making terrifying ghost films are nonbelievers. As skeptics, the producers aren't really interested in spirit encounters because they doubt their authenticity. In their quest to make the stories interesting to themselves, they introduce a fear factor.

I strive to present a balance. I don't want my readers to be *frightened,* I want them to be *fascinated.* And if that fascination is sometimes accompanied by a chill, I think that's fine. It's natural for us to be a *little* spooked by the unknown, and that's not a bad thing because it adds to the intrigue.

Even as I report stories of hauntings by benign spirits, I'm aware that I don't have a full understanding of all otherworldly beings. I've made a choice to investigate and report on what appear to be *nonthreatening* hauntings—to focus on *ghosts* and *not* unsavory entities that I have no interest in learning about. I trust my instincts, and if I sense something is off when I'm visiting a haunted place, I don't stay long. I am not scared, but *cautious.*

For instance, I would not engage with a Ouija board for any reason. I was given one for Christmas when I was ten, and while nothing bad happened when we played with it back then, I've now heard too many accounts of Ouija communication opening doors to unwelcome entities. My opinion on this topic has shifted dramatically since *Coast to Coast Ghosts* was published in 2001. In that book, I quoted experts on their varying opinions on the spirit board and advised readers to make up their own minds. While I *still* think individuals must decide for themselves, it would be unfair to my readers to fail to warn them about something that I perceive as very dangerous.

On that note, some experts advise that ghost hunting and alcohol are a bad mix, and encourage explorers to avoid overindulging. Psychic medium Nancy Myer warns that "excessive use of drugs and alcohol" can lower our resistance to "negative spirits" when visiting haunted locations.

Ghost hunting has become an increasingly popular hobby, but it is actually *our* world and *not* the Other Side that poses the most dangers. Railroad tracks, abandoned buildings, bridges, and treacherous roads are places ghost hunters are wise to avoid. Consider the tragic news reported by Charlotte, North Carolina's, WBTV on August 27, 2010. A group of ghost hunters hoped for a glimpse of a legendary phantom train, and in the wee hours of the morning, they ventured onto a railroad trestle in Iredell County. While some managed to run for safety when a real train suddenly appeared and bore down upon them, a twenty-nine-year-old man was killed, and two people were severely injured.

WBTV shared a press release from the Iredell County Sheriff's Office: "The group of people did not immediately run from the real train because they believed the train was—in fact—the 'ghost train' and posed no real threat."

The deceased man's family said that he had sacrificed himself for his girl-friend who could not run as fast as he could. He slowed his pace to match hers, and right before he was hit, he said, "I love you" and pushed her off the trestle. Though injured, she survived.

The tale of the phantom train stems from North Carolina's worst railroad accident. It was August 27, 1891, when passenger train number nine derailed while crossing the Bostian Bridge near Statesville. The engine and a string of cars landed in a crumpled heap, ninety feet below, killing twenty-three people.

Legend has it that a woman saw the ghost train on the fiftieth anniversary of the accident, and while evidence of legitimate sightings is elusive, that hasn't stopped the droves of excitement seekers who show up on the anniversaries of the fatal accident. A number of newspapers, including *The Herald-Sun*, reported in August 1991 that four hundred spectators watched from a field below the trestle on the one-hundredth anniversary of the tragedy. The crowd was disappointed when the phantom train failed to appear.

I'm not surprised when ghosts don't appear on schedule. It seems that most spirit encounters are unexpected. Sharon Henderson certainly wasn't expecting to see a ghost on a long-ago summer evening in 1977. She was working as a counselor at a horse camp in the foothills of Battle Creek, Washington. Only healthy food was available at the camp, but Sharon had a sweet tooth and often drove into town to stock up on junk food.

"I always stopped at the same convenience store and bought candy," she remembered. On that night, as she pulled into the parking lot, she felt an overwhelming sense of dread. She tried to shrug it off. "I was only eighteen, but it took a lot to unnerve me," she stressed. "I'd traveled around the country by myself and knew I could take care of myself."

Yet, she could not shake her apprehension. She glanced around the parking lot, looking to see if anything was amiss. Everything seemed to be in order. "There was not a person in sight," she confided. "I thought, *this is ridiculous! I want candy!*"

She pulled into a space near the store's entryway and put the car in park, but the engine was still running as she glanced up. She was startled to see a figure standing outside the store's front door. It appeared to be *guarding* the entryway! The apparition was translucent and manifested from the shoulders up.

"I could not tell if it was a man or woman, but I clearly saw a head and shoulders," said Sharon. The figure shook its head, as if in warning. The message was clear: Sharon was not to enter the store. She backed out of the parking space and turned the car around. "I glanced back one more time just to be sure I wasn't being unduly silly, but the figure was still there. That's when I got really scared. It was as if it were saying, 'No! Go away!'"

But it was not the figure itself that frightened her. There was nothing menacing about the mysterious being. Sharon instinctively sensed it was protecting her from an unknown danger. She sped through the parking lot and drove back to camp.

The next day, she heard shocking news. The convenience store had been robbed. A gunman had been there at the same time as Sharon. He had shot and killed the clerk. Sharon was horrified and overcome with guilt. She wished she could have done something to help. But a teenage girl was no match for an armed killer.

It's possible that the victim was already dead when Sharon drove up to the store. It's possible that the ghost she saw was that of the victim, warning the teen not to blunder in. No matter the identity of the being that saved her life, it was a very good time to be *Haunted in America.*